AF323117

# Memoir of a Cold War Soldier

# Memoir of a Cold War Soldier

By Richard E. Mack

The Kent State University Press

KENT, OHIO, AND LONDON

© 2001 by The Kent State University Press, Kent, Ohio 44242
All rights reserved
Library of Congress Catalog Card Number 00-036878
ISBN 0-87338-675-2
Manufactured in the United States of America

05   04   03   02   01      5   4   3   2   1

Library of Congress Cataloging-in-Publication Data

Mack, Richard E., 1924–
    Memoir of a cold war soldier / by Richard E. Mack
        p.   cm.
    Includes bibliographical references and index.
    ISBN 0-87338-675-2 (cloth: alk. paper) ∞
    1. Mack, Richard E., 1924–   2. Korean War, 1950–1953—Personal narratives, American.   3. Vietnamese Conflict, 1961–1975—Personal narratives, American.   4. Soldiers—United States—Biography.   5. United States. Army—Biography.   I. Title.

DS921.6.M33  2001
951.904'2'092—dc21                                             00-036878

British Library Cataloging-in-Publication data are available.

**For** *Margaret, Mary, Rolly, Elizabeth, and Rick, with love.*

Mid cannons' roar and rifles' peal,
We'll chant a soldier's song.

—*"The Soldier's Song," national anthem
of the Irish Republic*

# Contents

# List of Maps

# Abbreviations & Acronyms

| | |
|---|---|
| ALS | Army Language School |
| AOR | area of responsibility |
| ARCOM | Army Reserve Command |
| ARVN | Army of the Republic of Vietnam |
| ASTP | Army Specialized Training Program |
| BAR | Browning automatic rifle |
| BOA | battalion operational area |
| BOQ | bachelor officers quarters |
| C&GSC | Command and General Staff College |
| C/S | chief of staff |
| CIDG | Civilian Irregular Defense Group |
| CINCSO | Commander in Chief, Southern Command |
| CO | commanding officer |
| COA | company operational area |
| COMPHIBLANT | Commander Amphibious Command, Atlantic |
| COMPHIBTRALANT | Commander Amphibious Training Command, Atlantic |
| COMUSMACV | Commander, U.S. Military Assistance Command, Vietnam |
| CONUS | continental United States |
| CP | command post |
| CRAF | Civilian Reserve Air Fleet |
| CW | continuous wave (Morse code) |
| DCSINTEL | Deputy Chief of Staff, Intelligence |
| DLI | Defense Language Institute (formerly Army Language School) |
| DOD | Department of Defense |
| FAC | forward air controller |
| FO | forward observer (artillery, mortar) |
| Huks | Hukbalahap partisans (Philippine Islands) |

| | |
|---|---|
| I&E | information and education |
| I&R platoon | intelligence and reconnaissance platoon |
| IG | inspector general |
| JCS | Joint Chiefs of Staff |
| KATUSA | Korean Augmentation to the U.S. Army |
| KIA | killed in action |
| LFTU | Landing Forces Training Unit |
| LMG | light machine gun |
| LNO | liaison officer |
| LOD time | line-of-departure time |
| LST | landing ship, tank |
| LZ | (helicopter) landing zone |
| MACV [USMACV] | U.S. Military Assistance Command |
| MIA | missing in action |
| NAMS | Naval Amphibious School |
| NATO | North Atlantic Treaty Organization |
| NCO | noncommissioned officer |
| NKPA | North Korean People's Army |
| NSDM | National Security Defense Memorandum |
| NVA | North Vietnamese Army |
| OBAM Battalion | ordnance base automotive maintenance battalion |
| OC | officer candidate |
| OP | observation post |
| PAVN | People's Army of Vietnam (same as NVA) |
| PF | Popular Forces |
| POT (Staff) | Plans, Operation, and Training |
| PRC | People's Republic of China |
| R&R | rest and recuperation |
| RF | Regional Forces |
| ROK | Republic of Korea (South Korea) |
| RR | recoilless rifle (57 mm) |
| SA | senior adviser |
| SSI | Strategic Studies Institute |
| TACP | tactical air control party |
| TD | tank destroyer |
| TOC | tactical operations center |
| TOT | time on target (artillery) |
| UN | United Nations |

| | |
|---|---|
| USAFORSCOM | U.S. Army Forces Command |
| USAREUR | U.S. Army Europe |
| USARSO | U.S. Army South |
| USAWC | U.S. Army War College |
| USCOB | U.S. Commander of Berlin |
| USMA | U.S. Military Academy |
| VNAF | Vietnamese Air Force |

# Reflections on Early Experiences

It is June 1930, the day before classes ended for the summer at Margaret Park elementary school in Akron, Ohio; my mother, Elizabeth Giblin Mack, arrived at Mrs. Smith's first-grade classroom with my grandfather, Albert Eugene Mack, to attend the class skit, "A Day at the Circus." My grandfather lived with us in a bungalow that my father, Harold A. Mack, was buying on time. It was common to have grandparents living with their children during the Depression. My sister, Gertrude Helen, married Tom Wheeler in 1949; they later moved to San Diego, California. I had no other brothers or sisters. My father worked for Goodyear Tire and Rubber Company as a production supervisor. He had an eighth-grade education; my mother, however, had attended Cornell for two years.

But now back to the circus. I remember telling my mother how nice it was that they had selected me to play the role of the elephant. I believe my mother and grandfather were anxiously looking forward to see me acting in my first play. I remember that following the skit I was asked, "Which part of the elephant did you play, Dick?"

When I responded that I had been the back legs and the tail, I remember, my grandfather said that I had done a fine job and that next year maybe they would let me be the head and trunk. My grandfather reminded me that it was at that end the elephant had his large memory. My second-grade teacher didn't have a circus play, but I don't believe being relegated to the hindquarters of an elephant at that early age contributed to any developmental regression.

On the other hand, I cannot remember anyone accusing me of being a bright child. I can recall, though, hearing people say in so many words that I was persistent, to the point that I would pester people to get answers to my questions or would find my own solutions. I am sure that on occasion I was referred to simply as a "pain in the ass."

During my formative years, I was impressed with the fact that a penny was something of value—a symptom of the Depression. Nowadays, people drop their pennies in the bowl at the cash register—a symptom of affluence. My normal routine was distributed between Margaret Park School, Saint Peter's Roman Catholic Church, the YMCA, Boy Scouts, and the "Fulton Street Gang," all tempered by the strict guidance of my result-oriented parents.

Of those who made great impressions on me, Mrs. Cora L. Covey, the principal of Margaret Park School, stands tall. She had a firm yet understanding manner. A disciplinarian, she had the knack of achieving good deportment with the least amount of effort and pain. An example that strikes me as characteristic of her influence was the three-foot piece of garden hose we "learned" she kept in her office. Students truly tried to avoid a trip to her inner sanctum. There were tales galore describing the hose in detail and how she wielded it on the bottoms of the incorrigible. However, I never met anyone who had actually experienced Mrs. Covey's hose or had ever seen it. Her ploy would conjure up thoughts of child abuse by not a few parents today.

The influence of Saint Peter's certainly left an impression on me. The weekly catechism conducted between masses gave me a foundation in the world of right and wrong. This foundation, coupled with what I learned at my mother's knee, provided me a compass for maintaining moral direction over a lifetime. It also left me with a belief that little can be done to instill the oft-repeated military code of Duty, Honor, and Country, in the absence of the earlier moral direction.

I always felt that I was especially fortunate to have had friends among the Lithuanian families at Saint Peter's. It forever amazed me how industrious and well ordered these families were. The fact that few of my Lithuanian friends' mothers could speak English, forcing the children to learn both English and Lithuanian, impressed me. I remember my mother's saying that to be bilingual as a child was a gift from God; my mother herself had studied German and could speak the language fluently. She often said that it was a shame that the study of foreign languages in our high schools seldom produced the ability to speak them. During and after World War II, the armed forces and the State Department had to provide language training in order to meet operational needs.

My other friends lived on Fulton Street, and although they were known as the Fulton Street Gang, they were not of a violent nature. Each year the sixth through eighth-grade boys in the gang met on the Manchester Road side of Summit Lake for their annual swim across the lake, most without suits or shorts.

Naturally, our parents didn't know about the swim. At the time the lake was befouled by the drainage from the local Goodrich and Firestone plants, and we were lucky never to come down with an illness, let alone drown.

I believe my first struggle with maturity came when I was a seventh-grader: my father told me that I had better knuckle down and get better grades if I wanted ever to get ahead in the world. He had never attended high school but had worked as a tire builder and a supervisor at Goodyear, and later as an insurance salesman for the Metropolitan Life Insurance Company. Strikes in the 1930s, often violent, would require him and other supervisors and foremen to remain in the factory to continue tire production. I believe he had deep sympathy for the workers, who during strikes would surround the plant, preventing all entry and departure. At the same time, many of his friends were unemployed or were engaged in Works Progress Administration projects, earning a subsistence living. I believe that the empathy I had for soldiers was ingrained in me by my father.

In any case, I can remember the evening when my father told me, as I was reading the sports page in the *Akron Beacon Journal,* that I wouldn't "start growing up" until I began reading the front page and the business section. From then on at the dinner table, I had a daily quiz on the important news of the day, as well as the business news. When the topic of Adolf Hitler and Benito Mussolini came up in dinner-table conversation, which was most of the time, my parents expected me to enter into the discussion.

In 1939, when I was fourteen and a sophomore, we moved, and I enrolled in Buchtel High School, in a more affluent section of Akron. My mother believed that the change in schools would prompt me to set higher goals. She was probably right; she knew the value of education. There were three teachers at Buchtel High who provided me with lasting motivation: Mr. MacDonald, my geometry teacher; Mrs. Ruth, my German teacher; and Mrs. (Dr.) Reidinger, my English literature teacher.

I had a dreadful time in geometry during the first grading period in 1939. Mr. MacDonald rightfully gave me an F, which was not well received at home. During the next period I studied my rear end off and on the final examination received an A. Mr. MacDonald wrote on the examination paper, "Dick, I knew you could do it; you have intestinal fortitude." When I showed the examination to my mother, I asked her what intestinal fortitude meant. She responded that was what you need to survive when everything and everybody seems to be against you; then she told me it was another way of saying, "You have guts." That episode I never forgot.

I was in no way enamored with English literature. To Dr. Reidinger, English literature and her students were her world; she was a well spoken woman with uncommon common sense. I knew she had pinpointed me as not having great interest in *Beowulf,* "Evangeline," and the readings we were assigned nightly. She would require us to write a short synopsis of our nightly readings, no longer than eight short sentences.

About two weeks into the course, I composed a poem as the synopsis of my reading assignment. When she returned my homework, she had appended a note saying that this would be a boring world if there weren't people who responded to it in an unorthodox manner. I had done that by expressing myself in poetry, and for that received an A. I learned something about what the "boss" wanted and continued with the poetry synopses throughout the year.

Mrs. Ruth had a map of Europe and Africa in her classroom, and each day for about five minutes she gave us a presentation in German (and then in translation) of what was happening in Europe and Africa. Her motive, as far as I knew, was to connect the German we were studying with world events. As a soldier in Europe a few years later, I appreciated the insight I had gained from her in the classroom.

My mother was a lover of classical music and the classics in general. As a result my sister and I were more familiar with Sir Lancelot, Guenevier, and King Arthur and the Round Table than with Red Riding Hood, Little Miss Muffet, and Jack and the Beanstalk. Perhaps I saw something of my mother in Dr. Reidinger.

Akron high schools were organized into morning and afternoon sessions. Freshmen and sophomores went to school in the afternoon, juniors and seniors in the morning. Each session was four and a half hours, as I recall.

By the time I was a junior in high school, I was working at a drive-in steak station on Copley Road, called the Farmerette. My hours daily were from 6 P.M. to midnight, Saturdays from 10 A.M. to 2 P.M. I earned twenty-five cents an hour. The owner spent his evenings at a bar across the street, so I had early experience of managing a small enterprise.

My job fit in well with my school schedule, as I could study during the afternoon. Being on the high school cross-country team, I could also attend the practice sessions in the afternoons, and also the meets, which were always early on Saturday mornings. I was encouraged by my "save and have" parents to open a savings account and thus learned another lesson: being prepared for the "rainy day" was an important aspect of my father's job as a life insurance salesman.

By the time I had graduated from high school in 1942, there was no question in the minds of most American males that they had an obligation to serve in the armed forces. That is not to say that everyone was pleased to receive a "greetings" from the selective service board. Patriotism comes forward at an early age, enhanced by community, church, school, and even politics, and should be continued in tune with the times in succeeding decades. Patriotism in 1942 was defined in the simple statement, "To serve in the country's defense."

I enrolled at the University of Akron in June 1942, where in addition to the academic subjects I took ROTC (the Reserve Officers Training Corps), my very first experience with the Army. I immediately felt a sense of pride when I put on the uniform. Close-order drill and lectures on varied aspects of Army life were the centerpieces of ROTC training for freshmen. I was never impressed by instruction, which was conducted by a lieutenant who rambled. It appeared to many freshman that we were guinea pigs who provided a means for the Advanced Class students to exercise their leadership abilities.

I received my induction notice in December 1942, a scant four weeks after my eighteenth birthday. The draft board delayed my induction until I finished the semester, and then I found myself on a train bound for Fort Hayes, in Columbus, Ohio. It was on a rainy March 8 that I sat, in an old railway car clouded with cigarette smoke and anxiety, listening to the train's wheels clicking along the track. The only one in my car who had the foggiest notion of the adventure we were on was a draftee who had spent time in the Civilian Conservation Corps (CCC). Most of us listened as he explained in a loud voice what we should expect when we reached Forts Hayes. The anxiety continued, regardless.

During our short stay at Fort Hayes we had a crash course on the Army. Then we boarded the train (its destination a military secret), wearing wrinkled field uniforms and three-quarter boots and leggings, carrying duffel bags full of clothing on our shoulders. Our arms ached from inoculations.

We now knew that officers wore bars on their collars and that enlisted men wore stripes on their sleeves. We knew we should salute officers and that the sergeants with the most stripes seemed to be the ones running everything. We had taken aptitude tests and had our first "kitchen police" (KP) experiences. A private first class, or PFC, who had interviewed me had said that my classification test score made me eligible for aviation cadet training and that I should so inform the First Sergeant at my first unit. He also had me sign a paper acknowledging that I had taken the loyalty oath required of all recruits.

Now here we were, entering one of a long line of railroad coaches with straight-back seats, soot stained inside and out. For the next three days, we would ride the rails to Camp Bowie, Texas, near Brownwood, where we would take basic training in the 652d Tank Destroyer Battalion. The officers and non-commissioned officers of the battalion were already there. As we passed through the gates of the Tank Destroyer (TD) Training Center, we couldn't help but notice the large mural of a tiger's head with its jaws tightly clamped around a tank. We would soon find this was the TD shoulder patch we would be wearing. Next we saw the barren stretch of land and the patchwork of tar paper–covered buildings where we would be living and training for the next two months. Here and there were more substantial, yet bleak, buildings used for headquarters, logistics, and medical purposes.

I soon found myself sitting on my duffel bag with about a hundred other trainees. A captain wearing crossed sabers (the cavalry insignia) on his collar announced that we were now members of the battalion's reconnaissance company and intimated that we should be proud to serve in it. At the moment, with the temperature over ninety degrees, sweating, covered with soot, and wanting nothing more than a glass of water, we fell far short of being proud of anything. After the first days' training, however, we sensed the first bit of *esprit* forming.

The training included drill, map reading, marksmanship, first aid, and the like. We also applied sticky grenades to the underbellies of tanks; received greater than normal communications training, including Morse code; received daily training in armored car (M-8) maintenance; and spent many hours in nighttime reconnaissance patrols. Considerable time was devoted to 57 mm and 37 mm antitank gunnery.

The focus of our training was primarily on what had been learned during the North African campaign. Several of the officers and noncommissioned officers had served in North Africa, and they played an important role in the training. We were reminded that what applied to desert warfare might not be applicable elsewhere, but the doctrine was still to hit enemy tanks fast and hard and then maneuver out of range. Speed was essential!

The eighth week of basic training consisted of a forced march from Camp Bowie to Fort Hood, Texas; it took five days. Fort Hood had been developed to an extent far beyond Camp Bowie, especially the troop facilities, motor parks, and ranges. The battalion was issued the new M-36 Slugger tank destroyer and commenced training with it on the ranges. The M-36 contained a 90 mm gun, mounted in a light, open turret on a tank chassis. What it lacked in crew protection it made up in firepower, speed, and mobility, compared to its predecessor, the M-10A1, which mounted a 76 mm gun. There were thirty-six tank destroyers assigned to each TD battalion. Without question, tank destroyer training was challenging. It was very intensive, requiring considerable physical stamina, and the officers and NCOs were top notch.

While at Fort Hood I applied for the aviation cadet program. I spent two days at Kelly Army Air Corps Field taking tests, which I passed. As was the case with thousands of eighteen-year-olds, my urge to become a pilot was partly the work of the Air Corps's first-class public relations campaign. A few days after I returned to Fort Hood, ten of us were told to report to the orderly room at six in the morning. The next night I was in Camp Maxey, near Paris, Texas, awaiting transfer to the Army Specialized Training Program (ASTP), which had been established to ensure an adequate number of trained engineers after the war.

A week later I was at North Texas State Teacher's College in Denton. One of the first things I did was to tell the detachment commander that I thought a mistake had been made, since I had applied to the Aviation Cadet Program and not ASTP. To my surprise I was reassigned to Shepard Army Air Field, near Wichita Falls, to await assignment. I spent several weeks there, watching P-51s taking off and landing, hoping that eventually I would be in the cockpit of a fighter plane. Finally I was assigned to the Army Air Corps Student Training Detachment at Texas A&M, in College Station. My fellow students and I, designated as Aviation Students (A/S), commenced a five-month college program, which included a month of ground and flight training in Piper Cubs at nearby Bryan Airfield.

All of this came to an end in late March 1944, on a Saturday morning, when we were assembled in Guidon Hall to view a filmed presentation by Gen. Hap Arnold, commander of the U.S. Army Air Corps. He notified us that we were to be reassigned to the ground forces, because of the likely need for greater numbers in those branches. His pronouncement was the mother of all morale busters, but it was also a test of one's ability to persevere, to continue to march— traits of extreme value in the military.

It wasn't long before I found myself at the Mississippi Ordnance Plant (MOP) near Jackson, assigned to the 3166th Artillery and Fire Control Company of the 616th Ordnance Base Automotive Maintenance (OBAM) Battalion. The battalion was just organizing and was about to initiate eight weeks of basic training; I was a member of the 40 mm antiaircraft director repair section. I completed my "second" basic training, which was neither challenging nor conducted by officers and NCOs who possessed training skills. Luckily, the battalion would never see combat.

In December 1944, the battalion arrived at Camp Kilmer, New Jersey, and boarded a Victory ship for the trip to Europe in convoy. Initially the battalion was stationed in Ashchurch, England, repairing tanks and wheeled vehicles, in a factory-type setting. Then we were transferred to Etretat in France, where we found ourselves up to our armpits in tracked-vehicle evacuation and repair.

Mack in Marseilles, France, in May 1945, at the end of World War II. The battalion to which he was assigned was being shipped to the Pacific in support of the "pending attack" assault on Japan, which never took place.

When the war in Europe ended, on May 8, 1945, I had been in the U.S. Army for over two years, and aside from the German buzz bombs and the v-2 missiles in England, I hadn't been exposed to enemy fire.

Many of my high school classmates had not been as fortunate. Malcolm Graham had died in an airplane crash as an aviation cadet. John Fuchs had died fighting as an infantryman, and Lt. Harold Weaver had been killed leading a rifle platoon in 1944.

Our battalion had already been tagged to redeploy to the Pacific. Shortly after the guns went silent in Europe, we found ourselves riding the rails to Marseilles and boarding the ship that was to take us through the Panama Canal to Luzon, in the Philippines. I can't remember that anyone in our company contested being reassigned to the Pacific. We hadn't been in combat and hadn't accumulated the points required to get home. To their credit, the leaders in the battalion placed emphasis on our being among the few Army units to serve in two theaters during World War II.

Mack in the Philippines after Japan surrendered. His unit was bivouacked outside Quezon City and until February 1946 recovered Army vehicles for sale by the War Assets Administration.

On August 6, 1945, during our unescorted Pacific crossing, an atomic bomb vaporized Hiroshima. Three days later a second atomic bomb was dropped on Nagasaki. Upon landing in Luzon, our battalion set up in the outskirts of Quezon City, outside of Manila. We worked for the War Assets Administration, disposing of vast stocks of equipment that had been assembled in preparation for the invasion of Japan. Our battalion collected the noncombat vehicles for sale to Philippine citizens and companies, as well as to those of other Asian nations. Many combat vehicles and equipment found watery graves in Manila Bay.[1] In the fall of 1945, a "bring the boys home" campaign resulted in wanton destruction of material.

Gen. Douglas MacArthur decreed that for every American assigned in the Philippines, one Philippine citizen would be hired. Logistics units such as ours led a rather good life, with someone to make beds, do KP, shine shoes, build recreational facilities, and improve cantonment areas. Our closest involvement with combat was accepting the surrender of isolated groups of Japanese soldiers. Also, the Hukbalahaps (known as "Huks," partisans who had resisted the occupying Japanese under Luis Tarluc, a known Marxist) now commenced a terror campaign against the collaborators, who were being protected by elected Philippine leaders.[2] Units like ours initiated greater security precautions, in the event the Huks extended their attacks to our units, which they didn't.

One night, as I was watching a movie in our dayroom, the First Sergeant came in and read the names of three men who would leave in the morning for the replacement depot and the trip home. My name was on the list, and three weeks later, early in the morning of March 11, 1946, I was getting off the city bus in Akron, two blocks from home.

The euphoria of being home lasted only a few days. After three years in a disciplined environment, I had the satisfaction of knowing that I done my part, small as it had been, to defend my country. Still, when I compared notes with friends, I could see that though I had a lot of campaign medals, I had done nothing worthy of a decoration. After a week of visiting different bars every night with Dick Forbes and other friends, the subject changed from Army stories to the immediate future. The choice was whether to go to work or go to college under the GI Bill.

If ever there was an outstanding program, it was the GI Bill; there's no doubt that it ensured America's later position in the world. So it was that with several hundred other veterans I stood in the registration line at Kent State University. Former combat infantrymen, fighter pilots, submariners, POWS, men who had been wounded, and even a noncombatant ordnance type stood in that line. Not knowing exactly what I planned to do in the future, I selected mathematics as my major and German as a minor. My tuition, books, and equipment fees were paid by the government, and in addition I received a monthly subsistence payment of seventy-five dollars. I lived at home, and since I had no automobile, I generally hitchhiked to and from the university.

I had gone to the University of Akron before being drafted and while in uniform had attended North Texas State University and Texas A&M for short periods. The credits transferred from those institutions permitted me to graduate in June 1949.

But now I must backtrack a bit and mention two events that had great impact on my future. The first was when I met my wife, Margaret Mary Burkley, in April 1946 while on a double date. Marge was a student at the University of Akron; upon her graduation in 1948, she would work as a home economist for the East Ohio Gas Company. I continue to be amazed at how lucky I was to meet Marge, with all her fine qualities; she became a premier Army wife.

The other event was when a Maj. John Carter, U.S. Army, infantry, introduced himself to Dick Forbes and me in the temporary student union building during the winter of 1946–47. Major Carter was visiting Kent State prior to organizing a Reserve Officers Training Corps program for the fall of 1947. He took time to explain ROTC to us, emphasizing that for veterans it was possible to go directly into the advanced class and upon graduation to receive a commission as a second lieutenant. At Kent, commissions would be in the infantry branch only, at least initially. Carter had been an infantry platoon leader, company commander, and battalion operations officer in the southwest Pacific during World War II. He was a very likable person and was obviously bent on seeking eligible veterans who could apply for the advanced class.

During the next month I met with Major Carter several times, and in late spring 1947 I registered to take ROTC in the fall of that year. During my service years I had had hopes of becoming an officer, as evidenced by my aviation-student stint and also an application for the Infantry Officer Candidate School program while in the 616th OBAM Battalion. After joining ROTC, I began examining my prospects after graduation; in comparison to teaching school or working my way up to management in industry, an Army commission was appealing. It looked like it would be a challenge in a changing world, and I liked that. I made up my mind to compete for a regular Army commission, and I was fortunate enough to receive one upon graduation in June 1949. Marge and I were married on July 2, 1949, and soon began our Army life, in which we were to be sometimes together, sometimes not.

In July 1949 I was ordered to report to Fort Knox, Kentucky, for an interim assignment as a platoon leader in an armored infantry company until the Officer's Branch Immaterial School, a required junior officer orientation course, began in August at Fort Riley, Kansas. Marge remained in Akron until mid-August 1949, when we traveled with a friend and his wife and daughter to Fort Riley. Marge and I rented an apartment in Junction City and lived quite the austere life, with minimal furniture; our bed was a mattress and steel frame, our bureau was a steamer trunk, and our dining-room table was a card table, to which we added a used couch, two folding chairs, and orange-crate end tables. We bought our first automobile in Junction City, and with that felt we were slowly edging toward affluence.

The students attending the Fort Riley course were 1949 graduates of the U.S. Military Academy and ROTC; all had received regular commissions. Aside from the fact that the West Point graduates knew each other better and formed some cliques, there was very little emphasis on the sources of commissions. If there was any animosity between West Point and ROTC, it existed only to a very small degree, among the wives. As an example, one evening Marge and I had the officers from our platoon and their wives over to our apartment. Most of our guests happened to be West Pointers. One of the academy wives asked Marge if she could see her *Howitzer* (the Military Academy yearbook). Marge responded that she was sorry, but we didn't have a *Howitzer,* since her husband had gone to college. The wife was miffed, but the academy graduates roared with laughter.

The course, an introduction to the branches of the Army, included classes in military justice, communications, weapons familiarization, map reading, and other basic subjects. I believe that the course was most beneficial in the aspect of meeting peers with whom you would serve again in the future. The West Pointers were all assigned to combat branches; ROTC officers were in the combat branches initially for two years, with some permanently commissioned thereafter to the logistics and administrative branches. In December 1949, we received our orders to the Basic Infantry Officer's Course at Fort Benning, Georgia, an intensive five-month course that emphasized infantry weapons qualification and company and platoon tactics and administration.

After spending the Christmas holidays in Akron, Marge and I drove south to Fort Benning, where we were able to find quarters in the Camellia Apartments, just off the post. The majority of the Basic Class lived there, so Marge got her first opportunity to meet the wives of the students in the course.

The year 1950 was to be one of joyous events and also a major surprise for new lieutenants who had never really commanded at any level. The training we received revolved around the expertise needed to operate efficiently at the infantry platoon and company level. I found that there was one aspect of the tactical training at the Infantry School in which I took a special interest; it was known as "marching fire." Later in the year, this tactic proved to be very effective for me, when it was necessary for my platoon to engage an enemy objective and limit the effectiveness of its defensive fire.

The tactic called for the use of fire and maneuver to get within fifty to seventy-five yards of the objective, under supporting artillery and mortar fire; at that point the platoon would rise to its feet along a selected line and move forward, directing continuous, aimed fire along the military crest (just below the topographical crest) of the objective. In essence, the platoon leader had to use the weapons he controlled to take over the role of the supporting guns and mortars, whose fire was now shifted farther to the enemy rear. Such platoon-level force multipliers as glistening bayonets, accurate and increasingly rapid small-arms fire, and reduced bursting radiuses for ordnance the unit controlled made the enemy reluctant to expose himself. I found out later, researching a monograph on marching fire at the Infantry Officers Advanced Course, that this tactic had been used very successfully during World War II.[3]

Fire-and-maneuver was essential when working your way to an assault position, but the culmination of an attack on other than fortified positions required the platoon's total firepower from the selected assault line, up and over the enemy position. Fire-and-maneuver and "bounding overwatch" use only a part of the platoon's firepower during the last critical moments of the assault. I had no idea I would be employing marching fire in combat within a few short months.

Much of the training was intensive hands-on experience in the field, applying the concepts presented during classroom and map exercises. Emphasis was placed on the squad level, as a basis for the knowledge required in platoon leadership. We also fired most infantry weapons, and our results were recorded.

The basic course included several future generals, namely, Joseph Kingston, Jerry Lauer, Homer S. Long, Marion Ross, Sinclair Melner, and Robert Thurman. The class also included Lt. Sam Coursen (USMA, 1949), who would win the Medal of Honor, posthumously, in Korea.[4]

Marge visited the prenatal clinic a number of times. We knew the day would arrive when I'd have to get her to the hospital in a hurry. The time came unexpectedly as I was returning from mass on Sunday morning, April 25, 1950. Suddenly a car approached from the other way, the driver waving wildly. As we passed I saw it was Sam Mann, a Fort Benning schoolteacher, who lived next door to us. Seeing Marge in the car, I made a U-turn and headed toward the post. By the time I got to the hospital, Marge was already in the maternity section of the hospital. Our first child, Mary Louise, was born shortly afterward. The joyous event I mentioned earlier had now taken place. Mary Lou could not have been more fortunate: she had a truly nurturing mother. Marge and I had found the post salvage yard and the craft shop a godsend for the production of our first furniture, including a small dining room table, end tables, night stand, and a coffee table. Now a cradle, made from packing-crate lumber, made the apartment more like a home.

In early May I received my orders to report to the First Cavalry Division in Japan. I had received the assignment that had been my first choice. We did not have concurrent travel; Marge and Mary Lou would have a three-month wait until housing became available. Ironically, that would have been a short wait, compared to what actually happened. On June 25, 1950, upward of ninety thousand troops of the North Korean People's Army (NKPA) and a sizable force of T-34 tanks invaded South Korea.[5] Marge and I were not the only ones surprised!

# 2 The Pusan Perimeter

If the invasion of South Korea came as a surprise to Marge, my classmates, and me, it should not have been a surprise to the administration, and in particular to the military leadership, in Washington and in Japan. The higher the level of administrative and military failure in defining and carrying out foreign policy, the greater the cost to those charged with executing that policy. The cost in Korea, a small country about the size of Utah and resembling Florida in shape, was extremely high. The result was the "Forgotten War."

For me and many like me at the lower echelons of the Army, orders were amended. We were to travel light, leave our autos at home, consider all dependent travel to the Far East on hold, and proceed directly to Camp Stoneman, California, for movement to Japan. We assumed Korea was to be the final destination. Most of us little understood the meaning of the changes in major power relationships and the arrival of the Soviet Union as a nuclear superpower, or of the impact of a communist takeover in China and the earlier U.S. withdrawal of military forces from Korea.

For most of us this information would not have had any great effect on our attitudes, other than causing us to ask ourselves how, a mere five years after our country had played a major role in defeating Germany and Japan, we could be threatened by a small communist state on a new battlefield. As I moved closer to Korea, I hoped someone at a high level in our country was asking questions.

When we arrived at Camp Drake, Japan, the Eighth Army Replacement Center, it was more than apparent that we were in a life-and-death situation. Ironically, the expansive officers' club at Camp Drake had a less than determined air; senior Army officers, obviously staff functionaries in the Tokyo area, still played their Sunday afternoon games of bridge, their biggest challenges being their next finesses. I had the distinct impression that we, not the North Koreans, were the problem for these officers; we were about to upset their years of pleasant service in a conquered country. This was confirmed when a colonel in mufti came to the bar and through his silky white mustache demanded that we quiet down and act like officers and gentlemen, so that others could enjoy the club.

Prior to our arriving at Camp Drake and entering the replacement pipeline, a number of actions had been taken to stem the NKPA attack. First of all, on June 30, 1950, President Harry S Truman had authorized General MacArthur to deploy ground forces to Korea. On July 4, the first U.S. commitment, the battalion-sized Task Force Smith, had deployed near Osan, forty miles south of Seoul, to slow the NKPA advance as the U.S. Twenty-fourth Infantry Division was being deployed. On July 5, Task Force Smith had been attacked by a North Korean division, supported by thirty T-34 tanks; the task force had expended its ammunition and fought its way toward Taejon, to the south. On July 7, the UN Security Council had passed a resolution authorizing a unified command in Korea; Truman had appointed General MacArthur as its commander. Through July 22, the Twenty-fourth Division had fought a gallant delaying action against superior NKPA forces until relieved by the First Cavalry Division, which Lt. Gen. Walton Walker, commanding the Eighth Army, had deployed along with the Twenty-fifth Division. By August 1, the Eighth Army was withdrawing into a perimeter around Pusan, a UN defensive line that was ninety miles long in the west and about sixty miles across in the north, generally following the Naktong River.

American divisions were being committed with extremely low percentages of their authorized strengths; with shortages in weapons and ammunition, particularly artillery, as well as of field gear and rations; and equipped with only light tanks. The lack of readiness was apparent as we prepared to depart Camp Drake during the first week of August 1950. I can remember being issued an M-1 "single-shot" carbine and two rusty ten-round ammunition clips. I asked if I could have an M-1 rifle—a five-hundred-yard-range, hard-hitting weapon—to exchange with a rifleman in my new platoon, since it was known that many riflemen were being armed with only the smaller carbine version, which had a shorter effective range. I didn't get one. There were also no first aid packs; "I could get one along the line." There were no compasses available; again, "Get one along the line." There were no carbine bayonets, and there were no boots, even in the clothing store.

On the morning I was scheduled to depart via train for Fukuoka, on the southernmost Japanese island, to take a small Japanese ship to Pusan, I was instructed that I would be escorting infantry volunteers from the Eighth Army stockade, the Big Eight. A warrant officer went with me as my assistant, and we ended up with two railway cars of armed prisoner volunteers. Their sentences were to be mitigated when they joined their units in Korea. As I recall, there were about ninety prisoners, at the time nearly the equivalent of a rifle company in foxhole strength. I had no problems with the prisoners.

Three days later the warrant officer and I were in Pusan, with our charges and their orders to combat units. After sitting for two days in a dilapidated, feces-strewn building, we finally were driven to a railhead to wait for a train to Taegu. Another replacement lieutenant was assigned to take half of the prisoner replacements to the Twenty-fourth Division; I would escort the other half to the First Cavalry Division.

After two false starts, the train headed north. About half of its windows were broken; as a result, smoke and soot poured into the cars. The other lieutenant told me that he had heard at least one member of the Basic Officer Class at Fort Benning had already been a casualty. When we arrived at the Twenty-fourth Division railhead, that division's replacements detrained. The lieutenant shouted, "Keep your head down!" I didn't know his name, and I never saw him again.

First light was appearing and it was raining when we reached the First Cavalry railhead at Taegu; I had my charges get off the train and climb onto a platform at the railroad siding. Most of the men took off their packs and headed for the nearest bushes to relieve themselves. I walked to the end of the building and jumped down to what appeared to be a main road running into Taegu. Immediately I could hear screaming coming from a building on the other side of the road. A few minutes later, two South Korean policemen dragged a woman from the building and sat her down on the ground. It looked as if she had been beaten severely, and she was bound; she struggled to free herself, to no avail. When the policemen saw me, they carried her behind the building.

It was 6:15 A.M. on August 9, 1950. There was an odor of kimchee (made of pickles seasoned with garlic), smoldering charcoal, and human waste—a blended smell that would always remind me of Korea, the Land of the Morning Calm. In later years it would be reminiscent of suffering, death, and cruelty; at the time, it was nothing less than sickening, until a fresh breeze lightened the stench a bit.

A few days' experience in Korea would make me wonder how a nation as backward as this could ever manage to advance into the modern world. Years later, when Pres. Lyndon Johnson visited Korea, he must have had a similar attitude. He was to tell President Park Chung Hee that he should remember that it had taken the United States almost two hundred years to get to where it was, socially, economically, and politically. Park's response was that Korea wasn't going to wait that long. He was right! I had not yet detected the determination of the South Korean people, and I probably hadn't fully by the time I was to leave this poor country, already subjected to a half-century of foreign occupation.

As the rain stopped, a group of children ran to us and watched some of the replacements open their c-rations to eat a cold breakfast. Several of the men offered crackers, cookies, and candy to some of the children; the whole group rushed forward with open hands. Minutes later, two Army trucks with First Cavalry insignia on their bumpers arrived, with a South Korean policeman in the first truck. With a circular swing of his arms the policeman chased the children away, some of them dropping their "treasures"; the soldiers immediately badmouthed the policeman. They had just witnessed one of the cruelties of Korea: childhood lost in the maze of war.

Twenty minutes later we were at the First Cavalry Division replacement company; the prisoner replacements were marched away by a lieutenant after I gave him the men's records. I was processed in ten minutes; the routine included filling out a "quickie" will and a hand-printed pay-allotment form, both in pencil, and a check to see if I had my "dog tags" (metal identification tags hung around my neck on a small chain). I asked a captain in the processing tent if there was any place I could get a drink of water. He responded that I had just learned my first lesson in Korea—don't let your canteen get empty. Welcome to the First Cavalry Division, Lieutenant Mack.

I was at least convinced that here everything possible was being done to get replacements forward without delay. There was no formal briefing for replacements, but the captain told me that the Eighth Cavalry Regiment, to which I was assigned, was at the moment engaged in a strategic withdrawal to the Naktong River. It had sustained heavy losses and needed every man it could get its hands on. He confirmed that the Eighth Cavalry, like the other regiments in the division, had only two battalions instead of the normal three—another post–World War II budget restraint.

A half-hour later, a warrant officer, three enlisted men, and I were bouncing along a very dusty road in a three-quarter-ton truck on the way to the Eighth Cavalry command post (cp). The terrain on both sides of the road was fairly flat, but to the north we could see higher ridges. We soon arrived at a turnoff, where there was a large group of trucks spread out in a field, with several squad tents erected nearby.

To the right of the road, behind a small knoll, there were two tents, several jeeps, and a number of antennas. The driver told us this was the Eighth Cavalry Regiment's cp. We were met by a captain who said he was the regimental adjutant (the staff officer who handled administrative matters). He directed the warrant officer and three men to one of the tents. After taking my records, he told me I would be going to the regiment's First Battalion, commanded by Lt. Col. Robert Kane. The battalion was in the process of setting up a defense on the Naktong River, after having fought its way back from a place called Yong-dong, where it had suffered heavy casualties.

About then a jeep came flying up the road, dust flying every which way. It had come to pick me up. Wishing me good luck, the captain departed for one of the tents, and I departed in the jeep. We finally reached the battalion, after a more than half-hour tour of the area. The driver was obviously lost, and it wasn't until I saw a small, one-story building with several vertical antennas sprouting from the roof that we found the CP.

The building turned out to be a former schoolhouse. The first person I met was a lieutenant from the headquarters company. He led me into the building to meet a captain, who stated that he was the battalion adjutant. At the far side of the room was a group of officers, all facing a map pinned to the wall. The captain took me over to where the group was standing and told the battalion commanding officer (CO) that a replacement lieutenant had arrived. Kane said, "Send him to C Company," without turning around.

I could see that the CO was pointing to the blue line on the map that was the Naktong River. I could also see that one segment of the Naktong was divided into three sectors, with a C marked in the center one—obviously C Company's sector. The battalion adjutant asked me if I had written home. I had, but I hadn't known the return address; he gave me a preprinted card with C Company's address on it. I wrote a short note on it and put it in a box marked for outgoing mail.

Ten minutes later I was at the foot of a high mountain, in the company CP. The company commander, a First Lieutenant Taylor, gave me a rundown on his map of his platoon dispositions, which were on the other side of the mountain. He told me he would point out where my platoon was located when we got to the observation post (OP) at the top of the mountain. Then he went into detail about the readiness of the company in general; he briefly covered these items:

- Because of the hasty deployment, some men wore only low-quarter shoes.
- About half of the riflemen carried M-1 carbines instead of M-1 rifles.
- There were no communications with the platoons on the river, as the distance exceeded the range of the SCR-536 radio. There was a plan to lay wire.
- Because of a shortage of C-rations, each man received only two meals a day.
- There was a shortage of hand grenades; each one had to count.

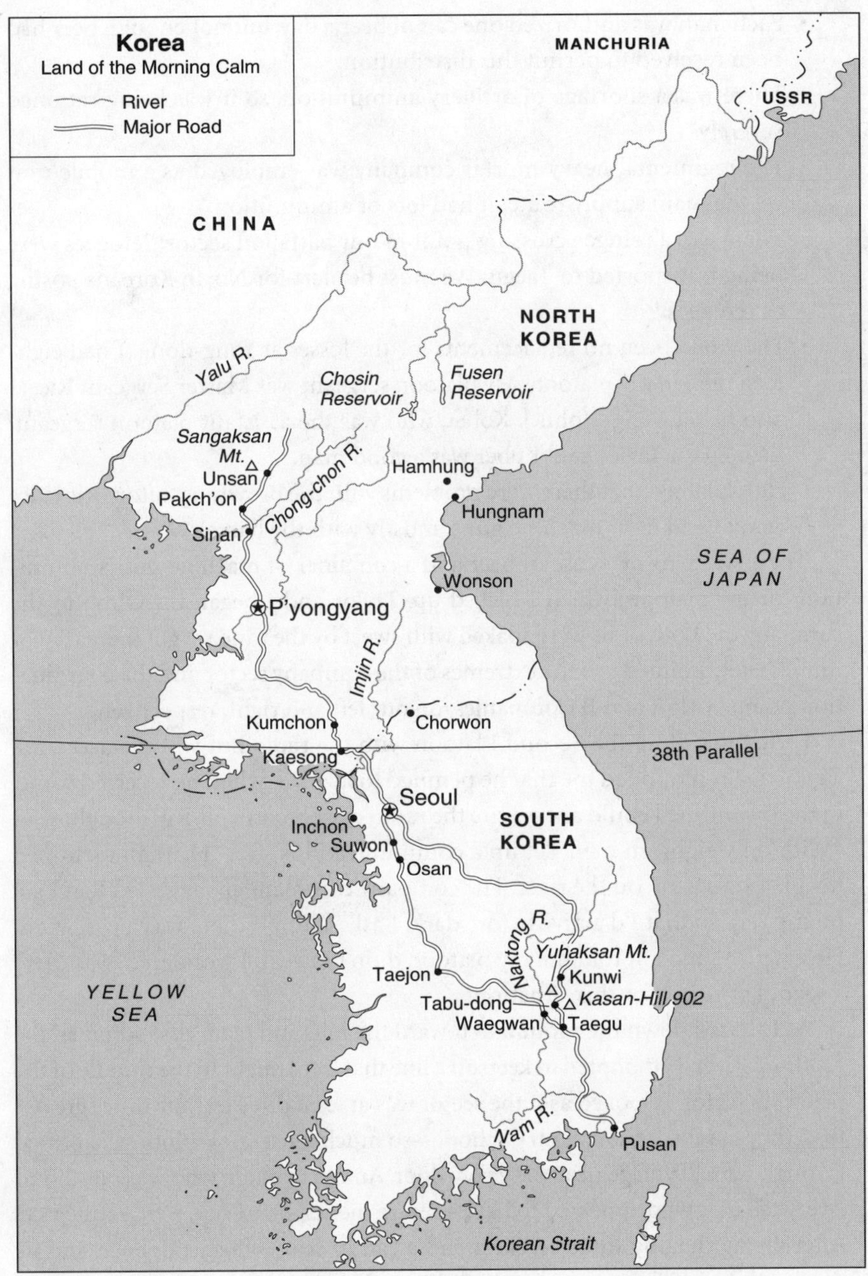

Korea
Land of the Morning Calm
River
Major Road
MANCHURIA
USSR
CHINA
NORTH KOREA
Yalu R.
Chosin Reservoir
Fusen Reservoir
Sangaksan Mt.
Unsan
Pakch'on
Chong-chon R.
Hamhung
Hungnam
Sinan
Wonson
SEA OF JAPAN
P'yongyang
Imjin R.
Kumchon
Chorwon
Kaesong
38th Parallel
Seoul
Inchon
Suwon
SOUTH KOREA
Osan
Naktong R.
Yuhaksan Mt.
YELLOW SEA
Taejon
Kunwi
Tabu-dong
Kasan-Hill 902
Waegwan
Taegu
Nam R.
Pusan
Korean Strait

- Each man was authorized one can of beer a day, but not enough beer had been received to permit this distribution.
- There was a shortage of artillery ammunition, so it was being rationed severely.
- The regimental heavy mortar company was employed as a mobile unit on the main supply route; it had lots of ammunition.
- There was a refugee crossing point in our battalion sector; refugees were being transported to Taegu. We must be alert for North Koreans posing as refugees.[1]
- There had been no replacements for the losses at Yong-dong. I had eighteen men in my platoon. My platoon sergeant was Master Sergeant Rice. I also had a M.Sgt. John J. Kober, who was the assistant platoon sergeant; Lieutenant Taylor said Kober was a good man.
- He explained that there were problems with the Browning automatic rifles (BARS) and light machine guns, mostly with the barrels.

There was part of a case of beer and a container of machine-gun ammunition for my platoon, which I picked up. Taylor and I began the climb to the company OP. Both of us were soaked with sweat by the time we got there. Taylor immediately pointed out the extremes of the company sector and the coordination points with A and B Companies, on our left and right, respectively.

I tried to call up the Second Platoon with the radio but was unsuccessful. Taylor again reminded me that he planned to lay wire when he received some; in the meantime I could always site the radio closer to the OP. My thought was, "With only eighteen men, set up a communications site?" He then identified my platoon sector, on the river. The company commander suggested that I get on my way, so that I'd arrive before dark. I asked him if there was a password. He gave it to me but told me my platoon didn't have it. I wondered, was there a school solution for this situation?

As I started down the mountain toward the hills and plain that adjoined the Naktong River, I attempted to keep on a line that led straight to the middle of the platoon's sector. It looked as if the sector was at least three or four times greater than they taught at the Infantry School—so much for school solutions. I passed through a small village near the valley floor. An old woman, who was blind, and a very tall boy, who appeared to have a severe mental handicap, were eating rice. After giving the boy some crackers and a can of fruit, which I opened and he devoured, I picked up a bowl and put some rice in it for him. The woman continued to eat her rice, and with that I continued toward the river.

I had lost sight of the river, but I continued on, guided by a peak on the high ground across the river. As the sun was touching the high ground on the other side of the river, I thought I heard voices. Moving cautiously, I realized that there were several Americans talking just ahead of me. The platoon sergeant (Master Sergeant Rice), the assistant platoon sergeant (Master Sergeant Kober), the platoon medic (Corporal Thacker), and the platoon messenger and radio-telephone operator (Private First Class Ramos) were lying down, resting their heads on their packs.

The four were stunned as I walked up and placed the beer and the container of machine-gun ammunition on the ground, the last rays of the sun glistening on my gold second-lieutenant's bars. I had two thoughts: one was that perhaps the reason I hadn't been able to raise them on the radio was that their set had been turned off; the second was that one NKPA soldier with a burp gun could have taken out the whole platoon headquarters. I introduced myself; Rice, the platoon sergeant, told me, in so many words, to get my ass down before someone shot me.

I took Sergeant Rice off to the side and told him that effective right then I was taking the platoon over, that he worked for me, and that he was never to address me again as he had just done. I also let him know that if he had a suggestion as to how to improve the efficiency of the platoon, I would be all ears, but he should put it in the form of a recommendation. It was dark when we returned; I had Rice get under a poncho with me, so we could turn on a flashlight, and show me how he had the platoon deployed. He sketched three strong points on a piece of C-ration carton (we had no map); they were positioned along the sandy shore of the Naktong. He told me he had five men in the left-flank strong point, and also the light machine gun; four men in the center strong point, with a BAR; and five men at the right-hand strong point. I asked him if the strong points were maintaining squad integrity (that is, if the men in each were all of the same squads); he wasn't sure about this. "We'll check out the strong points first thing in the morning," I told him, and I started preparing a foxhole for the night.

At first light, Rice and I moved along the back side of the berm on our way to the left, or southernmost, strong point. When we arrived I met the Third Squad leader, Sergeant Saito. I found that the left strong point had two rifle-men (both with M-1 carbines and each from a different squad), the machine gunner and assistant machine gunner, and Sergeant Saito. I told Saito that he should have the men dig deeper foxholes and make sure everyone was awake and alert during the day and that at least two were awake at all times at night. I asked the light machine gunner to lay his weapon on (that is, aim it along) the designated "final protective line." When he swiveled the piece so as to fire directly into the base of the hill across the river, I told him it would be better to

Sergeant Edmon, Sergeant First Class Saito, Corporal Rictwell, and Corporal Bartly, in Korea, early in the war.

tie in his fire with that of the Browning automatic rifle in the center strong point. Thereupon, I got down and swiveled the gun to the right and showed him how this would give him that famous "band of fire" the Army spoke of, which the enemy would have to run into if they attacked across the river.

It was obvious that Sergeant Rice was irritated that I had asked the question of the gunner and had shown him how to lay in his weapon. Rice's remark that the machine gun had been aimed at the trail across the river told me that he had forgotten how to employ this weapon in the defense. I explained how it was done as we moved on to the center strong point.

As we moved on to the center strong point, I asked Rice where the Third Squad's BAR was. He said it had been turned in for repair while they were in Japan and hadn't been returned. It was becoming very evident to me that the readiness of my platoon was questionable, which I told Rice. He told me that the enemy would have to get across the river before we would be in danger. I pointed out all the debris on the shoreline and the sandbars extending above the surface of the water, which was becoming more shallow every day. He had no response.

At the center strong point, I met Sergeant Bragg, the leader of the First Squad. Bragg had two riflemen, with M-1 carbines, and a BAR gunner. One of the riflemen was from the Second Squad, "because there are only three people left in my squad," Bragg explained. I went through the same routine with the First Squad, asking the BAR man to show me where his sector of fire would be if we were attacked from across the river. Like the machine gunner, he indicated a point target across the river, and I followed up by showing how to lay in the BAR on a final protective line.

I had yet to see an M-1 rifle and was about to say that I must be leading a carbine platoon, but I didn't say it. I had counted only seven fragmentation grenades in the First and Third Squads. I let Sergeant Bragg know that the platoon OP was directly behind him, about a hundred yards back, and that if we were attacked he could expect the platoon headquarters to move to his position to add to the defensive fires. Bragg said he would dig some additional foxholes for just that case.

Finally we got to the right-hand strong point and found Sergeant Bebb, the Second Squad leader, had his men stacking logs in front of their foxholes. I commended him on his initiative and was surprised to find that all of his riflemen actually had M-1 rifles and that his BAR man had laid in his piece across the beach in the direction of the center strong point. I recommended that he add sand to the log emplacements to reduce the visibility of the position, and then I told Sergeant Rice, "What a good idea Bebb had on reinforcing his strong point; let's have the others do the same." About all I got from Rice was a grunt. So I passed on the 50-percent-awake night time instructions to Bebb and told him what a fine job he was doing.

As we started back to the platoon OP, a round of small-arms fire cracked over our heads. We all flopped to the ground. This was my first time under enemy fire in Korea. I looked around and discovered that there were seven of us on the ground. I was a bit embarrassed, to say the least, because of the adverse impression it might have had on me.

When we got back to the OP, Rice told me outright that I was being too rough on the men. My only response was, "If we had been attacked last night, Sergeant, those guys across the river would have cleaned our clock. We are in a little better shape now, but we've got a hell of a lot of work to do." I detected a shrug of his shoulders. Later, Sergeant Kober asked if he could talk to me in private. Kober told me that half of the beer was gone. Then he showed me eleven cans, each with a small puncture in the bottom that had been made by a knife or a bayonet.

I got everyone in platoon headquarters together and told those who had bayonets to hand them to me, in their scabbards. Upon inspection of the three bayonets, I found that Master Sergeant Rice's had aluminum residue on its tip. He owned up to having drunk the beer the night before, so I took him aside once more: I told him he was relieved of his duties and to get his gear together. Rice and I started back toward the company OP to a point where we could communicate with it by the platoon's radio. I notified the company commander of what I had done and told him I had detailed the reason on a note that Rice would carry back. I also sent a sketch of a plan for daytime and nighttime positions. The plan called for the platoon to occupy in the daytime higher terrain that afforded better observation, and at night forward positions where we could hear and see a close approach of the enemy.

Before Rice and I departed, I told Sergeant Kober that he was now the platoon sergeant and that I wanted him to sketch out a plan for daytime and nighttime positions. When I returned, Kober showed me a sketch, which included position-occupation times. It was very close to the plan I sent back to the company commander, so much so that I said, "Let's follow your plan, Sergeant."

The plan called for the strong points to cover each other as they leapfrogged back to their daytime positions at first light, and to reverse the procedure before last light. Additional nighttime positions were prepared, to add flexibility as well as security. Even so, I was aware of the danger of having no map and no communications with the company OP, although we had intermittent radio contact from the daytime position. On the first day that we executed our new plan, our situation brightened a bit; I was notified that a sergeant first class and three replacements were on the way to me, laying wire as they came, and that an artillery concentration—a map reference point for adjusting artillery fire— was being placed on the far side of the Naktong. The company commander said he also had a map for us.

We watched the replacements as they came down the bald mountainside. Using binoculars I could see them laying the field line. An hour later, they were about five hundred yards away when Sergeant Kober said, "Hey look at this, Lieutenant!" Sergeant First Class Thomas D. Shea was arriving with not only the three replacements—Korean Augmentation to the U.S. Army (KATUSA)—and the field wire but also a sound-powered telephone, a BAR, two cases of C-rations, machine-gun ammunition, twenty cans of beer, and the promised map of the area.

Late that afternoon I talked to the company commander on the sound-powered telephone and coordinated the artillery concentration on the far bank of the Naktong. Then Sergeant Shea, Sergeant Kober, and I had a brainstorm on the defensive setup; I immediately saw that of the two sergeants, Shea was the more knowledgeable tactically, but Kober was more experienced in enforcing the rules. In due course Shea, at Sergeant Kober's suggestion, became the platoon sergeant, or as I would say, he was platoon sergeant for operations and Kober for administration. Regardless of the Army's scheme of things, it worked well for the Second Platoon, Company C.

Shea gave me the details on the Korean replacements: two spoke no English, and one spoke only a little. Shea recommended that we give them some on-the-job training in which we emphasized commands in English, like those to hit the ground, fire, crawl, run, and move out. The instructions were that each Korean soldier was to have an American foxhole buddy who accompanied him at all times. The Koreans were assigned one to each squad, and squad integrity was restored by returning soldiers to their regular squads. Shea had been a combat drill instructor in his last assignment and without doubt was skilled in instructing and organizing, a definite plus for building effectiveness in the platoon. In less than a month, almost a third of the platoon would be Koreans; they had fired their m-1 rifles, but not on a qualification course.

One night in the third week of August, at about 11 P.M., all hell broke loose at the strong point on the left. I could hear the experienced trigger finger on the machine gun firing three-round bursts on the final protective line. I crawled forward to the center strong point, and we heard voices and the sound of men splashing as they forded the river. I ordered the automatic-rifle gunner to tie his fire in with that of the machine gun and requested by sound-powered telephone that rounds be fired at the center artillery concentration; from there I could adjust the artillery fire onto the enemy in front of us. The rounds splashed across the river.

The enemy force appeared to withdraw when we fired our final protective pattern; all firing ceased, and it was quiet forward of our nighttime positions. Then we heard voices again and more splashing as they tried to cross once more. All strong points then fired their protective fires, and I again requested that the artillery concentration on the far bank be fired. The artillery forward observer back up on the company OP "walked" the bursting artillery rounds in front of our platoon and placed several illumination rounds over the river. On the sandbars in the river we saw several forms and at a distance a withdrawing NKPA unit. As I recall, about eight rounds of 105 mm high explosive were fired.

Twice more within the week the NKPA attacked across the river, each time supported by artillery and mortar fire. Our wire communications were cut, but the forward observer would walk his artillery and mortar fire in front of the platoons on the river as the infantry laid down their final-protective fires. The attacks were repulsed.

The payoff on the Pusan Perimeter was in denying superior NKPA forces the small enclave remaining to the UN; it was touch and go at times. If there was any grand strategy, it certainly was not something that could be noted at the platoon or company level. Only the personal guts and perseverance of the forward ground combat elements and aviation strike forces permitted us to hold on to a diminishing South Korea.

Slowly my platoon was strengthened as replacements arrived on the Naktong battle line. From the original strength of eighteen men, the platoon strength increased to thirty-two, including eleven KATUSA, two U.S. replacements, and myself. The KATUSAS at first were not fully accepted by the men, but as they became more effective, with Sergeant Shea's on-the-job training program, I noted a bonding between each KATUSA and his assigned American soldier.

We had received an additional SCR-356 radio, which permitted us to communicate via radio with the company OP through relay, when necessary. Because of the extended frontages that companies and platoons were required to defend, effective communications were an absolute necessity for effective use of artillery and mortars. Additionally, there was a pressing tactical requirement for two light machine guns in our infantry platoon, particularly to provide effective final-protective-line fire.

Atrocity reports increased during August. We soon learned that the NKPA routinely executed enemy wounded and prisoners. On August 17, forty-plus Americans from the Fifth Cavalry's Regiment's Heavy Mortar Company were executed near Hill 303, not far from Waegwan, and the next day six crewmen from the Seventieth Tank Battalion were executed nearby. I passed this on to my platoon and emphasized how important it was to avoid capture.

On the night of August 23, I received a warning order to assemble my platoon at the company CP, on the other side of the mountain, the next day. The First Cavalry Division was adjusting its line to the east of Waegwan. I had my strong points withdraw to their normal daytime positions. My platoon arrived at the company CP before noon on August 24. While there we learned that the Eighth Cavalry now had its Third Battalion, which would take over the First Battalion position on the Naktong. The First Battalion sector had taken on the name "Peaceful Valley," primarily because the NKPA's less-than-determined thrusts were being stopped at or near the river line.

At about 2 P.M. we boarded trucks and headed north, destination unknown. As we headed north along a tree-lined road, the convoy sprayed dust on a column of refugees sharing the road. After about an hour on the road, we entered a cut through the mountainous terrain, where we saw a road sign with the romanized letters "Tabu-dong." The trucks came to a halt at an intersection in the village; one road continued north, another west. The terrain was steep in every direction, but steepest directly to the north.

Company C had stopped in an open area between two one-story buildings. It looked like most people had been evacuated. An infantry captain we hadn't seen before was talking to a medical corps captain. When we were assembled, First Sergeant Thaxton called us to attention and introduced the new company commander, Capt. Tom Rounsaville. He had just completed the Advanced Infantry Officer's Course. We never found out what had happened to Lieutenant Taylor, the replaced company commander.

Captain Rounsaville told us the medics were going to check shot records to ensure we had received all the required shots. He said that if we didn't have our shot records, we would have to take a series of shots. Most didn't have their shot records, including me, so we would have sore arms that night.

As the platoons dug in for the night, we received our attack order for the next morning. Our mission was to attack up Yuhaksan Mountain, the high ground to the north, and relieve South Korean units in the valley on the other side. We would jump off at first light; the Second Platoon would lead the attack and relieve a ROK unit near Sabu-dong, in the valley below Yuhaksan Mountain. (See the Pusan Perimeter map.) All night there was the sound of outgoing artillery and occasionally incoming NKPA artillery, probably targeted on the trains area containing ammunition, supply, and other logistics or the regimental CP. Most of us had a restless night, if not from the thought of our role in the battalion attack in the morning, then from the soreness of our arms from the shots.

The next morning my platoon, being in the center company of the battalion attack, led out without any support; there was no specific information on the enemy. I had placed "on the point" two Americans and one Korean; they were the tip of the arrow. The point was the most advanced element in the company column, and the men there displayed great courage with every step up the steep, rock-strewn, tree-covered Yuhaksan. I continued to be amazed at the matter-of-fact bravery of such men. You realize that they hadn't been nurtured on such platitudes as the flag or Mom's apple pie but focused rather on the survival of their buddies, an attitude that is the greatest possible force multiplier.

Suddenly, as quick as lightning, the KATUSA on the point fell to the ground with a bullet in his head. The two Americans hugged the earth for dear life, fearful that the enemy would fire on them. Their courage returned, and they fired, though they saw no targets.

The company commander, at the rear of the column, received my contact report and ordered me to assault. Minutes later I moved out with two squads of the platoon, and we advanced by fire and maneuver (the squads moving

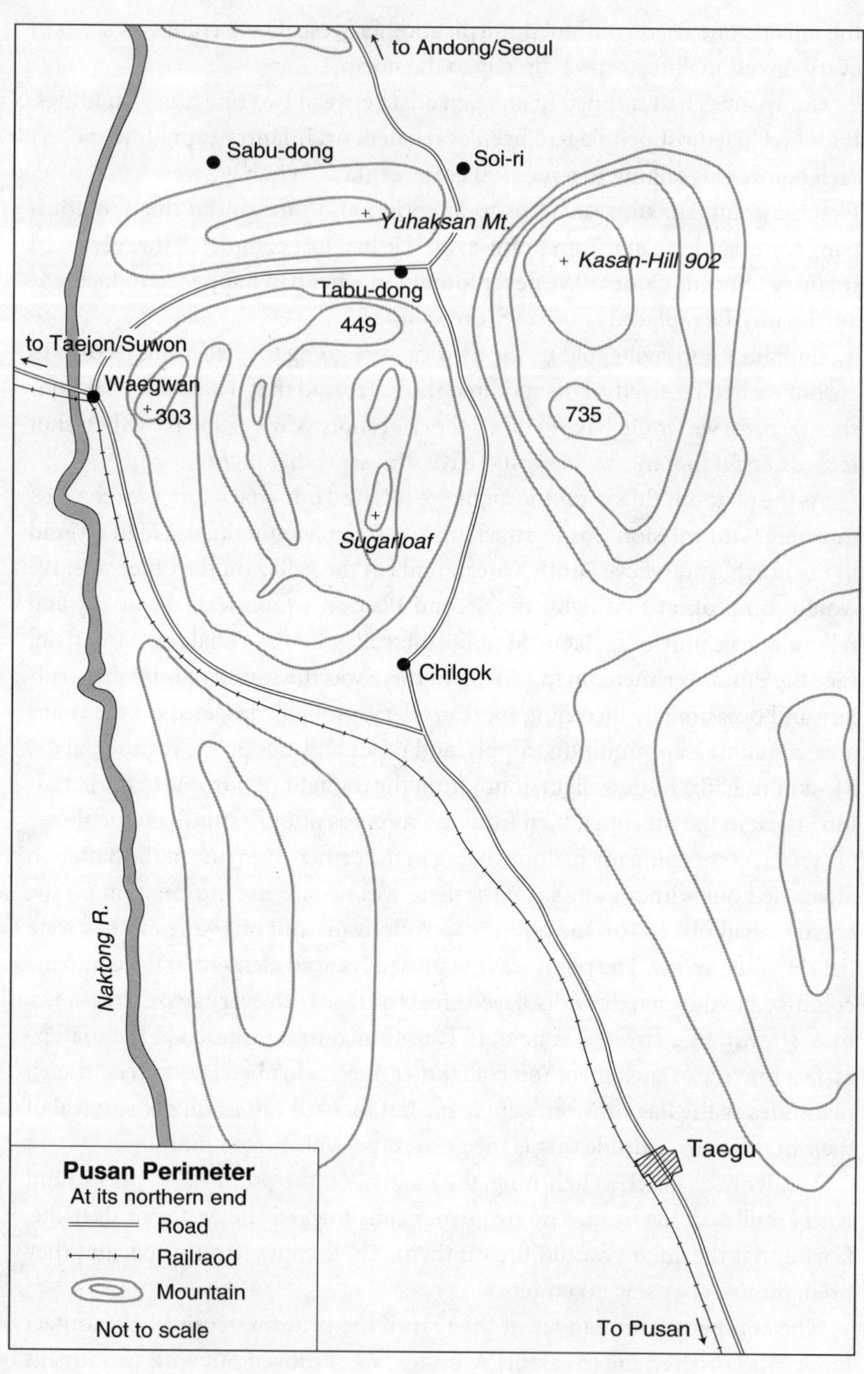

to Andong/Seoul
Sabu-dong
Soi-ri
Yuhaksan Mt.
Kasan-Hill 902
Tabu-dong
449
to Taejon/Suwon
735
Waegwan
303
Sugarloaf
Chilgok
Naktong R.
Taegu
Pusan Perimeter
At its northern end
Road
Railraod
Mountain
Not to scale
To Pusan

forward alternately, as the other covered it with rifle fire). A private shouted, "There are the bastards, to the right of the gully!" With that, two BARs and several rifles spit rounds to the right. Five NKPA soldiers darted up the mountain. Moving the third squad forward, I kept the platoon going as the trees thinned out. Suddenly, several NKPA soldiers rushed away over the crest of Yuhaksan, and we moved slowly after them. The sun now glistened on the platoon's shiny bayonets, and under our automatic-rifle and rifle fire the enemy continued to run. The platoon crossed over the crest and reorganized defensively, still firing.

Ten minutes later the company commander reached the crest, jumped into a foxhole dug by the NKPA unit, spread out his map, and pointed out the trace each platoon was to follow down the mountain. The captain had the only map of this region in the company, so each of the platoon leaders looked for reference points to follow. I picked out a small finger of the mountainside extending into the valley that I could use to guide my platoon toward Sabu-dong and the South Korean unit I was to relieve. Two men began improving the company commander's foxhole, and we three platoon leaders collected around the map, orienting it to our view of the valley. Rounsaville showed his displeasure, shouting at us, "Will you peckerheads spread out before you draw fire?" I had met the other platoon leaders for the first time at Tabu-dong.

From there my platoon and I moved down the mountain for about fifteen minutes. Half a mile from the crest, we saw several enemy moving rapidly toward the valley floor on a finger of land curving to the east. I asked for permission to take them under fire with the 60 mm mortar squad and the 57 mm recoilless rifle (RR) squad attached to my Second Platoon.[2]

The company commander gave permission but told me to coordinate with the platoon on that flank, which I did. I gave the mortar squad leader my approval to fire a registration (preliminary aiming) round on the withdrawing NKPA unit. The puff of smoke and the sound of the explosion came from about a hundred yards beyond the enemy soldiers. The squad leader "dropped fifty" and fired three rounds "for effect." Then I had the 57 mm recoilless rifle squad fire two rounds. At seven hundred yards it was difficult to determine casualties, because of the dust from the exploding rounds, but as it cleared we could see enemy soldiers being assisted and the NKPA group moving at a slower pace. I let the platoon leader on my flank know that the enemy was about six hundred yards in front of him.

We continued our descent toward the valley floor. Soon Shea told me he saw movement near a walled-in village to our left, Sabu-dong. It was the South

Korean company we were looking for, and I sent Sergeant Kober back up Yuhaksan far enough to report our contact and location via radio. The ROK company commander, a Lieutenant Chun, told me he had field wire laid to the top of the mountain, and he also provided me a tracing of a map on a scale of one to fifty thousand (my most cherished souvenir from the Korean War). He had marked the location of several strips of mines which he had laid and pointed out safe lanes through the minefield.

I could see that there was no way I would be able to deploy in the same positions Chun had used. The Second Platoon had thirty-four men now, whereas the ROK Company had three platoons of about thirty men each. Instead, I deployed a squad on each of three fingers of land that projected into the valley and placed my OP and the two weapons squads with the center squad. Forward and to the west of the platoon, on the valley floor, was the unoccupied village of Sabu-dong, with the minefield just north of it. Shea and I saw two NKPA bodies in the minefield.

Finally Lieutenant Chun said, in perfect English, "Nice to meet you, Lieutenant Mack. Good luck! Is there anything else I can do for you?" I requested two things. I asked him, first, to notify our company commander where the communications wire was so we could have sound-powered telephone communications, and second, to leave some 60 mm mortar ammunition. Chun gave us fifteen rounds of mortar ammunition, and he assembled his company in preparation to climb back up Yuhaksan Mountain.

Late that afternoon, August 25, it began to rain; we erected covers over our foxholes and camouflaged the positions with foliage. Sergeant Kober had already started checking out the foxholes, for each one making his standard comment, "Dig it deeper."

This had been my first opportunity to observe ROK troops. It was obvious that they were well disciplined, but there was no way to assess their effectiveness. As the ROK company assembled, I sent a three-man patrol back to the company CP with the platoon dispositions, to alert the company commander that Lieutenant Chun was about to withdraw through the company CP area, and to make sure the company knew about the Korean communications wire. Suddenly Shea shouted to me that North Koreans were getting off trucks on the other side of the valley and moving up the back side of the ridge on their side of the valley. I focused on Shea's sighting with my binoculars and saw a truck, momentarily backing up; several North Koreans off-loaded a large mortar and carried it up the opposite side of their ridge. The truck then went north on the Kunwi-Sangju road. I had Shea move up higher on Yuhaksan and report the mortar to the CO with the radio.

To ensure that the enemy ridge area was watched continuously, I set up a schedule involving all seven NCOs and myself, each having a three-hour stint. At last light on August 25, I heard Ramos, his ear to the sound-powered phone, say, "Roger, Charlie Two here; loud and clear"; he handed the telephone to me. I told the company commander about the North Korean heavy mortar and requested that artillery fire be placed on the suspected heavy mortar site behind the enemy ridge. He responded that I should use the 60 mm mortar attached to my platoon, even when I reminded him that the target was out of its range.

About 2:00 A.M. on August 26, my platoon received heavy mortar fire, which we believed to be coming from behind the enemy ridge. The platoon on my right flank also reported the heavy mortar fire and confirmed my estimate of the mortar's location. The enemy had an excellent view of the Company C positions. I could hear the low-pitched *ka-rumpf!* and see the flash as each round was fired. I again requested a fire mission, this time giving the approximate coordinates of the mortars. The company forward observer (FO) took the request, and minutes later 105 mm artillery rounds were dropping on and behind the enemy ridge. The enemy mortars stopped firing. I had no casualties in my platoon.

About 5:30 A.M. on August 26, I received an order to lead a reconnaissance patrol to the foot of the enemy ridge, withdrawing if I drew fire. I took Sergeant Bebb's Second Squad, less two riflemen who remained on the center position. We headed for Sabu-dong, which we thoroughly searched as we passed through. The village was abandoned, but we noted one fairly tall building that contained tons of rice. Some of the rice had been gathered in large cloth sacks, as if it were to be transported on the two A-frames leaning against the building. The KATUSAs filled their packs with rice.

At the north end of Sabu-dong there was a well-worn path that led toward the enemy ridge; I noted fresh shoeprints in it. The roof of the last house in the village had been partly blown away, and there were two dead NKPA soldiers inside. Before leaving the village I observed the enemy ridge and its approaches, but I could see no movement.

Unknown to me, Sergeants Shea and Kober, following our progress from the platoon's position, thought they saw enemy movement three-quarters of the way across the valley. There were ten NKPA soldiers west of the trail, apparently setting up an ambush for the patrol. Shea also saw a small NKPA unit approaching Sabu-dong from the west. Our patrol was now midway across the valley. The North Koreans at the suspected ambush position were exercising maximum stealth. Shea had the mortar squad fire on the ambush position after pointing out where our patrol was. The first round went over the ambush, but after an adjustment, three rounds were fired for effect. The NKPA soldiers, none of whom were dug in, rose almost in unison and with much yelling ran for the NKPA lines.

When Shea's first mortar round burst, my patrol hit the ground, thinking it was an enemy "incoming." But when the next three rounds landed and the NKPA soldiers began shouting, I knew it was friendly fire. I had my patrol fire on the running enemy; the BAR man was to fire two magazines. Two North Koreans fell. Regrouping my patrol, I commenced the return back across the valley, planning to bypass Sabu-dong to avoid getting ambushed. About fifty yards from the village, one man yelled, "Wait! I want to get some persimmons!" and jogged toward the village. I turned and called, "Get your butt back here!"

As I turned, I perceived movement behind the village wall and signaled the patrol to get behind a rice-field dike. Then I saw two enemy soldiers stand up. One fired his burp gun, and the other threw a "potato-masher" grenade; I was struck in the shin by two fragments. I crawled toward the wall, concealed by the tall grass on the dike, and about twenty yards from it I threw a grenade. It exploded just behind the wall. From the OP, Shea saw several enemy soldiers run toward the valley.

We were starting back to the platoon position when a man yelled, "Morgan's not with us!" Morgan was the man who had gone for persimmons. With that I shouted to Shea, who was coming to meet us, that I was returning to Sabu-dong to find a missing man. We moved cautiously back to Sabu-dong and found Morgan not far from the persimmon trees, face down. He was alive but wounded. We entered the village and found that my grenade had killed an enemy soldier. We used a wooden door to carry Morgan back to our lines. He was conscious, but he had suffered a spinal wound and had no movement in his legs.

It was to take six hours for four men to carry him to the top of Yuhaksan. He was later evacuated to Japan and then to the United States. One of his buddies in the platoon later received a letter from him indicating that he was regaining the use of his legs.

Back at the platoon OP, I extracted the grenade fragments from my leg and made a report to Captain Rounsaville. I told Sergeants Shea and Kober that I planned to take a patrol into Sabu-dong in the morning and destroy the rice stored there and thus plug one source of food for the NKPA. That night, at 2 A.M., a heavy mortar round landed behind the 57 mm recoilless rifle squad position. I requested a fire mission. As I put the telephone down, our side of Yuhaksan was blanketed with at least fifteen heavy mortar rounds. I could see the glare as friendly countermortar artillery rounds struck behind the enemy ridge. Then I heard Sergeant Bragg's squad, on the left flank, begin firing at a rapid rate; tracers from the BAR formed a barrier across the front of the platoon. As soon as rounds starting cracking over our heads at the OP, I ordered the Second and Third Squads to begin their final-protective-line fire and requested support from the company, to be fired in front of our position.

I could now hear enemy voices shouting orders. Like many forward positions in Korea, we did not have barbed wire with which to hamper an assault. With our automatic weapons laying down the final-defensive-line fires, it was up to every man to take out individual enemy soldiers. With a brief whine and a thudding crash, friendly artillery rounds fell in the prearranged concentration areas fifty to seventy-five yards forward of our position—there is no more beautiful sound than that of your own "outgoing." The enemy's determination to seize our position subsided almost immediately, and when a few illumination rounds began to cast weird nighttime shadows in front of us, we could see no movement.

Once again that night the enemy attacked, and once again we "lit" our final-defensive fires; I ordered our 57 mm recoilless rifle squad to place two rounds on what appeared to be an enemy concentration on our right flank, between the First and Second Platoons. The second attack was weak; the enemy then dispersed and hurried back across the valley. Our artillery dropped on the retreating enemy, but without known results. We soon learned that not all the enemy had retreated; to our surprise, there was firing against our right flank, but again the enemy did not assault the position. We fired the last three rounds of ammunition for our 3.5-inch rocket launcher ("bazooka") and also the 57 mm recoilless rifle to break up their formation before they could attack. Once again our artillery was probably the argument that convinced the estimated NKPA company to withdraw. A half-hour after the last attack, we heard two explosions on the enemy side of Sabu-dong. We found out the next day when we went into Sabu-dong that two more NKPA soldiers had "bought the farm" trying to cross the minefield.

At first light, I sent two men up Yuhaksan to repair the landline to the company CP. The telephone had been inoperative for several hours. The two men would have run into a trap had it not been for an artillery concentration that had been fired between the company OP and the Second Platoon during the night. During the night the enemy, while it kept us busy to the front, had sent a small unit to our rear. My two men found five dead NKPA soldiers at the break in the landline; it appeared they had been using the line to guide them to the company OP when our artillery had killed them and broken the wire. After repairing the line my men started back to the platoon.

At about the same time the two men were approaching the North Korean casualties, Sergeant Shea and I, with a seven-man patrol, were entering Sabu-dong. We had counted two North Korean dead in front of the platoon and now saw the two enemy casualties in the minefield. As we came to the building containing rice, we found another dead North Korean; he had been carrying a large sack of rice on an A-frame. I noted five other partially filled bags and one that had been hit by a 60 mm mortar the night before. The attack on our position could have been a cover; that is, they could have been keeping us busy while they gathered rice and while the small unit got behind us. Fifteen minutes later, the building containing the rice was in flames.

Shortly after I returned to my OP, the two line-runners returned. I contacted the company commander and told him about finding the NKPA dead and about burning the rice in Sabu-dong. I also reported the NKPA casualties during the early-morning attack on my position and recommended that a patrol be sent from the company OP to see if there were infiltrators between us. The captain was perturbed that I had destroyed the rice and told me to let him worry about the infiltrators. Then he told me not to initiate any more patrols forward of my position and ended with an abrupt "Out."

He soon called me back and reminded me that I was still responsible for making contact with the other two platoons on my flanks. I figured he didn't want me to misinterpret his order concerning patrols forward of our position. That night on the telephone, the company First Sergeant told me he was trying to get the company commander to check out the platoon positions. (I now had a good working relationship with the First Sergeant and avoided compromising his candor.)

Later in the day I saw seven North Koreans descending into the valley, about six hundred yards to the east of my OP; they were between my platoon and the platoon on my right flank. I requested a fire mission, but initially the company commander denied it because the target was too close to our lines. I replied that if he were at my OP he'd see the large gaps between platoons; I was surprised when the captain replied, "One round on the way—adjust." He put the forward observer on the line. Moments later an 81 mm mortar round landed to the rear of my last sighting. After I gave the FO an adjustment, the target area turned gray with dust; when it cleared, I could no longer see the North Koreans. I reported that we might have evened the score on the "sons of bitches"; the company commander reminded me that that kind of language was unauthorized on a military net.

Less than five minutes later, I heard automatic rifle fire in Saito's squad on the right flank. Kober reported that he had seen two North Koreans running "ass over tea cups," and he thought that was what Saito was shooting at. As the enemy was too far away by then to engage effectively, Kober shouted to Saito to cease firing. Shortly thereafter, the company commander told me to maintain contact with the platoons on our flanks. I told him that we had visual contact with both platoons and that we sent a two-man contact patrol every other day. There was no comment, other than "Out!"

It was relatively quiet on August 28; the rice in Sabu-dong continued to burn, the smoke rising in a column that could be seen for miles. When our resupply detail returned, it brought ammunition for the mortar and for the recoilless rifle, rations, and mail, the latter boosting the morale significantly.

On August 29, early in the morning, we received several heavy mortar rounds, and, expecting an attack, I put the platoon on 100 percent alert—keeping the platoon awake and battle-ready. But when no attack occurred by 3:30, I reduced to 50 percent. At about the same time, Sergeant Shea pointed out on the distant Northern skyline in the direction of Kunwi a distinct lightening behind the enemy ridge. The light came from many vehicles, of which the lead ones finally became visible at the end of the enemy ridge near Soi-ri. When I attempted to notify the company, the First Sergeant told me the CO had told him to awaken him only if the North Koreans were attacking the OP. I told the First Sergeant he should report the lights to the battalion. The First Sergeant advised me that only the CO contacted the battalion but that he'd notify the battalion operations sergeant.

Otherwise, for the most part, August 29 was a dull day—no mortars, no attacks, nothing; for the infantrymen it was a fine day. Late in the morning Shea saw what he believed to be an armored vehicle sticking its nose around the edge of the enemy ridge on the road. A fire mission was requested, but none was fired. Sergeant Kober also spotted about twenty North Korean soldiers at the foot of their ridge, heading toward Yuhaksan. The group stopped abruptly at a stream that ran through the valley. We were surprised to see them enter the stream, apparently to take baths. The bathing party ended abruptly when three 60 mm mortar and two 57 recoilless rifle rounds landed among them. Four bathers were seen being evacuated, and others, sans uniforms and weapons, ran toward their ridge. When I reported the incident, the CO responded that artillery would have been more appropriate!

Early on August 30, lights similar to those seen the night before were seen on the skyline in the direction of Kunwi. Later we heard the roar of distant engines, as if vehicles were taking positions on difficult terrain. This second movement of heavy vehicles looked like a buildup for a major attack. I reported this to the company, only this time I told the operator on duty to wake up the company commander, which he did.

When the captain got to the telephone, I reported what we were seeing and reiterated that we had now seen the North Koreans using vehicle lights two nights in a row. I told him that it looked like the NKPA were preparing for a big push. As soon as I said this, he let me know that if there was any significant buildup, word would come down the chain of command. This was a sign of the apathy that seemed to have set in. Too much emphasis was being placed on information concerning enemy threats being disseminated from above, probably all the way from General MacArthur in the Dai Ichi Building; not enough attention was being paid to observations from the frontline units. Rounsaville was adamant that if he were to report what I said to battalion, it would soon be looking for a new company commander. There was a crisp "Out," and the line went dead. Looking at Kober and Shea, I told them, "I think they believe we're seeing things." Then I told them that we had better prepare the men for a fast withdrawal.

It was especially quiet in the valley and on the enemy ridge during the day on August 30. Smoke still rose from the burning rice in Sabu-dong. It was another dream day for infantrymen; I had the men shave, wash their socks and underwear, and take quickie baths in one of the streams flowing through our position. About noon the First Sergeant called and said there was mail; we sent a "mail patrol" of three men.

At about 1:00 A.M. on August 31, North Korean heavy mortar fire began falling on the forward side of Yuhaksan, mostly hitting the area adjacent to the road to Tabu-dong. First Cavalry countermortar fire whined over our heads and fell on the back side of the enemy ridge; the enemy mortar fire stopped. Next we saw at least six North Korean self-propelled armored artillery vehicles move down the Kunwi road to the cut in Yuhaksan, near Tabu-dong. Again their road lights were on, definitely reflecting not only arrogance and confidence but also the lack of around-the-clock U.S. air support early in the war.

I reported the enemy artillery sighting to the company; a sergeant told me the company commander was keeping the battalion informed, but when I asked him if they knew where the enemy artillery was located, his only comment was that they couldn't see it from the OP position. I gave the sergeant the coordinates of the enemy artillery and told him to give them to the company commander. The enemy self-propelled guns then returned behind the ridge, just as our artillery began falling where they had been. I notified the company commander of their move, and shortly the friendly outgoing stopped. The captain acknowledged my original report, saying it had been a good one.

At about 5:00 A.M. we heard the rumbling of T-34 tanks at a distance on our right flank, moving down the road toward Tabu-dong. I could make out the figures of North Korean infantrymen accompanying the tanks when artillery flares were fired. Again I alerted the company commander, specifically that there were an estimated ten T-34 tanks and at least two companies of infantry with them, and gave him the coordinates. As I talked, the enemy column stopped and moved into forward revetted (that is, protected with earthworks) positions, which had probably been prepared under the cover of darkness. I gave the new coordinates to the captain, repeating them to make sure they were clear. He replied, "Good reports, Mack; I'll take it from here."

Several minutes later, the area where the North Koreans had been before was lit up like a Christmas tree as the division artillery fired a "time-on-target," or TOT, mission—a salvo in which all rounds were fired so as to land at the same instant. Sergeant Shea and I were completely amazed to see the error that had been made in target identification. I quickly checked the corrected grid coordinates I had given and found I had provided the correct new location of the enemy tanks. Then I notified Captain Rounsaville that the wrong target had been hit. He accused me of being unable to read a map; eventually, however, the FO called in the corrected coordinates, and another mission was fired.

Later, the battalion executive officer investigated the incident, and I, along with others, was interviewed. The executive officer found that the mistake had been accidental and not one of negligence on anyone's part. He apparently saw the report I had provided after making a damage assessment, for which I had had a good vantage point, following the second TOT. The assessment included three self-propelled artillery pieces severely damaged and two T-34 tanks with their guns pointed toward the ground, the tracks of each appearing to be damaged. Alongside the tanks there were an estimated eighteen forms, apparently enemy dead.

On August 31, late in the day, Shea and Kober both reported that they had seen increased activity on the enemy ridge and they had heard more heavy vehicles moving about behind it. Along the ridge it appeared that some antiaircraft positions were being reinforced and sandbagged. I reported this to the company commander, and we awaited a fire mission, which never came. It began to rain very hard. I had the feeling that what we had seen so far meant we were truly within a ring of fire. It looked to me as if the NKPA were going to let us sit on this damn mountain and circle behind us up the road to Tabu-dong.

It was 1:00 A.M. on September 1 when Sergeant Kober wakened me from a peaceful dream of being back in Georgia with Marge and Mary Lou. He shook me as we were walking around Camellia Apartments. It didn't take long to realize why he was waking me up. The top of the Yuhaksan near the pass was being pounded by artillery, round after round, and we could see the enemy ridge outlined by the continuous glare of the NKPA cannonade. Kober remarked that he hoped the incoming didn't tear up our communications wire to the company.

I contacted the company, and a sergeant told me they were receiving artillery fire. I told him to let the company commander know as fast as possible that even through this rain we could see a parade of tanks, self-propelled artillery, and trucks heading into the cut at the eastern end of Yuhaksan.

The line went dead. I kept blowing into the sound-powered telephone to get a response, but to no avail. As Shea, Kober, and I sat there looking to the east, where the road came into view prior to entering the pass, we saw our artillery and mortar rounds falling among the enemy tanks and infantry, but the procession continued into the gap. Now and then an enemy tank burst into flames, probably the result of hits on its unprotected external fuel tanks. We saw tracer rounds emanating from the unseen friendly lines, and also streams of tracers coming from the lower reaches of the enemy ridge near the road, as well as from the tanks. At daylight we saw NKPA casualties lying along the road, and here and there someone attending to them.

There was no doubt that the Soviet T-34 tank, which had served the USSR so well during its "Great Patriotic War," was now serving the NKPA well. I was more convinced than ever that our Achilles' heel would be the defense of Yuhaksan Mountain and that the NKPA had no intention of attacking us on the north side of this massif. It was becoming very obvious, as the enemy drove relentlessly against our defense and through the mountains, that the NKPA was dead serious about breaking through our thin lines. I hoped that someone up the line was looking for a better place at which to blunt this obvious North Korean drive to roll up our forces.

I must have sounded like one pissed-off lieutenant to my sergeants when I said, "Here we are, sitting on our butts, with no communications, with these bastards trying to exert their will, while we watch." Once again I sent two men up Yuhaksan to repair the field wire, telling them to be watchful for any enemy who might be setting up an ambush. After they left I stood and looked up the valley to the west, a probable route into our positions at the foot of Yuhaksan Mountain.

Earlier, when I arrived in Korea, I had heard that when the ROK II Corps had fallen back along the Sangju–Kunwi–Tabu-dong–Taegu road, which led directly to the UN combat operations and logistics center in Taegu, General Walker had sent Col. "Mike" Michaelis's Twenty-seventh Infantry Regiment, "the Wolfhounds," to plug the gap (referred to as "the Bowling Alley") where the route ran between these high mountains. Anywhere within a mile or so from there, you could hear the sounds of artillery reverberating up and down it; "bowling alley" was an accurate description of this terrain feature.

It was about dark on September 1 when the men who had been running down the wire returned with details about the situation in the company CP. They had continued on to the company OP, to make sure that their repair had corrected the problem. They returned with new batteries for the platoon radio, a bundle of mail, and a report on the casualties in the company CP.

Luckily, it appeared that there had been minimal casualties. Sergeant Thaxton had told them there was no talk of withdrawing from Yuhaksan but that if that happened, the Second Platoon would cover the withdrawal of the platoons on its flanks. Hearing this I told Shea and Kober that I wanted everyone in the platoon to have their packs ready so there would be no delay when we got the word. When we checked out the new batteries in the radio, we found that by moving less than a hundred yards up the ridge we could get radio communications with the company. Having communications relieved my mind greatly.

My morale went up even more when I opened a letter from Marge in which she placed the latest picture of Mary Lou—so close but so far away. Many years later the term "single parent" would be coined, but we should never forget that single parents have been around for a long time, especially the wives of soldiers at war.

Just after dark, the enemy commenced firing its heavy mortars once again, some of the rounds landing on the ridge along Yuhaksan. This time, however, the enemy mortars had been displaced forward into the valley on the south side of their ridge. My first thought was that their displacement forward meant a plan for an attack. I told Shea, "It might be a mistake, but let's give them a little countermortar fire with our 60 mm mortar." A few minutes later, 60 mm rounds were falling on the enemy heavy mortar positions, and with that the firing stopped. We jumped into our foxholes as the enemy sent a few rounds of artillery against our one 60 mm mortar. We sweated it out in what were by now substantial foxholes. No one was hurt. We had five 57 mm recoilless rifle rounds left, and I gave my approval to firing two of them at the enemy heavy mortar positions.

When I reported firing on the enemy heavy mortars, the company commander told me he hoped I'd never do that again. I accepted his comment without comment. As I sat there after midnight on September 2, I heard the low groan of armored vehicle engines clanking down the road toward the pass at the extremity of Yuhaksan. I saw the fiery exhausts of the vehicles, and I heard the enemy artillery and mortars as they fired on First Cavalry units defending the pass. I now saw what appeared to be muzzle flashes from infantry weapons moving up the eastern extremity of Yuhaksan toward the First Battalion positions.

I called the company commander and was about to give him the coordinates of the enemy infantry when he said "Wait" and put the FO on the line. I told him it looked like enveloping enemy infantry could also be heading for our platoons near the valley floor. When I mentioned this to the FO, he put Captain Rounsaville back on the line, who told me to keep my ass where it was until I had an order to withdraw. There followed a sharp "Out!"

About mid-morning on September 2, three F-80 Shooting Star jets screamed over our position heading toward the cut between Soi-ri and Tabu-dong. My platoon messenger handed me the telephone. It was the company commander, very annoyed that I hadn't had the phone to my ear. He told me to get all my men in their foxholes, since we were to receive air support soon. I informed him I already knew about the air support, since the first jets had just passed over my position. I blew into the telephone, but he was gone.

For the next ten to fifteen minutes, the jets and then three F-51 Mustangs (as the propeller-driven P-51 was now designated) bombed and strafed the tanks and infantry in and near the pass. We saw several tanks on fire and infantry scattering. As one F-51 came out of a dive at the cut, it suddenly shot straight up, the front of the aircraft engulfed in flame. We all watched to see if the pilot jumped, but no parachute was visible, and the aircraft fell behind the enemy ridge. A tip of flame and a plume of black smoke rose behind the ridge. I contacted the company commander again and told him that antiaircraft artillery (AA) on top of the enemy ridge was firing on the support aircraft. He acknowledged my report, but no fire was delivered on the enemy AA units.

For the remainder of the day there was an artillery duel between UN forces and the NKPA. Occasionally I saw a T-34 tank race out of its revetment, fire down the road several times, and return. I got the FO on the telephone, and he requested a fire mission that blanketed the revetments, starting a fire on one of the tanks.

Toward evening, I received word that Company A was receiving fire from infantry moving from the east. We could hear the firefight, but then all was quiet. Around midnight on September 3, I heard incoming rounds hitting the top of Yuhaksan once again. I talked to the FO on the phone, and he said that the enemy had control of the road south of Tabu-dong; our resupply route was gone. The First Sergeant then got on the telephone and told me that the platoons on my flanks had been ordered to withdraw and that my platoon was now the rear guard for the company.

Once again the telephone line was out, so I sent Sergeant Kober up the mountain until he could contact the company with the radio (again we had a radio problem). It began raining very hard, and as he told me later, he found it difficult to negotiate the rock-strewn mountain in the dark. He finally established contact with First Sergeant Thaxton, and then he and the three men with him waited, staying alert, for a withdrawal order. Kober heard firing to the west; knowing the company CO wanted to know about any attack in that direction, he contacted Thaxton again.

The First Sergeant now told Kober that the First and Third Platoons had arrived at the company OP and that the Second Platoon could now withdraw. Kober looked at his watch and saw it was about 3:30 A.M. About 4:00 A.M., Kober arrived back at the platoon with the order to withdraw. The rain was descending in torrents, and the sound of fighting in the east and west seemed even closer.

I sent the messenger to the right-hand squad to instruct it to withdraw to the platoon OP. I had Sergeant Shea instruct the left-hand squad to withdraw up its finger of the mountainside to where it joined the finger where the OP and the Second Squad were located. Yuhaksan wouldn't be ours much longer. We had gone a ridge too far.

# 3   **Withdraw and Attack**

Every man in the platoon was soaked to the skin as we began slogging up Yuhaksan. Sheets of cold rain impeded every step and caused us to slip and slide in the dark. The only direction that made any sense was up. When we reached the junction of the two finger ridges, where we were to be joined by Sergeant Bragg's First Squad, it had not arrived. Could it have passed through the junction and moved farther up the mountain?

We could have shouted, but in the heavy rain and wind no one would have heard us, and if anyone had, it would probably have been the North Koreans. So I had the platoon sit down, putting two men above and two below as security. It wasn't long before I had a platoon of sleeping men, getting what little comfort they could, their ponchos warding off the rain while the water flowing down the mountain swirled around and soaked them beneath. They had been awake for more than twenty-four hours.

Bragg's squad arrived about 5:15 A.M., and I had him give his men a break; they seemed to fall asleep as soon as they sat down. Then, mercifully, the rain subsided, and a mist took its place. By 6:30 the mist was very thick; we were actually in the clouds, I believed. I instructed the platoon to fall into column, move quietly, keep intervals, not to talk, and not to lose contact with the man ahead. Sergeant Kober took up the rear, to make sure we didn't have any stragglers. The men were so exhausted that it was quite possible that one or two would just say "F—— it" and sit down. Slowly the sun burned through the mist, and by 8:30 we were almost to Yuhaksan's ridgeline. When we reached the top, I found a clearing and looked down into Tabu-dong. We had arrived at what appeared to have been Company C's OP; there were empty ration cartons and signs that NKPA artillery had paid a visit.

Looking down at Tabu-dong, I saw a column of men climbing the smaller mountain to its south. I made my first attempt to contact the company on the radio and was surprised when the company commander's radio operator responded. He told me that they were just starting up the mountain south of Tabu-dong. Suddenly, we began receiving small-arms fire from the west, along the ridge. I placed a machine gun and 57 mm recoilless rifle among outcroppings of rock, to protect our rear. I requested artillery, but I was no longer on Lieutenant Chun's map, so I was unable to give coordinates of the enemy position. I used our identification panel (vari-colored canvas, five foot panel, normally used to identify ourselves to friendly aircraft) to mark our position, and the FO was able to direct fire to our west. Five minutes later the artillery rounds fell on the ridgeline, a hundred or so yards to our west. I told the FO I was starting down the side of Yuhaksan and to give us one more volley to keep the enemy off our back. He did, and I withdrew my machine gun and recoilless rifle. In record time we rejoined Company C.

Captain Rounsaville told me that the battalion commander had given up my platoon as lost but that he'd had faith we'd find our way home. As we started up the mountain south of Tabu-dong toward Hill 449, I looked back at Yuhaksan Mountain. Sergeant Shea remarked, "We really did go a ridge too far." I agreed with him and added, "But I sense we'll be back up this way again, Sergeant." We would be!

As the platoon moved in the company column up the spine of a ridge that overlooked the road junction at Tabu-dong, part of another company delayed the North Koreans with 75 mm recoilless rifles, machine guns, mortars, and artillery, all of which had seen use in World War II and were well worn. The North Korean Thirteenth Division had complete control of the pass, on the direct route to Taegu. Yuhaksan to the west and the ancient fortress of Kasan (Hill 902) to the east gave the North Koreans observation to the south toward Taegu and control of the fast route to that town.

As we looked down on the road immediately south of Tabu-dong, we could see trucks, jeeps, and trailers being searched and looted by NKPA soldiers. The looting may have been a blessing, because it gave us time to withdraw to more defensible terrain and in fact to escape the ring of fire within which the North Koreans had attempted to trap us. "Killer" Kane had succeeded in slipping us out of a cul de sac—though we weren't completely out yet.[1]

As the day progressed, the North Korean units began moving south on the Taegu road, a narrow valley section that was an extension of the Bowling Alley.

A company-sized unit turned west from the road and began to ascend Hill 449 toward us. The mortar FO with Company C directed 81 mm mortars on the enemy column, which stopped momentarily. Then a small number of North Koreans continued through the mortar fire and started uphill. As they came closer to the top, I had my platoon open its final-protective fires. The attack halted without an assault, with the exception of two or three men who continued to climb. The company commander ordered "Cease fire," but one of the enemy continued toward my platoon; he was taken under fire by one of my riflemen and killed.

Darkness came on fast, and it began raining again, making observation difficult. All platoons in Company C intermittently began final-protective fires, and 81 mm mortars began falling on the road below. I continued to be amazed at the stamina and determination of ordinary soldiers, who, weary as they were, faced a great variety of situations, all of which placed them in harm's way. The efficacy of U.S. foreign policy continued to depend squarely on the sights of M-1 rifles and carbines. After our last final-protective firing, Shea, Kober, and I went to each man and checked his ammunition status, reminding them all that we had to make every shot count, since there would be no resupply. The battalion's basic load of ammunition was down below on the road, captured by the North Koreans.

At about 9:00 P.M., the alert was given that the battalion was to continue its movement to the south. The battalion had infiltrated the NKPA line, and there was a small opening to the south through which it could still extricate itself and set up on more defensible terrain. The headquarters company commander and several others had been seriously wounded and were being carried in their ponchos. Second Platoon led Company C and had responsibility for maintaining contact with the company ahead. The column was one man wide and extremely long. The accordion action of the column as it stumbled along a ridge on a pitch-black, rainy night resulted in several losses of contact with the platoon behind mine. Sergeant Shea was continually falling back to restore contact with it.

At one point, considerable small-arms and automatic fire could be heard from the head of the battalion. Company C was ordered to send a platoon to clear a blocking position set up by a North Korean unit. My platoon was selected, and I took two rifle squads forward; the battalion operations officer guided me to the vicinity of the blocking position. I deployed my squads among the many boulders on the ridge, from where I could see the intermittent enemy firing on a rise to the left of the trail. Rounds began ricocheting off of the rocks, and then the enemy fire ceased.

The first morning light refracting through a mist revealed a concealed route to what appeared to be the flank of the enemy position. I hurriedly moved the squads toward the enemy flank; apparently the movement was undetected, since the enemy did not resume fire. There was room for my two rifle squads to extend on line, side by side. Although we were still a distance from the enemy position, I ordered the squads to fire on it, and then we moved forward toward it. I was surprised to find when we reached the position that the enemy had withdrawn, leaving a Maxim machine gun and several dead behind.

I reorganized my squads on the blocking position and sent Ramos to let the operations officer know the route was now clear and to bring the rest of my platoon forward. Moments later the enemy made a feeble and unsuccessful attempt to retake the position; the platoon arced grenades into their midst. By then, my platoon was down to about one or two clips of M-1 ammunition per riflemen. At about 8:00 A.M. on September 5, the battalion ascended a long saddle leading up to the foothills north of Chilgok. Taegu was not far down the road.

My platoon had received General Walker's "stand or die" order of July 26 before I had arrived in Korea. Withdrawal, strategic or otherwise, was unacceptable. General MacArthur confirmed on July 27, 1950, that withdrawal must cease. I neither saw nor heard any overt reaction to these orders; our own withdrawal continued. High command was learning its first lesson; stand or die orders early in the war failed to consider that in a case-by-case basis withdrawal was a means of trading space for time needed to build the UN forces.

After three days of retrograde movement from Yuhaksan Mountain, there was little doubt that the shortening of the defense line, enhancement of the supply line, and the introduction of additional UN forces, in conjunction with the lengthening of the NKPA supply lines and their increased vulnerability to air attack, had increased the UN ability to defend the Pusan Perimeter and to build up slowly an offensive capability. The NKPA made the strategic mistake of trying to press the UN forces all along the line rather than to apply the principle of mass and drive us into the sea with a major concentrated thrust. They missed an opportunity to disrupt our operational and logistics capabilities, which would have had a high probability of forcing us out of Korea. As the Eighth Cavalry Regiment backed away from sizable NKPA forces, it was trading terrain for a better defensive and ultimately offensive capability.

An advance is a positive note in battle. A withdrawal, for whatever reason, is viewed by the soldier as a delay in victory and leads to morale-busting drudgery. General Walker's "stand or die" order was beyond doubt intended to define the conditions his defense must attain, as he awaited the reinforcements he needed to go on the offensive. His sense of flexibility permitted adjustments in the line, as it should have. Regardless, there was a drop of morale in my platoon. As we prepared our position on a hill north of Chilgok, my men were edgy and quarrelsome; a note of fear seemed to have invaded their voices.

To a degree my own disposition was much the same, except that I realized I had to rise above it if I were to be an effective leader. My responsibility was to maintain my platoon's effectiveness and build esprit, mine included. At the platoon level the leader has to act as a member of the team, and this should never be forgotten. This required me to adopt healthy personal relationships with my men, an egalitarian attitude, and high personal standards, and also to accept personal risk. Weapons inspections, detailed defense planning (good foxholes, final-protective fires, and observation techniques), offensive training and planning, and emphasis on the health and welfare of the men are the means of promoting healthy attitudes, especially during periods of low combat activity. Discipline at the combat-platoon level is a matter of establishing cohesiveness in an environment of extreme violence. Leadership at this level is personal.

As we dug deeper, cleaned our weapons, and did all the other things infantrymen do in the defensive mode, our minds wandered toward home, and anxiety built over events many miles away. One soldier, a private who had just received two letters at mail call, became so upset by his misinterpretation of his wife's and his best friend's letters that he temporarily "lost it" and sat outside his foxhole during an enemy artillery barrage. The wife's letter announced that she was pregnant; his best friend's letter mentioned he had taken the man's wife to a movie and a bar and that they had had coffee in the wife's apartment. The man suspected that his friend was responsible for his wife's pregnancy. Sergeant Kober told him to write his wife and find out which month she was in, and to avoid mentioning his suspicion. Two weeks later the man received a letter from his wife that pinpointed conception while he had still been home. He thanked Kober for his suggestion. When Kober told me about this, I commended him for what he had done. I knew well that he was keeping a sharp eye on morale. NCOS play a valuable role in maintaining stability in the Army, and as in this case, they need a few social-work skills in addition to their military ones.

Early one morning, Company B, Eighth Cavalry, located on a low hill to our east and forward of Company C, received extremely heavy artillery fire. The NKPA had concentrated their artillery on units south of Tabu-dong, using the protection of the surrounding mountainous terrain. At first light, Sergeant Koburn, Shea and I scanned the Company B position; we could see that several wounded and dead had been collected near the road. Jeep ambulances arrived to carry the casualties away. Sergeant Shea commented that Company B was always getting pasted by the enemy because all the gunners had to do was "use the glitter of the trash in Company B's area as a reference point." I told Shea he was absolutely right and that that was reason enough to keep our area policed.

Looking out past Company B's hill to the Tabu-dong–Taegu road, I could see a column of eight U.S. medium tanks and accompanying infantry, moving north; they began to pass from view, masked by B Company's hill. As the last tank disappeared, the *crunch!* of NKPA artillery landing on the tank-infantry force could be heard, and the smoke and dust of exploding enemy rounds rose above the hill. Slowly the tanks reappeared the way they had come, backing down the road, firing their main armament as they moved.

Infantrymen reappeared as well, also withdrawing. I could see several men being assisted by others and two loading a limp body onto a tank as it backed up. As we watched the rearward movement of the tank-infantry force, several F-51 Mustangs buzzed the platoon's hill, pulled up, and flew directly toward Hill 902, the ancient fortress of Kasan. One after the other, the pilots peeled off and dove to the west toward the NKPA's artillery, self-propelled artillery, and tanks in the valley near Tabu-dong. Smoke and dust rose against the backdrop of the distant Yuhaksan Mountain, now just a hazy outline. We hoped a goodly amount of the NKPA's armor and artillery had been disabled.

We knew that the infantry was going to have to retake the high ground around Tabu-dong. The Second Battalion, Eighth Cavalry, had fought gallantly to prevent the enemy from gaining control of Hill 902, but it was now in NKPA hands, and its recapture was a high priority. The key to success, however, would be the recapture of Tabu-dong and control of the route to Andong and the north.

From September 5 to 18, 1950, Company C sat on the low hill north of Chilgok in battalion reserve, with Company B to its right and Company A to its left. Aside from receiving daily enemy artillery fire and digging deeper for protection, the First Battalion patrolled and prepared for the anticipated attack northward. We watched the Second Battalion continuously attack up Hill 902 and be repulsed, often after exchanges of hand grenades and small-arms fire. We also watched the mad scramble to seize Hills 570, 755, and 1192, and the ground to the east of the Tabu-dong–Taegu road; elements of the Seventh and Eighth Cavalry Regiments, and D Company, Eighth Engineer Battalion, attacked relentlessly to consolidate these features. Fortunately, due to these actions the North Korean efforts to seize Taegu, a scant eight to nine miles to the south, failed.

Among the peculiarities of the terrain north of Taegu in the Pusan Perimeter were razor-edge ridges, mostly bald; they sloped steeply on both sides and made control of units attacking simultaneously on both sides of the ridge extremely difficult. The result was that company commanders often attacked in a column of platoons, the old "pile-on" concept. Too often these were one-platoon frontal attacks, the least desirable of offensive tactics. In contrast, using two platoons and directing them against the flanks avoided the enemy's principal defensive fires, attacked weakness, and took advantage of the safest route to the assault position. However difficult they were to control, having a platoon on line attack on the flanks avoided the "walk along the razor's edge" of ridgelines, extremely unhealthy places, thus reducing the vulnerability of the frontal attack.

On about September 13, a regimental chaplain, Fr. Emil Kapaun, visited our company and said mass for the troops. He was a fabulous individual, often seen riding a bicycle along rice-field dikes to his "parish." As often as not, his uniform was as tattered and dirty as those of the "grunts" he so respected. The respect was reciprocal.

The men of company C had just changed into clean uniforms. I had thrown my dirty fatigues, with my insignia of rank accidentally still attached, into the "recycle" pile. Later, I was sitting on the edge of my foxhole with Sergeants Shea and Kober when the battalion commander came by, inspecting the line. Looking down, he told me to dig my foxhole deeper, as he would any soldier whose foxhole should be improved. When he had passed by, I told the sergeants, "It's a damn good thing I wasn't wearing my insignia of rank, or I might have been fired!"

Sergeant Shea's response was, "Don't you wish, Sir."

There are two types of people who seem to fail consistently: those who seldom follow the rules, and those who always do. There is an absolute requirement that on the battlefield, the leader must follow. He must know what the rules are but be flexible enough to follow the best possible course of action to achieve the mission.

One day, as I sat with my two senior sergeants, I told them, "We have been sitting on our butts for some time now, and I am sure that soon this company will get an order to attack north toward Tabu-dong." I also told them that I had the feeling that our platoon would have the "honor" of leading the attack—in a column of platoons, as usual. I pointed to a sugarloaf-shaped ridge north of Company B and said there was always a chance that we would have to seize it. Sergeant Shea suggested that we should war-game a Second Platoon attack on the feature, which henceforth we called Sugarloaf. For the better part of three hours we went through all the details, from the time we left our present position until we seized the third knoll on the ridge. Shea put together a little sand-table display of the terrain, in a C-ration carton. We ended up by preparing the order that would be given to the squad leaders; our request for supporting fires; and a plan for the employment of our bazooka, machine gun, 57 recoilless rifle (RR), and 60 mm mortar, as well as for our communications (we decided we would lay wire). None of us realized then how important our war-gaming session would be.

Shea consistently came up with alternative ways to tackle problems. Comparing the actual with the "sand table," he pointed out three little draws, which offered cover, leading directly to the first knoll on Sugarloaf; he also pointed out the optimum positions for the 60 mm mortar and the 57 mm RR during the attack. Perhaps his best suggestion during the war gaming was to have the men drop their packs at the foot of Sugarloaf, to preserve their energy for the assault. We were fortunate to have this tactically proficient NCO in the platoon.

As we focused alternately on Sugarloaf and the model, our attention was drawn to Hill 902. Although it was nearly three miles away, we could see minute flashes near its crest. Through my field glasses I could see what I estimated to be at least a rifle company conducting an assault on the peak. The flashes we saw were hand grenades thrown by the NKPA defenders; evidently the assaulting units were heaving grenades in return. Then I noticed the North Korean defenders begin to withdraw up Hill 902, with artillery landing among them. Finally, attacking units, which we later identified as part of the ROK Eleventh Regiment, took over the ridge running from Hill 902 to the east.

We heard later that an officer from Company D, Eighth Engineer Battalion, which was being used as an infantry company, had been captured and mutilated in an earlier assault on Hill 902, again exemplifying the cruelty of the NKPA.

*Swish* . . . a round of enemy artillery sailed over our position and landed near Chilgok. We got into our foxholes, as a spotting correction could bring the next round onto Company C. Our war gaming was quickly put aside. Sugarloaf was not discussed until the next day, when Sergeant Shea surveyed Sugarloaf through binoculars. He asked me to look at the ridge, and at once I saw what he had seen. There on the first knoll was about a platoon of North Koreans, digging in forward of the crest. I could make out what looked like a heavy machine gun near the center of the position. On the third knoll, about a thousand yards north of the first, was what looked like a company, also digging in.

I contacted the company commander and told him about the sightings on Sugarloaf, getting a rather terse response. Captain Rounsaville called back a few minutes later, however, and told me I had been promoted to first lieutenant, ending with the usual "Out." It seemed to me that if a company commander encouraged soldiers to conduct constant visual reconnaissance, he would learn more about the terrain, a necessity in the infantry.

On September 16, we were informed that the X Corps, consisting of the First Marine Division and the Seventh U.S. Infantry Division, had landed at Inchon the day before. The marines had gone ashore on the island of Wolmi-do and in Inchon proper, with the Seventh Division following, in an assault that had been extremely time sensitive because of the critical tide conditions. We also learned that plans were under way for X Corps to link up with UN forces here in the Pusan Perimeter, where the North Koreans still were advancing all along the line. Naturally a linkup depended heavily upon the Eighth Army's attacking out of the perimeter; it might be possible to trap the NKPA between the Eighth Army and the X Corps. By this time, the NKPA forces had overextended their supply lines and their lines of communication had been under continuous air attack. The Inchon Landing, as a result, facilitated a breakout by UN forces from the Pusan Perimeter.

At first light on Tuesday, September 19, fog obscured the distant heights of Hill 902 and Yuhaksan Mountain, leaving the dew-covered lower ridges and hills sparkling in the occasional sunlight. I could see five figures forward of the first knoll on Sugarloaf. Looking closely with my binoculars, I decided they were planting land mines. With the exception of these five, no other enemy could be seen, either there or on the knolls farther to the north.

About 8:30 A.M., the company commander instructed me and my platoon sergeant to be at the company OP in fifteen minutes; he also gave me a warning order to be prepared to attack within an hour. After telling Sergeant Kober to have the squad leaders have their men prepare for a move, I headed with Sergeant Shea for the company OP, where I joined the other platoon leaders. The first remark by the CO was to the effect of "Will you guys spread out, away from my foxhole?" Then he told us the battalion commander had ordered him to attack the ridge in front of Company B—Sugarloaf, no less—and seize a position from which B Company could continue to attack toward Tabu-dong. He had made a hasty visual reconnaissance of the objective, and because of the narrowness of the ridge, he planned to attack with one platoon "up" and two "back" (that is, one making the initial assault and two in reserve). He would commit the reserve platoons as needed. My platoon would lead the attack and would be the only C Company platoon to attack.

One platoon leader asked if the enemy strength on the ridge was known. The company commander's clipped response was that the leader of the Second Platoon had seen up to a company of infantry on the ridge, with an outpost on the first knoll and mines planted forward of that. He himself had seen about a squad of infantry there; he had no additional information from above—a typical and probably accurate comment. The battalion commander had agreed with the estimate and had laid on an air strike for 10 A.M. We'd have limited artillery support and plenty of 4.2-inch and 81 mm mortar support; the lead platoon (mine), he added, would have a 60 mm mortar and a 57 mm RR squad attached. He ended by saying that there was plenty of field wire with which to back up the radio during the attack.

As soon as we returned to the Second Platoon position, I heard Shea telling Kober about how sketchy the attack order we'd been given was.

I had already told the attached weapons squad leaders to have their men pack up and report to my position. Each of the squads had four men, so the platoon would have forty men, including the KATUSAS, in the attack. I then assembled the squad leaders and my two senior sergeants at a point from where we had a clear view from the line of departure to the final objective, and of the route we would take to Sugarloaf Pusan Perimeter (see map). Our vantage point permitted me to point out in detail:

- Our route down the cut to the valley floor
- The three rice-field dikes to be used crossing the valley
- The planned use of supporting weapons
- The place where we'd drop our packs
- The three covered cuts we'd use to ascend Sugarloaf
- The attack formation
- The location of the suspected minefield
- The assault formation
- The assault line for the initial objective
- The three objectives, starting with the first knoll and continuing to the next two knolls

I summarized: we would cross the valley quickly on three dikes; Sergeant Shea would be with Bragg's squad on the left, and I'd be with Bebb's squad on the right, attacking up Sugarloaf in the same formation. The machine-gun team and recoilless rifle were to follow me, and the bazooka team was to accompany Sergeant Shea; Sergeant Kober was to bring up the rear with the mortar squad, prepared to select a firing position along the way. I told the rifle squad leaders to have their men fix bayonets when we dropped our packs. Earlier I had had each rifleman shine his bayonet until it glistened, which might encourage the enemy to withdraw rather than fight. Then I identified the position from which we would assault the first knoll—some scrub bushes about seventy-five yards from the flank of the first objective. I pointed out two additional knolls (objectives) we would plan to seize. My final instruction was to keep the men dispersed and to move forward fast if we came under artillery or mortar fire.

There was only one question: Shea wanted to know how in hell I had known we were going to get the Sugarloaf mission. My response was, "Dumb luck! Now let's get our men ready."

I took Shea and Kober to the cut that led to the valley floor and showed them the cover and concealment it would give us. As we returned to our position, three F-51s roared above us, heading not for Hill 902 but Yuhaksan. One after the other they strafed and bombed the NKPA positions. It was already 10:30, and we had not received any word concerning the attack. At 11:30 we were still waiting; the men grew fidgety, and their original eagerness was waning.

Finally, I called the company commander to ask when our air strike would arrive. He responded that I had just seen it, and that someone must have changed the target! I asked the forward observer to plan some artillery support; he reminded me that artillery was still rationed, but he promised that he'd get us sufficient 4.2-inch mortar support. Then I took another look at the bunkers on the third knoll, where the estimated enemy company was located. An antenna was visible near one of them. I was beginning to wonder if the earlier F-51 strike had indeed hit the wrong target.

About 12:30 P.M., the First Sergeant called and told me the company commander had just received word that the air strike had been called off but that the battalion commander wanted the attack to "jump off" in fifteen minutes. The FO came on the line and asked me to notify him when I reached the valley floor; he would place heavy mortar fire on the first knoll and then on the second knoll. Then, looking at my watch, I told the platoon to "saddle up," and we started for the line of departure.

(What follows was obtained during a frontline interrogation of an NKPA prisoner, captured after Sugarloaf was secured. The interrogation was conducted by a South Korean soldier who was fluent in English. The prisoner was Sublieutenant Sun Yun Sok, a forward observer, who during our attack had been sitting on the bunker on the third knoll with a company commander from the North Korean Thirteenth Division. Sok had spotted for artillery pieces and mortars that were deployed just south of Tabu-dong.)

The North Korean company commander, Senior Lt. Yu Jae Hun, was responsible for defending the high ground parallel to, and west of, the Tabu-dong–Taegu road. He had seventy men in his company, including several South Koreans pressed into the NKPA. Desertion among volunteers was high, even though summary execution was the penalty when they were returned. Food was scarce north of Yuhaksan, and there was very little south of the mountain. Hun had placed a platoon on the knoll at the end of Sugarloaf; the platoon leader's orders were to defend it to the death. Hun had authorized him to lay a minefield in front of his position. Hun had great confidence in this platoon leader.

On September 19, Lieutenant Sok noted increased activity in the C Company area, as well as in B Company, and pointed this out to Lieutenant Hun, sitting with him on the bunker. Hun was offering Sok a Russian cigarette when suddenly Sok handed him his field glasses and pointed urgently at a column of Americans moving along their ridge and then disappearing into the cut that led to the valley floor. Hun said excitedly, "There are thirty to forty Americans heading in our direction. Execute a fire mission immediately." Hun alerted his company.

(In his interrogation, Sok was to report that Hun would later execute the platoon leader on the first knoll for failing to stop the Americans, and that when last seen, Hun himself had been severely wounded.)

So it was that as the last man of Second Platoon entered the cut, moving toward the valley, the first enemy mortar round exploded near the entrance. Luckily the last man in line, Sergeant Kober, was protected by the cover the cut provided. For three or four minutes North Korean artillery and mortars pounded the Company C position.

"Hey Lieutenant, the battalion commander wants you!" Ramos shouted, holding out the sound-powered phone. "Killer" Kane asked me if I was going to be able to seize a jump-off position for Company B. I told him we were going to try like hell to do just that, to which he responded, "That's the spirit!" Then he said, "I have the regimental commander [Col. Raymond D. Palmer] and the division commander [Maj. Gen. Hobart Gay] breathing down *my* back. Good luck, Mack." As I remember, he also included the Eighth Army commander's name as well. As I recall, my only reaction was that he knew my name now and that he was breathing down my back!

I led the platoon down the incline, under cover, until I reached the valley floor. The enemy artillery and mortar fire ended, though I fully expected they were adjusting it to meet us as we entered the rice fields. Making a hurried visual reconnaissance, I told Shea that things looked a lot different than they had from above. I called the FO and told him we'd move out when his first round landed on the objective. Then I called the three rifle-squad leaders forward and pointed out the dikes they were to use crossing the valley. A couple of minutes later the FO reported, "Rounds on the way!"

Unexpectedly, sheets of paper fluttered down on the platoon from an enemy artillery round bursting overhead; I picked several up and quickly noted that they were propaganda leaflets, enjoining us to surrender. I told the platoon to pick them up if they wanted, since the sheets were bigger than the "TP" in the c-rations.

The squad leaders led their men to the dikes across the paddies and started crossing rapidly, as the support weapons positioned themselves as we had planned. (Three lateral dikes separated the paddies.) Our own artillery whined overhead as we moved out and landed on the first knoll, exactly where we wanted it. I yelled to Sergeant Shea that our FO was one smart artilleryman, and I warned everyone not to bunch up.

Partway across, I looked back and saw the platoon messenger, Ramos, far behind, loaded down with all the field wire. Shouting to Kober to get someone to help him, I yelled to Ramos to keep down in the dry paddy. Kober bounded toward Ramos with another man, and they relieved him of his pack and a roll of wire. Upon reaching the head of the platoon, Kober unreeled the wire on Ramos's back, mounted a new reel in the reel holder, and made a quick line-check with the company OP.

We dropped our packs at the foot of Sugarloaf and fixed bayonets. I signaled the platoon to start the attack toward the top, using the cuts for cover. I got the FO on the telephone again and, once he had us in sight (so he wouldn't accidentally hit us), asked for additional fire support on the first knoll. A few minutes later, 4.2-inch mortar rounds were landing above us.

Moving with the center squad leader, Sergeant Saito, and with Ramos following at my heels, I could see our three columns of bent-over riflemen as they slipped on loose rocks, batted mosquitoes, and cussed. The hot afternoon sun was drawing sweat from every pore; our fatigues began to turn white. Our steel helmets (often called "steel pots" by soldiers), though they offered protection, would bob up and down annoyingly, hindering sight, causing discomfort, and fueling tempers. The sun's one benefit today was that it made our bayonets glisten, but they couldn't be seen yet by the North Korean unit above us, and they would not be seen until we had passed over the folds of earth seventy-five to a hundred yards from the enemy position on the first knoll. I reminded everyone once more to keep away from the mined southern edge of the first knoll. I could still hear mortar rounds exploding above, and I yelled to Kober to set up our mortar. Ramos handed me the phone, and the FO told me the last mortar round was on the way.

When the stump of a tree on the objective became visible, I knew we would soon be seen by the North Koreans. Our 60 mm mortar started dropping rounds on the objective, and I shouted to Sergeant Bebb to keep his men in line with the other two squads. Finally, I alerted all the squads to be ready to move on line, in "marching fire" (as I had practiced at Fort Benning). The next instant there was a *crack! crack!* as an enemy Maxim machine gun commenced firing. I called to the 57 mm RR gunner to bring his weapon forward. Taking the weapon from him, as there was no time to orient him to the machine gun, I kneeled and fired one round of high explosive, which dispatched the gunner and his assistant and toppled the machine gun.

Noting that we had already reached the assault position, I yelled to the squad leaders to move on line, in marching fire. A moment later Sergeant Bebb was killed; I ordered his squad to move on line. By then all three squads were up, and we were proceeding on the first knoll from the flank; the crescendo of rifle and automatic fire increased as we closed in on the enemy position. A man in the right squad was hit and fell, and then a man next to me, as Shea and I guided the line up and over the flank of the knoll. Then one of the Koreans in the left squad was hit and killed. The platoon medic was busy, going to each of those hit at the shout of "*Medic!*" and attending to the wounded. We had about twenty-two glistening bayonets on rifles and carbines that were firing a round with each pace, which in itself probably caused a considerable number of the defenders to keep their heads down and not return fire, or to fall back to their next position.

Having gained the objective, I reorganized the platoon into a defensive position facing the next knoll. We quickly commenced firing on the retreating North Koreans, using our 57 mm RR, machine gun, automatic rifles, and an undamaged enemy Maxim machine gun. We saw several of them fall. The rest stopped at a knoll about eight hundred yards from what we believed was the main enemy company position. I reported back that we had seized the first knoll and had suffered two killed and two wounded. I was ordered to continue the attack to the next knoll, for which I requested fire support. The FO came on the line and said he would have 4.2-inch mortar support fired, which we were more than happy to get.

I had Sergeant Koburn move the 60 mm mortar to my location and have the squad register on the next knoll, where I could see North Korean soldiers digging feverishly into the rock-filled ground. Our 60 mm mortar fired a registration round, and I placed the 57 mm recoilless rifle where it could support the continuation of the attack. We had seen about ten North Koreans run as fast as they could from their company position to the knoll we were preparing to attack.

Remembering that Company B was to follow me, I called my company commander and asked him to inform Company B about the minefield in front of the first knoll. I fully anticipated the terse reply I received: "Anything else I can do for you, First Lieutenant Mack?"

There were seven dead North Koreans on the first knoll; we later buried them in three of their foxholes, driving a Russian carbine into each grave for identification. The First Sergeant told us he was sending a detail to pick up Sergeant Bebb and the Korean soldier. The wounded, who could walk, would accompany the detail back to the company OP.

The first 4.2-inch mortar rounds landed on the next objective; the enemy knoll suddenly erupted into a mass of flying rock and shrapnel. With that we commenced our attack. I put my whole force on one side of the ridge, executing a left-flank attack on the obviously hastily prepared defense so that we could be observed from the company OP. I hoped placing the machine gun and 57 mm RR fire on the right flank of the enemy position would prevent the North Koreans from reinforcing their left flank.

The thick dust offered concealment as we moved up to an assault position about fifty yards from the enemy flank position. Then we began receiving small-arms fire, and a man was wounded. As the medic ran to assist the man, Sergeant Shea and I aligned the platoon, and I again ordered marching fire. We moved across the enemy defense position from the left flank, and a rapid withdrawal of the North Koreans ensued, most of them running to the other side of the ridge, not toward their company defense position. There were several enemy dead and one wounded on the knoll. The foxholes were extremely shallow, so I had the platoon begin digging them deeper. Several minutes later Sergeant Saito shouted, "There they are!" and pointed to ten North Koreans circling back up the ridge about 150 yards north of our location. Four of them fell as the platoon fired on them.

It was then late afternoon, and I recommended to the company commander that B Company come forward and continue the attack, to prevent the enemy from reinforcing their company position. Again I received a terse response: "Stay where you are, Lieutenant, and let us worry about the tactics and strategy! *Out!*"

We worked quickly to prepare a position in event of a counterattack or heavy mortar fire, of which the North Koreans seemed to have an inexhaustible supply. As any infantryman knows who has reorganized against a counterattack, a newly seized enemy defensive position usually faces opposite the direction from where the counterattack is anticipated. While the foxholes may serve as protection against air, artillery, and mortars, new positions are needed to ward off a ground attack. So we feverishly dug a defensive position in the rocky soil where the North Koreans had barely "scratched" one earlier. Captain Rounsaville called to tell me that my unit was to be attached to Company B as soon as it arrived on

Sugarloaf. I suggested that he tell Company B that there were not sufficient foxholes for a company at this end of Sugarloaf, and it would have to dig in when it arrived. Again I walked into a terse "Anything else? *Out!*"

I scanned the NKPA company on the next knoll; I could see one soldier smoking and another moving along a trench. I knew then that the North Koreans were still there, and I thought it had been an error for Company B not to have followed closer; we could have kept them running.

I went back to work on my foxhole, when with a *swish!* NKPA artillery rounds skimmed over our ridge and landed to the rear of Sugarloaf. We had seen Company B leaving its position fifteen minutes earlier. Now I was amazed to see the company exposed, in column of twos, on the Tabu-dong–Taegu road; the enemy artillery hit all about them. Several of Company B's men were on the ground; the company now made a mad dash across the dry paddy, some dispersing, some running for Sugarloaf.

I quickly ordered my men into the foxholes they were preparing, telling Sergeant Shea to bring the 3.5-inch bazooka and the 57 mm RR up on line while I organized our automatic weapons. I fully expected a counterattack, but it didn't materialize. It was almost dark when the B Company commander and his advance party arrived. His best estimate was that he had lost six dead and eleven wounded from enemy artillery. He said nothing more. He was emotionally drained.

His First Sergeant, holding an SCR-536, then told him that his First Platoon was approaching the first knoll. When I heard this I shouted, "Stop them! They are walking into a mined area!" The First Sergeant ordered into the radio, "Freeze in place! You are near a mined area!" I then learned that the information about the mines had never been relayed to Company B. Sergeant Kober went with the First Sergeant to the first knoll to guide the platoon around the danger.

I recommended that one platoon of Company B remain at the first knoll, where they could use some of the North Korean positions. The captain told me to remain in the position I was preparing and that he would have a platoon dig in on both of my flanks. He planned to put his 60 mm mortars just forward of the first knoll and told me to have my mortar squad join his section.

I kept my platoon at 100 percent alert until his two forward platoons had dug in; most of their positions were little more than slit trenches. For two hours the line was lit up by the sparks from entrenching tools hitting rock. The captain established his OP next to my foxhole. His first message to battalion was that he was getting dug in on Sugarloaf.

The first enemy heavy mortar rounds descended on our end of Sugarloaf about 8:30 P.M. The earth shook as the rounds dug deep craters and found a partially dug slit trench, killing the two occupants. There were no casualties in my platoon. The enemy firing stopped for a short time and then commenced again. One mortar round landed about ten feet in front of my foxhole, and a spray of dust and small rocks fell on me. Then there was one last heavy mortar bombardment, all of it on the first knoll, which a Company B platoon occupied. They reported secondary explosions in the mined area, which was confirmed at daylight. There were no casualties.

The Company B commander notified his platoon leaders that there would be a meeting at his command post, about 150 yards behind his OP, at 11:00 P.M. I was told I should attend; at the meeting I met a First Lieutenant Walthauer, who had been at Fort Benning but whom I had never met before. He had arrived in Korea about a week after me and had tried to be assigned as the Eighth Cavalry Regiment's intelligence and reconnaissance (I&R) platoon leader. I made sure that Walthauer knew there was a North Korean company on the knoll forward of us.

The captain then gave us his plan for the next day, which essentially called for one platoon to attack frontally while two platoons enveloped the enemy position, on order. The plan did not appear to recognize that there was an enemy company defending the prepared position on the next major knoll, nor that the enemy had all-around security. The only mention of my platoon was that it was to be in reserve. I nudged Walthauer and said, "Here we go again with the pile-on concept." He just shrugged his shoulders. The captain said Lieutenant Walthauer's platoon would lead the attack and assigned the right and left platoons to the enveloping phase. He said he would give his final orders at 5:30 A.M., September 20, at his OP.

When I got back to my platoon, I told Kober and Shea about the meeting and found I wasn't the only skeptic. As we looked north, we could see a cigarette being lit here and there, even though it was raining lightly, less than a kilometer to our front. I mentioned to my two sergeants that because we no longer had communications with Company C, I could go as far as to seek a council of war with the CO of Company B. The unnecessary casualties Company B had suffered that day had sent me a message.

During the night, several volleys of enemy artillery whistled overhead, heading for the battalion or regimental headquarters, or the trains area. I dozed on and off and finally took the 3 to 5 A.M. shift, relieving Sergeant Shea. The rain had stopped, and the stars and moon were visible. Peering through the blackness with my field glasses, I began to make out the enemy knoll. Then slowly a mist took over from darkness and obscured the position.

At 5:30, Walthauer, whose platoon had occupied the first knoll, came forward to my position with the company commander to make final preparations for the attack. When the captain realized that the enemy position could not be seen, he decided it would be foolish to try to coordinate an envelopment and decided simply to attack in a column of platoons. He told Walthauer that if he got in trouble, he'd just send another platoon through his.

The Company B FO requested an artillery fire mission on the enemy position, to start at 6:10, when Walthauer's platoon was to cross the line of departure. Walthauer was to have follow-on fire support from the battalion 81 mm mortars and the company 60 mm mortars. Because of the mist, Walthauer would control the supporting fires, using the company radio frequency.

As I sat there I saw Walthauer look at his watch and say that the artillery should be falling on the objective soon. Then he led his platoon down the center of the ridge. Immediately he told his platoon sergeant that he wanted a column of squads on line (that is, one squad behind the other, the men of each squad in line abreast), so he could deploy the platoon for the assault more easily.

What happened during the attack and final assault was reported to me by a surviving sergeant, who had been severely wounded.

After advancing over five hundred yards on the ridge, up and down several small rises, the platoon received heavy small-arms fire from the flanks and front. Two men were killed and three wounded. The platoon hit the ground; Walthauer got them back on their feet and continued the advance. He then began deploying the platoon for the assault and requested 81 mm mortar support. When he saw the rounds bursting a great distance from him, he probably realized he was far from where he should begin the assault.

Nevertheless, he kept his platoon in the assault formation. The line sagged as the men walked over undulating terrain. Walthauer then called off the 81 mm mortar and asked for 60 mm mortar support, to avoid walking into the larger bursting area of 81 mm mortars. Because the distance to the objective was difficult to determine, the 60 mm mortar fire fell behind the target. The enemy line now executed all of its defense fires on his platoon. Walthauer was killed immediately; his messenger was severely wounded, and the radio was destroyed. The platoon sergeant was wounded in the arm, and part of his jaw was shot away. The sergeant said that some of the men returned fire and moved toward the enemy position, some hit the ground, and men still standing were hit.

A sergeant returned to the company with sixteen men, by following a route that afforded some cover. The platoon had started the attack with thirty-four men. Another wounded man walked back in later in the day, telling how he had played dead, and how the North Koreans had shot wounded Americans and then searched their bodies for valuables. The company commander became almost a basket case as he heard what the North Koreans had done to his men. The wounded platoon sergeant became unconscious through of loss of blood; a "buck" sergeant, the only NCO in the platoon not a casualty, took his place. The Company B First Sergeant organized a detail to evacuate the wounded and killed.

I detected an intense somberness in my platoon as they watched Walthauer's men return, some dragging their weapons. I had my men deepen their shallow foxholes in the rocky earth and had my medic help the other medics in stabilizing the wounded. Using my field glasses, I could see several members of Walthauer's platoon lying in front of the enemy position. The 4.2-inch mortars fired three missions on it, with the hope of caving in the enemy bunkers.

The captain assembled the platoon leaders at my position, because of its good observation. I was advised that I would participate in an attack on September 21, the next day. Walthauer's platoon now consisted of two squads, and a staff sergeant from another platoon acted as platoon leader; that platoon would not participate in the next attack.

First the company commander told us that he had been threatened with relief from duty if we didn't eliminate the NKPA company in front of us. General Gay had passed the word to "Killer" Kane that he expected the battalion to link up by the next day with a Seventh Cavalry unit that was heading south from Tabu-dong. The captain then told us that if anyone had an idea how to seize that knoll up ahead, he should feel free to let him know. I recommended that we use a minimum of two platoons to envelop the enemy position from both flanks, using the covered approach routes lower on the ridge. I pointed out how, using the folds in the terrain, sufficient cover could be found to move both platoons almost to their assault positions. At the same time I recommended that the reserve platoon advance along the right slope to a small knoll halfway to the objective, from which it could reinforce the other two platoons if need be and in the interim lay down a "base of fire" to keep the enemy from reinforcing either flank.

The captain said that my plan had a lot of merit, and then he detailed an attack order that included many of the elements I had mentioned. He designated my platoon as the reserve platoon, with the initial mission of deploying to the small knoll, setting up a base of fire to be executed on order; it was also to be prepared to reinforce the other platoons or, if necessary, assault the enemy's right flank. He then presented his plan for the other two platoons to advance and assault the enemy company's flanks. He told his forward observer to lay on supporting fires to commence at 6:10 A.M., the line-of-departure time.

I got my sergeants and squad leaders together and gave them their orders. The men were to get their packs ready but leave them here to be picked up later. There were no questions, so I sent the squad leaders back to their squads.

It was a sleepless night for Company B. There was some heavy NKPA mortar fire near midnight. The captain had a hole prepared for him and his radio operator near mine. I heard the radio operator say that he now knew how Pickett's men felt after their attack at Gettysburg. The night was punctuated with the sounds of nightmares among those few who had managed to block out the world with restless sleep. Fear of what tomorrow might bring is ever present in the minds of infantrymen in combat. A few succumb to the fear, but more often "grunts" carry it within them, in silence. I was no different from the dirty-socks infantrymen I led.

Sergeants Shea, Kober, and I were up at 5 A.M. on September 21. Most of the men were awake, huddled in their slit trenches under ponchos to keep the cool fall air at bay. A few were eating their C-rations; we were now back to three C-ration meals a day, or as some would say, you now had a greater choice of what you wouldn't eat.

There was no shaving; water was scarce, and I had already sent a detail to fill canteens from a small stream in the valley. Slowly the men assembled their packs, the contents of which separated them from human bankruptcy. Many carried a plastic bag or a used machine-gun-ammunition case to store their valuables: wives' and girlfriends' pictures, letters, writing paper, a pair of panties or a bra, a small Bible. All were irreplaceable items.

I assembled the NCOs near my OP and gave them the attack order, and then I brought the platoon up behind the OP and had the men clean their weapons. As they worked I gave them an overview of the part we would play in the attack, pointing out the little knoll on the rise about halfway to the objective. I reminded them that they should take full advantage of any cover, stay low as we moved forward, fix bayonets when we got to that knoll, and be prepared either to lay down a base of fire on the right side of the position or move out rapidly to an assault position. Then I told them, "We'll make it OK, as long as we work as a team."

I said a prayer to myself for the platoon, wrapped my rosary around my hand, and placed my trigger finger inside the trigger guard. As I did so, I noted the sun was rising to our right rear, placing the glare in the enemy's eyes. It was about 6:50 A.M. when the first artillery rounds dropped on and about the North Korean position and Company B moved out in the attack. The attack had been delayed for an air support mission, which had failed to materialize.

The company commander was still at my observation post, talking by radio to his platoons alternately as they advanced to the flanks of the enemy company. He told his forward observer to follow up the artillery with lots of 4.2-inch mortars on the objective and then told the 81 mm mortar forward observer to alert his fire-direction center to be prepared to support also. The captain already had his 60 mm mortar section leader ready to drop the first round down the tube when given the command. He was ensuring that his company received every bit of fire support that was available.

As the artillery mission ended, the platoon enveloping to the right received its first fire. It was about three to four hundred yards from the objective. The platoon leader reported that he had one man wounded and that he was moving by bounds toward an assault position. The company commander then ordered me to move my platoon to its position as soon as I could. The platoon on the left had not been fired on and perhaps was undetected.

As we reached the small knoll, we could hear the 81 mm mortar rounds burst on the enemy position. I contacted the company commander and told him I was prepared to lay down a base of fire on the right side of the objective, for which he gave permission. I initiated the base of fire, and I could see the right-hand platoon renew its advance, now that it had the 60 mm mortars protecting it, until it began receiving enemy fire again.

With that the right-hand platoon was given an order to lay down a base of fire, and I was ordered to begin advancing to an assault position, to tie in with the left-hand platoon in the assault. The 60 mm mortar section continued its fire on the enemy after the 81 mm mortars ended their support; this, together with the heavy fire being placed on the enemy by the right-flank platoon, permitted my platoon to close on an assault line and tie-in with the left-hand platoon.

When ordered to commence the assault, my platoon and the platoon to our left moved to and across the enemy company position, using marching fire; the captain had ordered his platoon on the right to cease fire. Shea and I kept our platoon aligned with the Company B platoon as we crossed over the right half of the enemy company position. The bunkers were in shambles from our fire support. Momentarily, I could sense a rise in the platoon esprit as we secured the enemy position and saw the North Koreans in flight. An NKPA officer who had been wounded was captured. He was the company commander.

Unknown to us, down on the road to Tabu-dong, General Gay and Lieutenant Colonel Kane were shaking hands with a sergeant from Company C, Seventh Cavalry Regiment, who led the platoon that had completed the encirclement of the North Koreans. The road to Tabu-dong was open.[2]

The North Koreans had left the American casualties from the day before where they had fallen. Four had been executed. Lieutenant Walthauer and several others had had their valuables looted. All boots and weapons had been taken.

Late in the day, many North Korean prisoners were taken, most in mufti and without weapons. One prisoner was Sublieutenant Sok, the North Korean FO whose story I've mentioned. The men searching Sok found Lieutenant Walthauer's military ring and wallet on him. The Company B commander, standing before the kneeling Sok, called over an English-speaking Korean soldier, and they interrogated Sok well into the night. The next day all of the prisoners were evacuated, and the dead NKPA soldiers were buried inside one of the bunkers.

Elements of the Eighth Cavalry Regiment were quick to move up the road toward Tabu-dong. Below Sugarloaf on the Tabu-dong–Taegu road, a Col. Lee Hak Ku, the chief of staff of the North Korean Thirteenth Division, gave himself up to two sleeping "grunts." Lee described the Thirteenth Division as an ineffective fighting force, with only 1,500 men; many were impressed South Koreans, who would desert at their first opportunity.[3]

My platoon returned to C Company on September 22. Taking a break on a congested road, I saw two new boots hanging from the lift handle of a jeep and exchanged them for my boots, whose soles were lined with C-ration cardboard. A perfect fit! Lousy logistics! Some with minimal combat experience, or none at all, might cite ethics here; my ethics at the moment centered on leading a rifle platoon without razor-sharp rocks slicing the soles of my feet. Shea, seeing a machine-gun muzzle sticking out of the jeep's canvas-covered trailer, "acquired" it, making the Second Platoon perhaps the only platoon equipped with two light machine guns, which was the authorized number. Seven other machine guns were in a trailer—more weapons than there were gunners. Reaching Tabu-dong, we remained for two days of maintenance and had our first hot meal in Korea.

Task Force Lynch (a specially reinforced regiment commanded by Lt. Col. James Lynch) from the Seventh Cavalry Regiment was to link up with the X Corps's Seventh Division. The Eighth Cavalry Regiment attacked north to Ansong, to protect the Seventh Cavalry's right flank. As a result of the Inchon Landing on September 15, the First Marine Division and Seventh Infantry units were able to trap and cutoff many NKPA units in South Korea. NKPA units were dispersed in their retreat and in general lost their conventional effectiveness, greatly facilitating the UN breakout by Pusan perimeter forces and link up with the 7th Infantry Division. On September 27, Company L, Seventh Cavalry, made contact with the Seventh Division's Thirty-first Regiment, south of Suwon near Osan, where Task Force Smith had made the initial U.S. contact with NKPA units in early July.

From September 22 until October 6, Company C had no contact with the North Koreans. It was raining hard on October 6 when the battalion arrived in Kaesong, the last major city below the thirty-eighth parallel. Company C dismounted from trucks in full view of NKPA forces that occupied the major ridge north of Kaesong, astride the thirty-eighth parallel. The company marched for two miles until it reached a large cement blockhouse, on a rise a hundred feet above the road. The company commander halted the company, and the platoon leaders followed him into the house, from which everything removable had been carried away by the North Koreans. The odor of urine and feces permeated the place.

On the second floor was a window with an excellent view of the high ridge to the north and Hill 209. There was also a lower ridge south of it, but north of the blockhouse, which rose from west to east for a kilometer. The CO selected the building as his CP, and this room as his OP. Then he pointed out platoon sectors and attached a 57 mm recoilless rifle to each platoon. (See the map of North Korea.)

My platoon sector was on the lower ridge extending about 150 yards to the west of a group of tile-roofed buildings. As we moved along the road that led to the sector, we passed several ransacked buildings. All of the wire had been taken from the utility poles. Here and there we saw a small group of "civilians" who eyed us curiously; I warned my platoon to keep their eyes open, saying, "The next thing you might run into is the NKPA." We reached our sector as the rain was dwindling to a drizzle. I designated sectors for my three rifle squads and for the "two" light machine guns, one at each extremity of the platoon. I placed the 57 mm recoilless rifle near my position, where its gunner had good observation. Before last light I surveyed the high ridge before us and saw several North Koreans, who were probably surveying us. I reported my sighting to the company commander and received a firm response: *"Out!"*

Unknown to me and my platoon, there were a number of high-level incongruities that would adversely affect UN efforts in North Korea. The Joint Chiefs of Staff on September 27 had sent General MacArthur a directive stating that he was authorized to conduct military operations north of the thirty-eighth

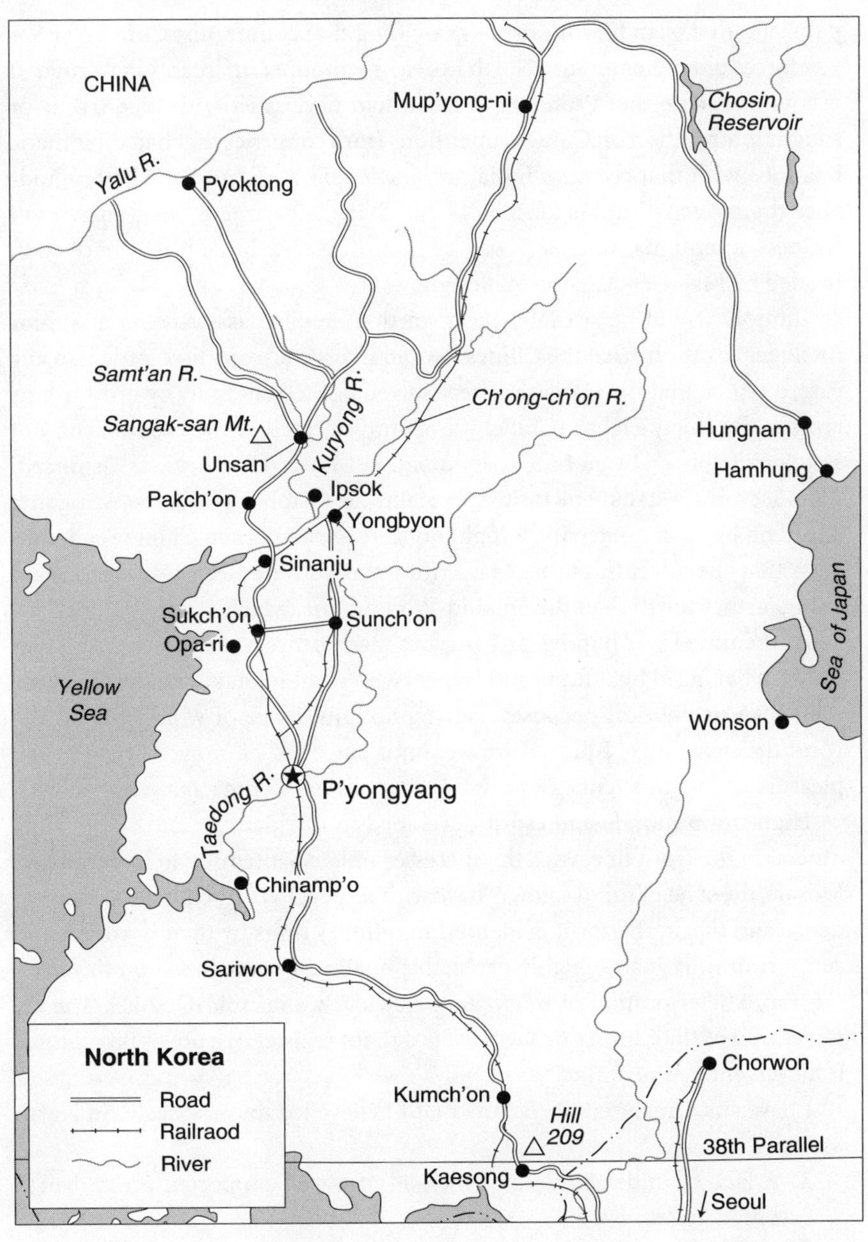

CHINA
Mup'yong-ni
Chosin Reservoir
Yalu R.
Pyoktong
Samt'an R.
Ch'ong-ch'on R.
Sangak-san Mt.
Hungnam
Hamhung
Unsan
Kuryong R.
Pakch'on
Ipsok
Yongbyon
Sinanju
Sukch'on
Sunch'on
Opa-ri
Sea of Japan
Yellow Sea
Wonson
Taedong R.
P'yongyang
Chinamp'o
Sariwon
North Korea
Road
Railraod
River
Chorwon
Kumch'on
Hill 209
38th Parallel
Kaesong
Seoul

parallel—that is, in North Korea—providing that communist Chinese or Soviet forces did not enter into North Korea or announce an intention to enter. It was unfortunate that President Truman had never met with MacArthur or sought information on Chinese intentions from countries that had diplomatic relations with that country. India, for one, could have provided better guidance than MacArthur. As for the CIA and State Department, their analyses of Chinese intentions were as flawed as that of MacArthur's intelligence staff, headed by Maj. Gen. Charles Willoughby.[4]

Rumors would persist later in Japan that credible assessments by junior intelligence officers that the Chinese would intervene were disregarded. In any case, a report that the Chinese were resolved not to stand idly by if UN troops crossed the thirty-eighth parallel was communicated to the U.S. secretary of state on October 3 by an Indian diplomat, K. M. Panikkar, but was dismissed. Mao Tse-tung's statement to Joseph Stalin on October 13 that he was going ahead on his own, preferring to fight on Korean rather than Chinese soil, suggests that the adventuresome MacArthur should have been restrained from going farther north than the Sinanju-Wonsan line, which was defensible.[5]

At the time I was hoping, as I am sure many officers at my level were, that we were being led by officers and leaders who wouldn't take needless risks for their own or political purposes. Having no knowledge of what went on beyond the next ridge, I prayed we were not pawns to be moved about at the pleasure of incompetents. I was wrong; my prayers weren't answered.

High troop morale and esprit developed in my platoon, and presumably others on the front line, with the successes of late September to late October. Morale, the state of mind soldiers have with respect to their courage and confidence and esprit, the spirit evidenced in military units by their devotion and support of unit goals—highly perishable qualities—were based on the obvious rapid deterioration of the NKPA, particularly after mid-October. The intervention of the Chinese or the Soviets did not register as a possibility for me, if it even entered my mind.

I have since analyzed the factors that I believe led to our disaster in North Korea:

A. A lack of understanding of the will of a well-supported proxy, North Korea, to survive.

B. A failure to believe in the determination of the People's Republic of China to protect its borders and to assist another communist nation under attack.

c. A tactical and strategic error in splitting the UN forces between the Eighth Army in the west and the X Corps in the east, at Wonsan.

d. The untimely crossing of the thirty-eighth parallel without further buildup of UN forces while the IX Corps, part of the Eighth Army, was involved in counter-guerrilla operations below the thirty-eighth, further reduced the UN (Eighth Army) capability in the west.

e. Having crossed the thirty-eighth parallel, failure to select a defensible line above Pyongyang from which to plan further military operations.

I was fortunate to not know of the high-level inadequacies that were to plague us as we crossed the thirty-eighth parallel and headed north. I can now say with a certain amount of confidence that our senior leadership was engaged in what amounted to trying to juggle soft gelatin. Perhaps a principal lesson that can be learned from the Korean War is that political decisions must be weighed closely against the probable consequences of military actions that result from them. We must never forget that we stopped communist aggression in Korea by fighting nose to nose with a determined army; still, our goal should have been to restore the border as it was on June 25, 1950.

The problem at hand on October 7 at 1:00 A.M., however, was surviving a heavy barrage on and about the company's cement blockhouse. Round after round screamed over it, landed near it, and slammed into it. The North Koreans were attempting to disrupt the preparations being made to cross the thirty-eighth parallel.

My platoon flinched with each terrifying scream of the incoming round. Several patrols from the First Cavalry Division patrolled to or across the parallel on October 7 and 8.[6] I received an order on October 7 to patrol forward toward a small hill lying between my platoon's position and Hill 209 to the north. Captain Rounsaville said that he had seen movement on the hill and suspected that the NKPA had an FO there. He instructed me to patrol until I received fire and then return. I had Sergeant Kober put together a six-man patrol for me to lead and instructed him to keep us under observation. Sergeant Shea was at the battalion aid station with diarrhea.

An eighteen-year-old patrol member remarked that he thought that by now the Army would have found a better way to find out where the enemy was located than letting him shoot at us. I had to agree, but unfortunately we didn't have one. I reminded him that we had to remember that at our level we didn't fight for abstractions; our motivation had to be to protect each other. If we did that, we would have the greatest chance of achieving success. He seemed to understand this. As I looked at each patrol member, I sensed that they understood why they were going on the patrol, whether or not they wanted to go. I may have asked myself whether I did myself.

It was about 6:45 A.M. when we moved out in single file through scrub trees and bushes that provided concealment. I had reminded the patrol that our mission depended on seven pairs of eyes and that I wanted everyone to let me know if they saw anything suspicious. We walked at a crouch, or crawled, for twenty minutes or so before the point man held up his hand. I crawled to him, and he pointed out a cave on the hillside. With my field glasses I saw that it was actually a bunker, constructed of logs, rocks, and dirt. Scanning the hill I sighted two other bunkerlike structures. I instructed the patrol to keep a close eye on the three bunkers, especially any movement around them. Then we continued crawling along folds in the ground, which gave us concealment, if not protection. Suddenly, the soldier who had questioned the reason for the patrol said he thought he saw movement in the bunker to the left.

I stopped the patrol once again, and we took a closer look. I was sure I saw movement in the bunker also; a light blinked on and off, as if someone was using field glasses, which were reflecting the sunlight. I made a wild guess that the bunker was an outpost forward of the defense line on the higher ridge and Hill 209. As I looked at the center bunker, I saw an individual in civilian clothes climbing up the hill from a Buddhist shrine near the base of the hill. He was carrying a bag over his shoulder. We were five to seven hundred yards from the bunker now, and I could see field wire stretched from the bunker port up the ridge.

I made a radio report to the company OP, giving the company commander the coordinates of the three bunkers and telling him that I saw a landline going up hill from the center bunker, and that someone in civilian clothes was climbing to the center bunker. The company commander put the FO on the radio, and I gave him the information. Then the FO told me the company commander wanted me to return.

I acknowledged the instructions, just as a patrol member emptied a clip from his M-1 rifle into four North Koreans charging down toward us. The patrol then fired in unison; two North Koreans went down, and a third fell almost on top of me, wounded in the arm. The fourth North Korean turned and ran back up the hill. I immediately commended the soldier who had initiated the fire for his quick reaction. By then the center bunker was being pounded by the 4.2-inch mortar company. I put a bandage on the wounded North Korean's arm, and we commenced our return. On the way I notified the First Sergeant that I was bringing in a prisoner and asked him to send an escort.

Remembering how we had nearly been ambushed at Sabu-dong, I told my patrol to keep their eyes open and to use all the cover and concealment available. Looking back up the hill again, I could see our mortars were still hitting the bunkers; I could also see several North Koreans running toward the main ridge.

It was 1 P.M. when I reached the platoon; Sergeant Kober told me I was to return to the company CP with a prisoner detail. There the First Sergeant told the other platoon leaders and me that he had heard from the battalion intelligence sergeant that the regiment had given our battalion an attack order.

When the company commander returned, he explained that the division didn't yet have authority to cross the thirty-eighth parallel but anticipated receiving it soon. He then told us that he had an alert order for an attack, which would permit us to plan for it. Pointing to a map, he explained that the Seventh Regiment was to attack west toward Paekch'on, across the Yesong River and then North to Ham'po-ri, above Kumch'on. The Fifth Cavalry was to attack east on the Sibyon-ni road and then envelop the North Korean Twenty-seventh Division on the road west to Kumch'on. The Eighth Cavalry, in the center, was to attack north to take Kumch'on, with the First Battalion seizing and securing the major ridge north of Kaesong and Hill 209. As part of the plan, we would move northeast of Kaesong on September 9 in preparation for the attack.

I saw Sergeant Shea standing nearby; he was feeling better, so we started back to the platoon. Just after we departed the company CP, a heavy barrage of North Korean artillery began hitting the Eighth Cavalry trains area; it was then adjusted forward to the blockhouse CP. We watched as our outgoing artillery fell on the three bunkers we had reported and then shifted to Hill 209, on the main ridge.

The best source of information for immediate ground operations, other than a mole within enemy councils, is a prisoner of war. Prisoners can provide critical information on enemy strengths, weaponry, locations, morale, plans, weaknesses, and vulnerabilities. Soldiers engaged in the capture of prisoners should receive feedback on the results of their sweat, to emphasize the importance of taking prisoners and expeditiously evacuating them through intelligence channels. This calls for a closer link between capturing units, information processing, and dissemination of intelligence to frontline combat units. That could easily have been attained in 1950, and it can certainly be made available to all combat units today.

To illustrate the point, Senior Sgt. Pak Ho Yup, the man we had captured, said he was a section leader in the Nineteenth Division. He had been responsible for security of the bunkers on the hill north of Kaesong, which we had reconnoitered. He would later tell an interpreter at the battalion CP that the bunkers had radio and wire communications for artillery targeting purposes. Pak also divulged that civilian line crossers visited the bunkers and brought military information on the UN forces, probably for operational use. Pak said he suspected that the line crossers were spies, who would return to the UN side. He also provided information on NKPA artillery and mortar locations. We received this feedback only because the First Sergeant was a friend of the battalion intelligence sergeant, who had used an English-speaking South Korean soldier to interrogate Pak. Henceforth, line crossers were turned over to South Korean authorities. An air strike settled the score with the bunkers.

My platoon assembled at the company CP after dark on October 8. We occupied a large room on the first floor of the concrete blockhouse. During the night of the 8th, we received particularly heavy NKPA artillery fire, several rounds hitting the upper floor and roof of the building. Effective counter-artillery and mortar fire silenced the enemy guns.

On October 9, we marched west about two miles to a small village to await the attack order. It didn't take long for local civilians to assemble along the road where we waited. I suggested that the Korean military police control the civilians in and about the village to prevent the enemy from receiving advance information concerning our attack plans. Captain Rounsaville responded that the North Koreans probably already knew we are going to attack; all they had to do was read our newspapers. He may have been right!

At about 4:30 P.M. Lieutenant Colonel Kane passed along the road with Company B, mounted on tanks. He and Rounsaville conferred over a map spread out on the drive train of a tank. The sum of their short conference, as given to us shortly thereafter, was that the company was to attack at 5:30 P.M., going up the finger nearest to us to gain a foothold on the top of the ridge. From there the company would attack east along the ridge to seize Hill 209. (See the map of North Korea.) The captain gave us his own attack order, stating that when we seized Hill 209, we would have accomplished our mission.

The top of the ridge could not be seen from the bottom at this point, because of the trees and foliage at the lower levels. The latest air reconnaissance showed that the North Koreans had dug a trench the length of the ridge, along with bunkers of both log and steel-reinforced concrete. At the eastern extremity of the ridge was a large reinforced-concrete bunker.

At 5:30 P.M. the company commenced the attack, with my platoon the second in line of a column of platoons. The First Platoon, leading the attack, penetrated the forested area and then came to open rocky slopes and the steep, rocky, undulating terrain and a series of cliffs that led directly to the main ridge. Before reaching the main ridge there were cliffs with vertical drops of thirty to fifty feet. As the First Platoon got to the brink of the first cliff, the point man was struck by enemy gunfire and fell into the deep precipice, to his death. By then it was pitch dark, the sky being overcast. The platoon leader went forward to the edge of the drop and requested 81 mm mortar fire on the main ridge; he then adjusted it to the next rocky peak. After that fire mission, the men of First Platoon began lowering themselves down the cliff under fire from enemy located on the main ridge, suffering one man killed and three wounded.

About 10:30 P.M., the First Platoon reached the last cliff before the main ridge. The first man to reach it was hit by enemy machine-gun fire and fell about fifty feet to his death. When the company commander received word of the casualties, he ordered me to attack through the First Platoon. I went forward, with Sergeant Shea guiding the Second Platoon behind me. When I got to the final cliff, I requested 81 mm mortar illumination over an estimated fifty-foot drop; as soon as I saw the difficulty of negotiating it, I told Shea that there was no way we were going to proceed by that route.

Instead, I moved the platoon lower on the backside of the cliff and maneuvered to the left in a wide circle to what appeared on my map, and from what I could see in the light of the illumination rounds, to be a gentler slope to the main ridge. I had Sergeant Kober set up a machine gun and fire several bursts onto the main ridge. The NKPA returned fire, giving me a better idea of where they were. We finally did reach a gentler slope, five or six hundred yards from the top of the main ridge and leading to a trench. I lined my platoon up, and we advanced cautiously the rest of the way to the top of the ridge. A Korean soldier was wounded on the way up. We ended up in a trench, the enemy having withdrawn to the east toward Hill 209, a few running down another ridge to the north.

Two North Korean dead remained in the trench. I then took Sgt. James Forester's squad, and we moved down the trench to the east. Receiving fire from behind the first bend, we threw a hand grenade ahead of us before continuing. Finally, we came upon a bunker; we threw two grenades inside. I returned to my radio and notified the company commander that I was holding up for the night near a bunker. I could see signs of ambush at every bend in the dark trench.

I told the squad leaders to maintain 50 percent alert and to have their men take up defensive positions on both sides of the trench. Shea and Kober stood with me as we looked back down into Kaesong. We could see NKPA artillery dropping here and there among the lighted areas in the city, which made good targets for NKPA FOS.

I had laid wire, and now I called the company commander to make sure he knew exactly where we were, in the event fire support was placed on the ridge. When I asked him about the resupply and feeding plan, his only response was

Sgt. James Forester and SFC Thomas Shea in Korea. Forester was a squad leader and retired as sergeant major. Shea was the platoon sergeant and later received a battlefield commission.

that he'd discuss that when we took Hill 209 in the morning. I asked about ammunition resupply; he said he'd take the chance that we could make it without more ammunition. My response was, "What risk are *you* taking, Sir?" The line went dead.

Next morning, Shea volunteered to make a reconnaissance to see how far the trench went along the ridge. As I recall, he started down the trench and continued until he arrived at a bunker, where an NKPA soldier unsuspectingly walked into the trench. Shea shot at him as he jumped out of the trench and ran down the north side of the ridge. Shea then ran past the bunker, where he had a good view all the way to Hill 209. He decided that he had gone far enough. It was about 7:45 when Shea started back to the platoon, checking each bend in the trench for any enemy he might have overlooked before. As he looked back, he suddenly saw three marine attack aircraft, Corsairs, circling to the east of Hill 209. The aircraft dove, one behind the other, and strafed Hill 209, continuing along the trench to the west. Shea jumped into a lateral trench and avoided being hit.

When I saw the strafing run begin on Hill 209, I had the men get into the lateral trenches and the bunker nearby. By the time I had unrolled our identification panel for the pilots to see, the Corsairs were on their second strafing run, but I got it spread out in time to wave it from behind a lateral trench. Sergeant Kober yelled to me that all three aircraft had pulled up sharply. We all saw them waggle their wings as they flew down the ridge one more time, without strafing.

I moved the platoon to where Sergeant Shea was waiting, not knowing whether he had been hit by the "friendly fire" or not. He had buried a dead NKPA in a lateral trench and bandaged a soldier he'd captured. I called the company commander and let him know we had come under fire from Marine Corps aircraft but had received no casualties and were continuing toward Hill 209. We were about to run out of trench, which meant we would have to move by fire and maneuver to a rise that was just before a saddle running up to Hill 209. All three rifle squads deployed and moved slowly, leap-frogging a squad at a time toward a bunker on the rise, five hundred yards away. Sergeant Forester was wounded as we advanced, and then one of our Koreans was killed. Forester continued to lead his squad.

There were several shots, and then the long-range firing of a machine gun from Hill 209 caused the platoon to hit the ground. Suddenly Private Steiner shouted, "*A sniper!* I see him!" Steiner stood and fired two rounds at a shape hunched behind two rocks. You could see a rifle fly up into the air as one of Steiner's bullets caught the sniper between the eyes.

I got the platoon on its feet. I noted that Forester's wound was now slowing him down, and I had Corporal Daniels take over the squad so that the medic could take care of him. We assaulted an open bunker from a flank and found no enemy in it. Finally, we were at the rise that was five or six hundred yards away from Hill 209 as the crow flies. We had an excellent view of the gentle saddle, with a trench, between us and the reinforced bunker on 209. I told Kober that I wanted him to control the fires of our machine gun, 57 mm RR, and 60 mm mortar; in particular, I wanted him to place fire in the bunker's port that looked over the trench along the saddle.

While the support was being fired, I would take two rifle squads to attack the bunker, using the trench to approach it, and leaving behind Sergeant Shea with one rifle squad in the event I needed reinforcements. First, I went with Sergeants Saito, Bragg, Shea, Kober, and Corporal Daniels to where we could have a good view of the entire trench to Hill 209. I requested artillery fire on the bunker, as well as 81 mm mortar support, as we advanced up the trench. Kober laid the 57 mm RR on the bunker port, and I pointed out to him where we would exit the trench for the assault. I had one light machine gun accompany us up the trench so that we would have sufficient firepower when we were reorganizing afterward and awaiting the remainder of the platoon. As the first rounds of artillery landed, we got into the trench and began our trek toward Hill 209.

Sergeant Kober had the machine gunner fire about two hundred yards in front of us, searching up the trench ahead of us until it was no longer safe to support us. He had the 57 mm recoilless rifle fire into the port on the trench side of the bunker when we were about a hundred yards from where we planned to leave the trench. Upon leaving the trench, we assaulted the bunker from the rear with marching fire and threw several grenades into the rear entrance. Looking down the back side of Hill 209, a man yelled, "They're getting away!" We saw about fifteen North Koreans running down the hill. Saito and Bragg had their BAR men fire on the running enemy, and two of them fell. Inside the bunker we found two dead North Korean officers.

I placed the two squads in a defensive position on the north side of the hill and waved to Sergeants Shea and Kober to come forward. I then called the company commander and told him we had seized Hill 209. As I was reporting the results of our attack, we began receiving heavy small-arms fire from the east side of the hill. There was a scramble to get my people into the bunker and into the lateral trench on the east side of Hill 209, and to return the fire.

Sergeant Saito yelled, "Don't fire! Don't fire! GIs attacking!" Luckily we had the panel with us; Bragg and I flapped it quickly up and down. Someone among the advancing GIs yelled, "Cease fire! Cease fire!" It was a platoon from A Company. A few minutes later the Company A commander, Captain Deringwater, came onto the hill, and he was very angry that we had taken what he believed was his objective. He calmed down after contacting our company commander.

Deringwater then told me that if anyone had been injured during his assault on Hill 209, he would have preferred charges against our company commander for not coordinating my efforts with him. I found out later that our real objective had been the rise to the west of Hill 209; it had been Rounsaville who had assigned us Hill 209 itself. The two company commanders agreed to drop the matter. Two friendly fire incidents were more than enough for one day.

Our company commander didn't come forward either to where we had gained initial access to the main ridge or to Hill 209. It was late afternoon on October 10 when a small column of Korean laborers, each with an A-frame, arrived on top of Hill 209. The group had our resupply, water, and breakfast, and it evacuated the Korean soldier who had been killed.

During the night of October 10–11, I did some real soul searching about the profession of arms, to which my family and I were committed. The fact that we had seized the objective, whether it was ours or not, left me with little of the feeling of accomplishment that one might have expected. My main feeling at the time concerned the sacrifices that ordinary infantrymen made and their great value to our nation's foreign policy. I felt privileged to lead, and join in a union of wills with, men who met beyond all doubt the highest standards of American manhood. What amazed me most was that these men took on the responsibility of citizenship without expecting gain, in a nation that exalted great wealth. I felt the same about the South Korean soldiers in my platoon.

The First Battalion, Eighth Cavalry, now centered its main effort on seizing Kumch'on. On October 12, the battalion commander was severely wounded while riding on a tank on the road to Kumch'on. A heavy airstrike on enemy defenses was not enough to get the battalion through. I was ordered to patrol west along the high ridge on which we had been attacking for the past three days. When we reached the northern extension of the ridge, along the road to Kumch'on, I was ordered to attack north to mop up scattered North Korean units. The first day we had no contact. On the night of October 12–13, about 10 P.M., a small enemy force attacked us in our night-defense position. We fought off the brief attack, with no casualties.

As we continued north on the ridge paralleling the Kumch'on road, we could hear the sounds of battle, as First Battalion units harassed the withdrawal of the North Korean Seventeenth and Nineteenth Divisions. We found little resistance to our attack. Finally, the other First Battalion units reached us, extending from the road to our location on the ridge.

On October 12, while en route to Kumch'on, the drive of First Battalion, Fifth Cavalry, to cut off the remnants of the North Korean Twenty-seventh Division northeast of Kaesong was stopped. The newly arrived British Twenty-seventh Commonwealth Brigade, also operating in conjunction with the Fifth Cavalry Regiment, unfortunately took a dead-end road northeast of Kaesong and so was not involved in the battle for Kumch'on. The Second Battalion, Fifth Cavalry, fought through an enemy blocking force; for his actions during that engagement 1st Lt. Sam Coursen, USMA 1949, a member of our Basic Officers Course, won the Medal Of Honor posthumously. On October 14, Fifth Cavalry units secured Kumch'on and linked up with the First Battalion, Eighth Cavalry, south of Kumch'on. However, the bulk of the North Korean divisions had escaped the trap set for them above the thirty-eighth parallel.

By mid-October the Eighth Army was in North Korea, less the IX Corps, still engaged with NKPA guerilla forces in South Korea. By October 26, the X Corps was in the Wonsan area, under General MacArthur's direct control. His rationale was that the Taebaek Range's ruggedness above the Seoul-Wonsan corridor presented logistics problems that could only be dealt with by a separate corps, with its own line of communications.

On October 11, General MacArthur announced his intention to place all land-based air operations at Wonsan under X Corps, as well as to reassign the ROK I Corps, the first Eighth Army unit to cross the thirty-eighth parallel, to X Corps. Jawaharal Nehru reported that Chinese troops were massing on the Manchurian border. President Truman made arrangements to meet with MacArthur at Wake Island.

# 4 The Final Thrust

Euphoria ran high in the First Cavalry Division, right down to the last tired man, who was already shivering in his summer field uniform as the Manchurian winds blew stronger north of Kumch'on. Farther north, the town of Sariwon was in shambles. An informal ICORPS competition between the Twenty-fourth and First Cavalry Divisions ended with the cavalrymen being first into P'yongyang, with one exception. The ROK First Division made it across the Taedong River first; the North Koreans blew the bridges, but the ROK First Division crossed using fords known to the division commander, Gen. Sun Yup Paik, whose home had originally been in P'yongyang.[1]

On October 20, the Second Platoon, Company C, Eighth Cavalry, entered the darkened city, elated by the thought that the end of the war was but days away. I felt very good about how things were going. I had been awarded the Combat Infantryman Badge, I had been promoted to first lieutenant four months ahead of time, there was a good chance I'd get a company when we returned to Japan, and it wouldn't be long before Marge and Mary Lou would be joining me. General Willoughby, General MacArthur's intelligence officer, announced on the same day that organized resistance on any large scale had ceased and that the North Korean military and political headquarters may have fled to Manchuria.[2] This first inkling that the war was ending, however, was unknown to us "grunts."

I was almost asleep on the ground with my platoon outside of the feces-strewn building where we were to be quartered when the First Sergeant called for the platoon leaders to attend a meeting with the company commander. Captain Rounsaville told us that the 187th Airborne Regimental Combat Team had jumped north of P'yongyang, between Sunch'on and Sukch'on, and that we were to depart with a task force to link up with it at 0600 on October 21.

Task Force Rodgers consisted of the First Battalion, Eighth Cavalry Regiment, a Seventieth Tank Battalion company, and a platoon of light tanks from the Sixteenth Reconnaissance Company. My platoon was to ride on the lead light tanks.[3] Lt. Col. William M. Rodgers, commander of the Seventieth Tank Battalion, led the task force. The 187th Regimental Combat Team's mission was to capture North Korean officials and withdrawing troop units, and to rescue American prisoners who had been evacuated by train from P'yongyang. However, most of the U.S. prisoners had been murdered by the NKPA, outside of a train tunnel as they prepared to eat.[4]

During the movement to Sunch'on, great numbers of North Korean soldiers willingly turned over their weapons, which were destroyed by grinding them under tank tracks. My best estimate is that several thousand NKPA officers and men surrendered to us. When we made contact with the 187th, we found that it had been spread thin, and its men were more than happy to see our tanks. The only major contact by Task Force Rodgers occurred when the task force set up a defense at night in an area under excellent observation from the surrounding terrain. The tanks circled, and the infantry dug in among them. In the middle of the night, all hell broke loose when a North Korean antiaircraft battery lowered the tubes of its 37 mm antiaircraft pieces and fired on the task force. The tanks "buttoned up" (shut their hatches), but after I climbed up on one tank and returned fire with the externally mounted .50-caliber machine gun, the tanks finally returned fire with their main armament. The irony of the situation was that the next day, as we continued toward Sukch'on, we passed the battery of guns that had fired on the task force; it had already been hit by an air strike, but it had retained enough combat-worthiness to wound a number of people and damage several tanks by lowering its barrels and firing on the circled task force.

Throughout the linkup, we noted that people waved American flags and cheered as we passed through the villages. I imagine there were Kim Il Sung representatives present, however.

The main military contact by the 187th Airborne was at Opa-ri, in the western area of the operation, where 187th Airborne units engaged a retiring North Korean regiment.[5]

My platoon was relieved of its role of riding the light tanks when we headed south on the return leg of our mission. We were bivouacking outside of P'yongyang when we met the new company commander, Capt. James Walton. Captain Rounsaville had been promoted to major. Our euphoria upon finishing our "final mission" outweighed our thoughts of this change of command.

Walton was an older officer, about forty, who had been on the division G-4 (logistics) staff. He told us they had promised him a company when he joined the division in Japan.

If we thought there was euphoria in the air when we came north into P'yongyang, it was nothing like that when we returned to the city on October 23. First we turned in all ammunition except that needed for guard duty. Then we began having three hot meals a day; a training schedule was being prepared, the Bob Hope Show arrived, the FO said that artillery ammunition was being out-loaded, and—the last but most definite confirmation that the war was over—it was reported that a victory parade was being planned for the First Cavalry Division in Tokyo. Traditional yellow cavalry neckerchiefs arrived, along with an order that they be worn, adding to the credibility of war's end, except for a little mopping up.

My former company commander, now the battalion's operations officer, came into my platoon area with a gift for me. He gave me his M-2 automatic carbine, telling me he wouldn't need it any more. When I told the company commander about the gift M-2 carbine, his only comment was, "Let me know if he ever wants it back!"

On October 26, after the Bob Hope Show was over, my platoon had its turn to use the quartermaster shower facilities. Rumors were now rampant that the Chinese were very vocal about UN units operating in the direction of the Yalu River. There were even rumors that the People's Republic of China was coming to the aid of North Korea and had already sent units across the Yalu. It didn't take long for the rumors to downgrade morale.

On the day after the Bob Hope Show, we were conducting close-order drill on a cobblestone street outside of the battalion compound when the First Sergeant notified us that Captain Walton wanted to see the platoon leaders as soon as possible. We learned that ROK units many miles to the north were under heavy pressure and that it looked like we would be heading north again; that was all Walton could tell us. The shower-tent rumor about the Chinese took more solid form. My exact thoughts escape me, but I'm sure I reviewed the communist maxim: when they attack, we withdraw and surround, then we decimate their forces and withdraw again. I can remember a sense of anxiety, after the morale "trip" I'd taken during the past few days. I also knew that I had to look at this positively, probably in the way my ordinance battalion commander had done five years earlier when we were notified we were going to be deployed to the Pacific.

In the west the Twenty-fourth Infantry Division and the First Cavalry Division were to attack north toward where the ROK I and II Corps were already engaged, reportedly with the Chinese, and barely holding on. In the east the First Marine Division had landed at Wonsan; the Seventh Infantry Division and subsequently the Third Infantry Division would land at Hamhung. The ROKs had already reached the Yalu River, opposed only by light NKPA resistance. As the NKPA remnants withdrew, they were sucking American, Commonwealth, and ROK forces into the pockets they created, which were dominated by Chinese forces. This I understood years later.

The probability of Chinese intervention became no longer a question in late October, when a ROK unit approaching the Yalu River was nearly destroyed by Chinese forces. Then the First ROK Division became heavily engaged, forty miles south of the Yalu. The Chinese Fortieth Army was identified, and U.S. X Corps and ROK units north of P'yongyang began picking up Chinese prisoners. Any of these events should have caused a prudent commander to put a hold on all northward movement rather than describing the situation as "not alarming."[6]

By October 27, the UN forces had a mere five days remaining to organize a defense, preferably from Sinanju to Wonsan, a narrow, defensible line that could provide the UN forces with the operational and logistical capabilities needed in the face of an overwhelming Chinese intervention. The UN forces could have had the psychological advantage of retaining the North Korean capital within their lines and could have held terrain that would have been a nonnegotiable dividend. However, judgment was the first thing to be overwhelmed. As it was, the consequence of not acknowledging that the Chinese were in North Korea in strength was the forced withdrawal of UN forces below the thirty-eighth parallel.

The company commander finally met with us at 2:30 P.M. on October 27. We would be moving north in the morning to relieve the First ROK Division in the Onjong area, northeast of Unsan. The ROKs had identified Chinese forces, but the UN command had considered these Chinese to be only volunteers, used as fillers or in support of NKPA units. The entire Eighth Cavalry Regiment was being deployed, and, Walton said, we would relieve ROK forces on the west of the Samt'an River.

Walton then told us that our immediate task was to reissue ammunition, rations, and test our communications equipment. M-1 ammunition would be reissued as unclipped rounds; each man would be issued some clips (that is, the metal holders that contained the ammunition in the rifles' receivers), but not enough for all our ammunition. Until further notice, riflemen were to retrieve their clips as they were used. He emphasized that all high-explosive ammunition and hand grenades should be checked for safety pins. Each man was to carry three days' rations. What a way to begin an operation: pockets jingling with loose rounds!

Walton ended by telling us we would load onto trucks at 5:30 A.M. the next day. There were no questions; we returned and gave our platoons the bad news.

My former company commander, now a new major, strolled up to me and with a quick motion and a long face returned my old M-1 carbine. I swung the M-2 automatic carbine off my shoulder and gave it to him. With that he departed, without a word. I looked over at Captain Walton; he remarked that it looked like we were going north. "What a goddamn fiasco this is!" I heard one man in the platoon say as he was issued a dozen empty M-1 ammunition clips, several handfuls of loose M-1 ammunition, and two fragmentation grenades. He stuffed the loose ammunition in his field uniform pockets.

I had everyone clip their M-1 ammunition, and those with carbines load their magazines. Luckily, the light machine gun ammunition was reissued already belted, in ammunition-carrying cases. I had my sergeants check every grenade and bazooka round to ensure that the safety pins were secured. (During the night, a grenade went off accidentally in another company, wounding three men.) Later in the evening each man was issued a sleeping bag and a field jacket. As I stood outside looking up at the stars, a cold wind blew across the stage where Bob Hope had performed. The cobblestoned street was filled with trucks. We could kiss away that victory parade in Tokyo for now, I thought.

On October 28 the presence of the trucks, and men milling around as we waited to get on board, drew very little attention. Two youths watched hopefully for a GI to hand him a can from his rations, which several did. There was a larger group of civilians standing just outside our building, probably waiting for us to leave so they could search the building for anything left behind—or were they trying to pick up information on our plans?

The morning air was cold, and frost was visible on rooftops as we sped through the outskirts of P'yongyang to the ford over the Taedong River, the same road we had used returning from Sukch'on. A section of three tanks pulled ahead of our column, raising a cloud of dust from the crumbling concrete roadway. We followed the road to Sinanju, crossed the Ch'ongch'on River, and then headed northeast at Pakch'on. (See the map of North Korea.) There was a distinct change in our reception by the population from a week before. There were no U.S. flags or friendly peasants waving to us. The NKPA had probably left behind cells to control the population and punish those who had welcomed us earlier. There were absolutely no NKPA soldiers surrendering or offering up their weapons.

Looking in the bed of the truck, I saw that most of the men had unrolled their sleeping bags and crawled inside to protect them from the very cold wind, exacerbated by the rate at which the trucks traveled. At Sinanju, where the British Twenty-seventh Commonwealth Brigade maintained bridge security, a British officer told us that many of the civilians had left the area and were probably refugees in P'yongyang. The terrain became more mountainous and the road narrower the farther northeast we went. About 3:30 P.M. we reached the Kuryong River, where the road wound around sharp river bends along a high precipice.

An hour later the convoy halted, and the battalion continued on foot. That night, October 28, Captain Walton led the company to a small rise off the road, about two miles south of Unsan. The wind began blowing very hard, and snow flurries swirled about the rise. Between us and Unsan there was a battery of 155 mm howitzers, which fired all night in support of the ROK Eleventh and Fifteenth Regiments near Onjong. Unknown to us, these regiments, separated by the Samt'an River, were slowly giving way before the Chinese Thirty-ninth Army's 115th and 116th Divisions. Also unknown to us, the ROK First and Sixth Division commanders were convinced they were fighting organized Chinese forces, but their warnings were being denied all the way back to Japan. We dug in; the soil had started to freeze.

On October 29, we were up at 5:00 A.M. and headed north to an assembly area above Unsan. On the way we saw our first Chinese prisoners; they were being escorted to the rear by members of the ROK Eleventh Regiment. The ROK guards said there were only Chinese up ahead. I passed this on to Captain Walton. Later in the day, in the assembly area, a South Korean soldier and I stopped two Chinese prisoners. Their escorts showed us captured rifles marked with Chinese characters.

Maps were issued, and my platoon provided security around a platoon of tanks. North toward the Sangak-san Mountain and even across the Samt'an River to the east, the sky was filled with smoke, which concealed all ground movement. The Chinese forces had set these fires, probably to constrain the use of UN airpower. The wind carried an odor of the fires to Unsan. As we sat near the tanks on the banks of the Samt'an River, there was a continuous column of refugees crossing it at a ford. I told Shea and Kober to remember where that ford was located. I was beginning to sense an attack, this time by the Chinese, and the ford might be needed.

A South Korean lieutenant who had been wounded in the arm walked through our position with two other ROK soldiers and a Chinese prisoner with a hand wound. The lieutenant had been to the Officers Basic Course at Fort

Benning and spoke very good English. He told us that his battalion hadn't had any contact with NKPA units but had been fighting many, many Chinese. He said he had been wounded as his unit withdrew; he also said they had killed many Chinese soldiers, who had attacked in waves.

I reported this information to Captain Walton. He hesitated to pass it on to the new battalion commander, Maj. John Millikin, who had earlier told him that the Chinese were just a few volunteers, per higher headquarters. I told my sergeants about the response and told them that I doubted we'd see any enemy other than the Chinese.

All of a sudden, a second platoon machine-gunner fired his carbine in the air and started running down the road toward Unsan. I told Kober to go after him, but the First Sergeant had already stopped him. Kober talked to him, and they both came back up the road. He got into his foxhole. I told him the platoon depended on him and his machine gun; we all knew he was a skilled gunner. I also told him not to disappoint the men in the platoon. Unfortunately, he would be wounded four nights later as we defended ourselves against overwhelming Chinese assaults; he was declared missing in action.

About 5:00 P.M. on October 29, the increasingly gray, smoke-filled sky immediately to the north became even more ominous as tips of flame became visible, as if more fires were being set. There was a continuous whistle of outgoing artillery, and more columns of ROK soldiers began passing nearby, some carrying wounded in ponchos secured to poles. Each column had a small group of Chinese prisoners with it.

Captain Walton then showed us how the battalion was to be deployed on the forested hills north of Unsan. We would not relieve the ROKs at their position but would establish a line through which they could withdraw. We would follow Companies A and B; our company was to be the battalion reserve. My platoon would plug a gap between A and B Companies.

Company C began its movement into the foothills north of Unsan at 5:30 P.M.; the company, less my platoon, was positioned on a rise south of A Company. My platoon was assigned a position on a finger of land jutting out from the rear of Company A and extending to the rear of Company B, past the gap between those companies. There was a small valley between us and the rear of Company B. It was dark as we began digging. I had the platoon dig additional positions extending east toward the road along the Sam'tan River. The ROK columns with escorted Chinese prisoners continued to pass through our lines.

During the day on October 30, a platoon of tanks and infantry headed north on the road to the west of the Samt'an River, but it received heavy mortar fire and withdrew. Also during the day I saw 105 mm howitzers being towed south on the road across the Samt'an, apparently withdrawing to new support positions, or so I hoped.

It was about midnight when Walton notified me that I was to report to the battalion at 6:00 A.M. on October 31 to receive a patrol order. I told Sergeant Shea to organize a small patrol for me, to include the Korean soldier who understood some English. I had him select the patrol's members since he would be charged with the defense when I was on patrol.

When I arrived at the s-3 (operations and plans) tent the next morning, Major Rounsaville traced a route he wanted me to follow to contact the Second Battalion. There was a one or two–mile gap between the two battalions, and he emphasized that I was to search for any evidence that the NKPA had used the gap. I asked him if that included the Chinese; as I recall, he responded that the Chinese, if any, were replacements in NKPA units, not organized units. I wasn't surprised at his response.

I returned to pick up my patrol and was told to see Captain Walton before I departed. As I was going up the draw that led to the company OP, I distinctly heard the crunching of dry leaves. I assumed a deer had heard me and dashed away; we had seen several in the area. I was wrong! Unknown to me, three Chinese soldiers, their tan, padded uniforms blending with the dead leaves, were standing frozen in their tracks at the sight of me. I was told at the company CP that the battalion communications line had been tapped and that the enemy was stringing wire from the tap to the north. What had happened was that an enemy wire-tapping party had made a wide swing around Company A in the direction of Sangak-San Mountain, perhaps to the Chinese 116th Infantry Division; a Company A outpost fired on them, wounding one, but all three members of the party escaped. The empty wire reels and splicing tools found near the scene were all U.S. Army equipment.

I was told that after contacting the Second Battalion I was to extend my patrol to the northwest toward Sangak-San Mountain, to see if there was any evidence of NKPA or Chinese units assembled in the area. Walton was as surprised as I was at the inclusion of Chinese units in the patrol order.

I returned to my platoon, picked up my patrol, and moved out at about 8:00 A.M., proceeding from the rear of Company A to the low ridge that separated the two battalions. At about 8:30 we crossed a trail leading upward to much higher ground. The trail showed signs that a small group had used it to move in a northwestern direction. I sent three men up the trail, but they returned after ten minutes, one of them with a toothbrush they had found. Other than that, they had nothing to report.

Continuing on our contact mission, we finally reached the highest point on a small ridge and halted to observe to the west. Looking down into a little valley, I could see what looked like a squad of Americans sitting in their foxholes about a kilometer away. At about 9:15, we made contact with the right-hand (easternmost) company in the Second Battalion. I told them that there had been no evidence of any enemy in the gap between the two battalions, except for tracks on the trail and the toothbrush.

We then departed from the Second Battalion, climbing up a tree-covered finger of land as far as the trail we had crossed earlier in the morning. Turning northwest on the trail, we headed up the ridge in the direction of Sangak-San Mountain. Unknown to us at the time, up ahead of us on the same trail were the three Chinese soldiers who had survived their earlier contact with Company A; they were still unreeling wire, which they apparently believed was still tapped into the First Battalion landline. The Chinese soldiers had crossed our path without either group realizing it.

When we started up the trail, I placed one man on a point as an early-warning measure. After about a half-hour or so, he held up his hand. Leaving the patrol behind, I moved up to the point man, who was now under the low branches of a tree. He pointed to three men in quilted uniforms sitting and talking; I moved back to the patrol and brought the Korean soldier forward.

The two of us moved close enough for the KATUSA to hear the enemy conversation. The KATUSA told me that he could not understand their language and then said, very softly, "Chinee, Chinee!" I waved to the patrol to come forward under the concealment of the trees on both sides of the trail. I saw the three Chinese soldiers had reels of wire and were testing the line. Then they started back down the trail. When they reached the point where my patrol was hidden, the eight of us overwhelmed them, pinned them to the ground, and disarmed them. Taking off their tennis shoe–type foot gear, we bound their hands with their shoestrings.

I left them with three men from the patrol, whom I had moved back a distance into the forest for concealment. Five of us continued up the trail, with me taking over the point detail. We had covered at least a mile or so without noticing anything unusual when at about 10:45 we came to a rise where the trail met another that branched off to the left into a large grassy bowl, and to the right into the forested area. I could hardly believe what I saw in my field glasses; there in the bowl, which was covered with a dry, broad-leaf grass, I could see four to six hundred Chinese soldiers, their padded winter uniforms blending well with the dry grass. I signaled the KATUSA to come forward and had him look at the Chinese soldiers to confirm their presence and perhaps to identify them as Chinese troops. His only remark was "Many, many, Chinee!"

As the KATUSA and I lay there looking at the Chinese soldiers, we heard voices of several Chinese approaching us from the bowl. I quickly signaled the patrol to get off the trail. The KATUSA and I rolled back under the low-hanging tree boughs. I believe you could have heard our teeth chatter. I then saw five Chinese soldiers standing at the trail intersection. The KATUSA whispered that they were "Chinee!" One of the five was doing all the talking, pointing in various directions; he was wearing a pistol and seemed to be in charge. Finally, four of the soldiers headed northwest on the trail that led toward Sangak-san Mountain. I watched the one I believed to be an officer walk at a brisk pace back into the bowl and into the wooded area, where a tent was visible. I noted that the forest on three sides of the bowl was burning, at a distance. The soldiers were in small groups and appeared to be cleaning their weapons.

About 1:15, I saw the soldiers form into columns and start up the trail toward us. The KATUSA and I moved quickly down the trail to where our three patrol members waited. I still had a clear view of where the Chinese would exit the bowl; I told the patrol to return to where the three prisoners were and wait for me. Shortly after they departed, the head of the Chinese column crossed the main trail and moved in an easterly direction into a thickly forested area. I tried counting them; my best estimate was still four to six hundred men.

It was obvious that I had better get back to the battalion, so I picked up my patrol. The wounded prisoner had died from his wounds, but we started back to the battalion with the other two prisoners. At about 3 P.M. we arrived at a point that had an unbroken view of the Namyon River valley. As I looked toward the river with my field glasses, I saw an estimated four hundred Chinese soldiers sitting inside the edge of a wooded area on the north side of the river. They were concealed from air observation; my estimate as to their numbers was in part a guess. I marked the location on my map.

It was 4:30 when I arrived at the battalion CP. I turned the prisoners over to the s-2 (intelligence officer) and went to the s-3 (operations and plans officer) tent with the KATUSA. I asked him to tell the s-3 that the soldiers we saw were Chinese and that they spoke Chinese. I then showed the ops officer on the map where the two groups of Chinese were located. I concluded by telling him that the two Chinese locations would make good artillery targets and that we had made contact with the Second Battalion without incident. I don't think he was impressed.

He dismissed me, and I arrived back at my platoon just as it was getting dark. My only comment when I told Kober and Shea about the patrol was that I might as well have gone out a few hundred yards and stayed there all day.

The night of October 31–November 1, 1950, was a very quiet and cold night. I slept until 3:00, when Sergeant Shea awakened me for the early-morning watch. There was so much mist I couldn't see the rear of Company B in front of us. As I sat there in my foxhole with a cigarette cupped in my hand to hide its glow, I reflected on how fortunate I had been to have had Shea and Kober to assist me in leading my first rifle platoon in combat, even with the unorthodox job descriptions I had given them. I felt deeply that the three of us had done everything in our power to produce a class-A fighting team, especially in that we had never risked our men by placing them unduly in harm's way. I was amazed how well our men accepted their miserable stake in life, with so little to be gained, and how well they displayed an honor that was distinguished by any standard.

Then I thought about the patrol I had conducted the day before. My temples began to throb as I realized that though we had risked our lives for information that should have been considered essential in the preparation for battle, should it come, that information would be disregarded. Then it occurred to me that our platoon—the whole regiment—might be in another ring of fire, for exactly the same reason that my patrol report would have little impact on the outcome in the Unsan area. The problem was personal arrogance and professional lack of interest—that summed it up for me. I ducked down in my foxhole, lit another cigarette, and cupped it in my hand.

As a final thought, I guess my concern was that I hoped we had not been betrayed through the operational and informational negligence that had characterized the whole U.S. strategic thrust into North Korea. At my level, I knew that I had but a slight bit of the "big picture," but it annoyed me. I thought, "It doesn't matter if the Second Platoon fights well, because the battle may have already been settled, and no one can change that." But I told myself I'd fight this platoon, and fight it well, regardless.

Sergeant Shea sat down on the edge of my foxhole with me, and we watched the mist clear until we could see the small fires on top and to the rear of Company B, as their people heated their coffee and c-rations; the littered position became more visible as the sun rose. Shea remarked that it sure was hard to get rid of a bad habit! I agreed and then told him my opinion that the whole regiment should be consolidating on a more defensible piece of terrain than this molehill. I told him about the gap between our battalion and the Second Battalion, and that I imagined the same existed between the Second and Third Battalions. Realizing that this talk could be demoralizing, I changed the subject.

As we sat there, Captain Walton called and told me that the battalion wanted me to conduct another patrol to the locations where I had reported Chinese the day before. He told me that I was to be specific as to the size of formations and the weapons I observed. He wanted the coordinates of the "center of mass" of enemy units I observed. Walton ended by saying he had been informed that ROK units had been issued padded uniforms, as well as the NKPA units, so I had to make sure I didn't misidentify the units I observed. Walton remarked that it appeared the patrol report I had provided on October 31 had been sent up the line to the commanders, who wanted me to disprove myself.

I put together another patrol of three men and the same KATUSA who had been with me the day before. I cautioned the patrol to be especially alert for enemy patrols that might be searching for the wire-tappers we had captured the day before. I also told them that the enemy was not the NKPA; the enemy was now definitely the Chinese.

Arriving at the vantage point from where I had observed the Chinese near the Namyon River, I searched the area to the north of the river, east of Obang-San Mountain. In the edge of a forest south of the Namyon River I saw what I estimated to be six hundred Chinese, which may have been a little high, and also saw a small column of Chinese south of the river, moving south, partially concealed by trees. I had the KATUSA and other patrol members confirm my sightings. The great distance, about a mile and a half, and the undulating terrain covered with trees made estimates difficult.

As we continued up the trail toward Sangak-san Mountain, we heard voices and the sound of several soldiers walking on the trail. We quickly and silently rolled under the tree boughs and held our breath. About ten Chinese soldiers came stumbling down the rocky trail, unaware of our presence. They stopped farther down the trail; it sounded like they were preparing a defensive or ambush position. Telling the patrol to remain concealed, I crawled slowly under the evergreens in their direction. I could see that they were in fact preparing a position, so my only thought was that we had to get back to the battalion as quickly as possible to report what we had seen. I decided not to go any higher up the mountain and rejoined the patrol.

We commenced moving south, with me acting as point, on a long, silent crawl around the Chinese soldiers. When the sound of the digging faded, I led the patrol back to the trail toward friendly lines. Just before a bend in the trail I heard someone coming up the hill, and then more voices, so I signaled the patrol to move off the trail and to take up firing positions.

Around the bend came three individuals in civilian clothing, each carrying a burp gun, with one carrying a pack. I thought they would see us, so I gave the order to fire. Two went down, but the third got away. I took the pack from one of the dead, and, in the words of one of the patrol members, "we hauled ass" before the Chinese farther up the trail could reach us. Finally, out of breath, we stopped briefly, and I opened the pack. It contained several documents in both Korean and Chinese. There was a sketch of the general Unsan area, with locations of what I took to be our military unit locations.

We were back at the battalion CP by 1:00 P.M.; I turned in the pack and reported the coordinates of the enemy formations. Finally I said that I had been unable to confirm the location of the Chinese units seen the day before higher up on the trail. I was not convinced that anyone believed that we had ever seen any Chinese troops. I was thanked for my report and the documents and told I'd better get back to my platoon.

As I was returning to my platoon, I went through Lt. Charlie Wright's platoon. Wright had the 3rd Platoon and had joined the company in P'yongyang after we returned from linking up with the 187th Airborn Regiment. Wright told me that this was his four-hundredth day in combat, most of it in World War II. Then he said, "I'll bet you five bucks you get it before I do!" A couple of stray rounds cracked over head as we shook on the bet, and I returned to my platoon. I gave Shea and Kober a rundown on the patrol, once again saying I was convinced we would be facing the Chinese.

On October 25, a Chinese prisoner taken by the ROK Fifteenth Regiment had reported that the Chinese had an estimated ten thousand troops in the higher terrain north and northwest of Unsan, North Korea, and another ten thousand to the east toward Huich'on. On the same day a tactical air control party reported to a Mosquito aircraft pilot that there were ten to twenty thousand Chinese troops in the general Unsan area. The pilot reported this to Eighth Army headquarters. Later in the day, I Corps received a similar report from the G-2 (intelligence) liaison officer with the ROK First Division.[7]

The contacts and sightings of Chinese units near Unsan and reported through the chain of command during the period from October 25 to November 1 should have been sufficient reason for a concentrated intelligence-gathering effort before the Eighth Cavalry Regiment was fully committed to the Unsan area.[8] Myself, I knew nothing of the growing Chinese capabilities until I was sent on patrol on October 31 and November 1. By then the Eighth Cavalry's alternatives had been reduced severely. There can be little question but that large Chinese units were in North Korea by mid-October. Small groups of ROK soldiers, many bandaged head to foot, tired and hungry, and barely capable of controlling the Chinese prisoners they escorted, marched quietly through my platoon positions to the rear, knowing well that there was a new enemy in Korea, regardless of what the American generals said.

It was about 5:15 P.M. on November 1, 1950. The sun was setting, and Sergeant Kober was calling out names as he passed out the mail. There were a few small packages, probably cookies for Thanksgiving. As I sat in my foxhole reading a letter from Marge, Shea suddenly said, "What the hell is that up there?" Looking up, I saw what at first looked like a shooting star, but then I noted smoke and flame trailing across the sky. Following the smoke trail southwest across the Samt'an River, I saw the source. Several Katushka rocket launchers, courtesy of the USSR, were firing on Eighth Cavalry command posts and trains area. The Company C artillery forward observer directed a fire mission on the Katushkas; it was but a matter of minutes before the artillery began dropping on the rocket launchers. One must have made a direct hit; the launcher exploded in a ball of fire. The remaining trucks with their launchers moved behind a low ridge.

The battalion was placed on alert, in event of a ground attack. It was not dark yet. About 7 P.M., the first *crack!* of incoming small-arms fire caused necks to draw in. It was coming from the direction of Company B, to my immediate front. My account of what took place now at the Company B position is based primarily upon descriptions given to me at the time and from discussions with Company B personnel while I was in the hospital, later.

The Chinese troops closed to within assaulting distance of Company B, undetected. It is questionable whether anyone could have detected them, since most of the Company B men were sitting on the edge of their foxholes, heating c-rations and coffee, or resting on the ground outside their foxholes. By now it had been dark for over an hour, and the unit had not gone to alert status. There were Chinese infantrymen within the defense positions almost immediately; the defenders jumped into their foxholes and began firing. Fortunately, the automatic weapons gunners were able to initiate their final-protective fires, which temporarily stopped follow-on waves of the assault. The fighting became hand to hand, a shoot-out with the enemy soldiers who had penetrated the company. A Chinese bugler blew the recall, and the attackers withdrew.

About a half-hour passed without a shot being fired by either side, with the exception of outgoing artillery and mortar fire, some of it falling immediately in front of Company B. A wounded Chinese soldier lay a short distance in front of the company, moaning. A KATUSA crawled forward and dragged him into his position. Later, the man identified his unit as a battalion of the Chinese 116th Division. There were Chinese dead in front of the company and probably more behind it.[9]

About 7:30 the eerie sound of a bugle sounded again, and small arms fire began in front of Companies A and B, accompanied by Chinese mortars falling throughout the First Battalion positions. Several fell on the Second Platoon. There was a large gap in the First Battalion left flank between Company A and the Second Battalion, as we had found during our patrol on October 31.[10] A regiment could move through this gap at night with little risk of detection. Unknown to us, the Chinese attacking Company A found the undefended flank of the company. The 116th CCF Division (unbeknownst to me at the time) infiltrated through the gap into Unsan and wreaked havoc on the tanks and vehicles using the road through Unsan. Also unknown to us, by noon of November 1 the Chinese had passed around the 8th Cavalry Regiment, presumably to the west, and blocked the main road six miles south of Unsan. This effectively blocked reinforcement of the Eighth Calvary Regiment.

Meanwhile, in our front, bugles sounded repeatedly as the Chinese units successively assaulted and withdrew; their lines were apparently reinforced after each surge. Eventually we could see muzzle flashes and hear the crack of small-arms rounds that meant the Company B line was beginning to melt. The Chinese attained a foothold on the ridge, and I could see and hear more and more flashes on the hill in front of us. I requested friendly mortar fire immediately in front of the Company B position; the firing from the hill died down.

At this point a young infantryman ran to my position and said, "I'm not going to be an eighteen-year-old hero! I'm buggin' out!" I grabbed the soldier by the collar, placed my .45-caliber pistol to his temple, and told him that if he tried bugging out on me, he'd be a dead coward. He got back in his hole and continued to fight. Ethics take on a different tone in battle.

Now we began receiving a high volume of fire from the Company B ridge. I could hear men shouting and running toward us in the small valley below us; I recognized the voices as Americans and shouted to the automatic weapons gunners to fire bursts of three above them, on the Company B ridge, and again I requested mortar fire on it. I was sure also that we were running low on ammunition.

As withdrawing Company B men ascended our ridge, a Company B sergeant ran about wildly, shouting, "Cease fire, there are friendly wounded up there!" As the sergeant came by me I grabbed him and told him that if he wanted to help, he should stop his people and get them into the holes to our right. I called for Shea and Kober, and we all helped the sergeant get his men tied in to our right. One of the men who came in said he was a lieutenant; he hurriedly organized a platoon from the men coming up the rise. I never saw him again after that.

I then yelled to the 57 mm recoilless rifle to fire on the Company B ridge, but I could get no response. I rushed to the 57 mm RR position, to the right, and ordered the gunner to fire on the ridge in front of him. He then spaced the last seven rounds he had along the ridge now occupied by the Chinese. The Chinese once again attacked our position, just as I was running back to my position. I felt a burning sensation in my left knee and leg; I had been hit. I fell face first to the ground. I got up just as an enemy mortar round went off nearby; raising my arm in reaction, I caught a piece of shrapnel in my left forearm. After a few more steps, I got into my foxhole.

The platoon medic, Corporal Thacker, crawled over to me and bandaged the knee wound and removed the shrapnel from my arm, put sulfa on it, applied a bandage, and jabbed a morphine syrette into my leg. Then, checking my arm wound with his flashlight, he found it was bleeding heavily; he applied a temporary tourniquet and rebandaged the wound. I told him to check the other wounded but to hug the earth while he did it.

I crawled to Sergeant Shea's position. He said there were no more Company B men entering our line, that we had stopped twenty or thirty from the company. The latest assault on our position was now recalled, as the bugle blew again. I told Shea to check the machine gun on the left to make sure it was firing on the final protective line; I checked the right flank myself. I also found the Company B men on the right and found that about fifteen men from the regimental mortar company and an engineer detachment had joined them. I could not find the lieutenant who was with the Company B men, but I did find the sergeant. I told him he was in charge of our right flank.

The added reinforcements stemmed the repeated assaults, but the enemy continued to keep our attention to the front. At one point, my machine gunner near the left flank stacked up a number of Chinese not far from his position; it was obvious he had become an objective. I crawled over to an automatic-rifle man and had him tie in his fire with that of the machine gun, which slowed down the surge toward the machine gun. Suddenly, as the machine gunner was putting a new belt in his weapon, the operating handle disintegrated, and his right thumb was shot off. The assistant gunner immediately began to fire into the assaulting troops with his carbine. The gunner wrapped the wound with a bandage from his first aid packet, retracted the bolt of his weapon with a round of ammunition, and got the weapon firing again. Once again the enemy assault ended.

My right-flank machine gun was no longer firing, and I crawled along a fold in the ground to its location. The gunner told me he was running low on ammunition, with only one full case left, plus the half belt in his weapon. I told him to fire only bursts of three and to have his assistant gunner use his carbine to protect the gun position. I managed to crawl back to my foxhole. The Chinese assaulted the line again. I added to the fusillade with my single-shot carbine, and I threw my last three grenades, shouting, "Grenade the bastards!" Again the bugle sounded, and the Chinese assault ceased.

When I stood up to watch the enemy withdrawing in the moonlight, I immediately sank back into my foxhole, my sight becoming blurry. Thacker again got into my foxhole and checked both of my wounds. He found my arm wound was still bleeding and had soaked my uniform: the tourniquet had loosened. He told me he was going to get someone to help me back to the company CP, and he left the foxhole.

The next Chinese assault was feeble. When it ended, Sergeant Shea got into my foxhole and told me I should consider moving back to the company CP while I could still navigate. It was obvious that the medic had gone to Shea. When he turned on his flashlight and saw the blood-soaked right side of my uniform, he became insistent, and I agreed to go with another walking wounded. I told Sergeant Shea that he was in charge of the platoon and also of the Company B men and others on our right flank.

The other wounded man, who told me he was from Company B, had helped me partway up the rise on the path that led to the company CP when the Chinese assault on the line began again; the man received another wound, this time in his upper arm. I fell to the ground beside him. I applied the man's unused bandage to his wound, and we continued to crawl. He finally said he could go no farther, so I told him I would have someone come for him. Finding him a fold in the ground where he would be protected from small arms fire, I continued up the hill. When I finally reached the CP, the first sergeant, Thaxton, told me that Captain Walton had been killed and that he was trying to get Lieutenant Wright to take over the company. He also told me he'd have someone assist the wounded Company B man. At about the same time the s-3 notified the First Sergeant to prepare to withdraw the company—no mean task at that point.

Unknown to leaders at battalion and lower level, Maj. Gen. Frank Milburn, the I Corps commander, had at 8:00 P.M., November 1, called a meeting of division commanders, including those of the First Cavalry and ROK First Divisions.

Before going to this meeting, Major General Gay, of the First Cavalry Division, sent a warning order to the Eighth Cavalry Regiment to make plans for withdrawing from the Unsan area. The order reached company level about the same time that I reached the company OP, about 11:30 P.M.

At the meeting, Milburn had announced that the corps would go from the offensive to the defensive. He acknowledged that we faced a new enemy, the Chinese, and that they were not just "volunteers" for the NKPA. His decision to execute a twelve-mile withdrawal was two or three days late.[11] Had an order to pull back to more defensible terrain been given just a day earlier, the Eighth Cavalry Regiment could have conducted an organized withdrawal, and it would not have suffered the extensive casualties, equipment losses, and disorganization that occurred when the Chinese attacked. Accusations will not bring back the lost men, but we should reflect on how this happened and what results when commanders lose touch with the battlefield situation.

As I made my way down toward the battalion aid station with eight to ten other wounded, everyone helping each other, none of us had an appreciation of the total situation in the area around Unsan. There was no question that the Chinese forces had positioned themselves so as not only to push us from our positions but also, and of greater importance, to block any attempt to withdraw, as well as any relieving force. It would be 1961 before the events at Unsan would be fully known, with the publication of *South to the Naktong, North to the Yalu* by the Department of the Army.

Major Millikin, First Battalion commander, planned to hold until the Second Battalion cleared Unsan. However, the confusion that ensued as the Chinese attacked, coupled with a complete breakdown of communications and the scattering of regimental units, permitted the orderly withdrawal—over the only protected ford on the Kuryong River to Ipsok—of only his headquarters, B Battery of the Ninety-ninth Field Artillery, and the First Battalion and Second Battalion vehicles and trains. Batteries A and C of the Ninety-ninth ran into Chinese roadblocks. Survivors scattered into the hills; they would filter into Ipsok for several days.

Early in the morning of November 2, I was in a field ambulance when it came under fire while crossing the river; after crossing, the engine failed. Two other wounded and I walked the rest of the night. Early in the morning, from a high hill southeast of the Kuryong, we saw fires in a valley and, reconnoitering, found a small unit from the ROK Fifteenth Regiment. The ROKs rebandaged our wounds and drove us to a clearing station in Ipsok. From there we were flown to the field hospital in P'yongyang.

In the meantime, Major Millikin, the First Battalion commander tried to withdraw the remnants of his battalion as a fighting unit, but the battalion split up into small groups, which crossed the sole ford of the Samt'an River. At 8 A.M. on November 2, Millikin reached Ipsok, where he found about two hundred men; about fifteen officers and 250 men of the First Battalion had become casualties. Millikin's decision to withdraw Company A, the remainder of Company B, and his trains early in the battle reduced his losses, although his battalion, like the Second, was no longer a combat-effective unit.[12] The Eighth Cavalry regimental headquarters, four tanks from the Seventieth Tank Battalion, and five artillery pieces crossed at the Kuryong ford and joined the division at Yongsan-dong on November 2.

The Third Battalion was the last unit to be attacked, and it suffered the most heavily. Its commander, Maj. Robert Ormond, who would die of wounds, had been able to hear clearly the battle to his north, while all was quiet in his area. His command post was located in a field east of the Namyon River and north of Camel Head Bend. The battalion's mission of protecting the regimental rear had been overtaken by the forced withdrawal of the First and Second Battalions, leaving the Third Battalion to fend for itself. Then the Chinese attacked. The battalion's units converged on the embattled command post and slowly established a perimeter. The Chinese forces destroyed tanks defending a Namyon River crossing, attacked the trucks to be used in withdrawing the battalion, and engaged the battalion perimeter in hand-to-hand combat.

By the time the Chinese soldiers had been driven out of the perimeter, the battalion had been reduced to six officers and two hundred men, with about 150 wounded in the command post dugout. By first light on November 2 the Chinese had withdrawn, and fighter-bombers attacked their positions throughout the day. This permitted the small battalion force to improve its position, gather ammunition and weapons from their trucks, and collect enemy and friendly dead.

The Chinese returned, but Third Battalion continued to resist. As casualties mounted, eventually to 250, they were placed in the command post bunker. Finally, on November 4, it was overrun. The chaplain (Father Kapaun), the s-3, and fifteen walking wounded were marched away as prisoners. Capt. Clarence Anderson, the battalion surgeon, volunteered to remain with the wounded rather than join the final attempt by remnants of the battalion to escape. Maj. Veale Moriarty, the battalion executive officer, rallied a group of defenders outside of the perimeter and led them across the Namyon River; when he reached Ipsok, he had assembled over a hundred Eighth Cavalry troops. The bravery of all these people was nothing less than extraordinary.

Mack, several days before being discharged from the hospital in Hokkaido, Japan.

The rest of the battalion split up into groups, but on November 6 they were surrounded and captured. By the end of the day the battalion had ceased to exist as an organized unit. This all happened near Yongbyon, today the location of a North Korean nuclear research facility.

The Fifth Cavalry Regiment had tried to break through the road block six miles south of Unsan to the Third Battalion until last light on November 2, but the Chinese had prevented the relief. The Fifth Regiment had suffered high casualties among its assault companies in the rescue attempt.

When I woke up in a hospital in P'yongyang, on the cot next to me was Lt. Charlie Wright, whose first question was, "What time did they get you, Mack?" He had won the bet! We were evacuated by air to Fukuoka, Japan, and subsequently to the Tokyo Army Hospital. In late November I was transferred to the U.S. Army Station Hospital in Sapporo, on Hokkaido, for physical rehabilitation.

The consequences of sending the Eighth Cavalry Regiment to relieve ROK elements were many and varied, not the least being that as of November 3 the regiment had lost over half its strength and was no longer combat effective. Many high-ranking officers probably now wished that the UN forces had never crossed the thirty-eighth parallel. The losses sustained at Unsan also included those of the U.S. Ninth Field Artillery Battalion and Sixth Tank Battalion, which had been supporting the ROK regiments. The Eighth Cavalry Regiment's losses amounted to well over six hundred men killed, wounded, and missing, twelve 105 mm artillery pieces captured, and nine tanks destroyed or captured.[13]

The battle of Unsan had not been inevitable. Before the Chinese 115th and 116th Divisions and the 347th Regiment attacked, enough had been known about their presence and strength to have justified a withdrawal to a more defensible and supportable position. The many reports provided by the ROK First Division to U.S. intelligence officers and commanders had confirmed the presence of large Chinese units. By the early morning of November 1, the only safe route of withdrawal was to the east, through the ROK Fifteenth Regiment area, but there would be no decision to withdraw for twelve hours: by then the die was cast. Again, the denial of the threat emanated from the Dai Ichi Building, and it followed the chain of command down to the Eighth Cavalry regimental headquarters. It's always easier, if not safer, to agree with the boss! Adding insult to injury, the action at Unsan was described at the time as an ambush of the Eighth Cavalry Regiment. Ambush, hell![14]

I arrived at the Army hospital in Sapporo just before Thanksgiving 1950. I was the only officer patient in the hospital, and I would be there for over three months. When I found this out, I asked the hospital commander if he could give me some duties, so that I could assist his staff. He asked me to plan trips to the ski slopes nearby, the athletic facilities at Camp Crawford, and the spa and rest hotel at Naborabetsu. He wanted to get the troops active to hasten their recuperation and, of course, their return to duty. In the next three months, I learned to ski myself. In early March 1951, I was placed on limited duty and assigned to Company 3, First Infantry Battalion, at the Japan Replacement Training Center at Camp Drake, which had become a very impersonal body depot. Perhaps the most challenging part of that assignment was maintaining control over the men, who, mostly draftees, experienced the anxiety of knowing they would enter combat within a few days.

After three months, I requested reassignment. By mid-June 1951 I was back in Korea with the G-3 staff (operations and plans) of the First Cavalry Division, which was by then in the Yongch'on-Chorwon valley area, conducting limited operations against the Chinese. General MacArthur had been relieved by President Truman in April 1951 over policy disagreements. The UN forces were now at the thirty-eighth parallel, under the command of Gen. Mathew B. Ridgway, a determined, objective leader. There was little doubt now that the U.S. strategy was "containment" and not victory in Korea. The Chinese entry into the war ensured that strategy for Asia as well. The focal point in Korea was the armistice negotiations, conducted initially in Kaesong and then at Panmunjom.

After several weeks as an operations duty officer, I was assigned as the liaison officer to the British First Commonwealth Division, which was commanded by Maj. Gen. A. J. H. Cassels. By the end of October, I had traveled the back roads from the Commonweath division to the First Cavalry well over 120 times. Then, one night in mid-November, I was notified I'd be returning to the United States within a week or so. That meant I would be home with Marge and Mary Lou by Christmas.

I had lived in a two-man tent with a New Zealand lieutenant for several months. When I told him my good news, his only response was, "Let's have a party." The officer's mess tent resounded with toasts, even as the British artillery was firing.

I boarded a General-class troopship in Fukuoka, Japan. We steamed under the Golden Gate Bridge in mid-December 1951. It reminded me of passing under the bridge almost six years earlier, with two differences: Marge and Mary Lou would be waiting for me, and there were no welcome-home banners or cheering crowds. It was already the "Forgotten War."

# 5 | **Between Wars**

On December 15, 1951, I met Marge, her brother John Burkley, and Mary Lou at the bus station in Akron. Marge was as beautiful as ever, and Mary Lou could now walk. It would take Mary Lou a few days to get to know who this guy was who had just shown up in the middle of the night.

There were still men suffering in the war in Korea. That fact was out of most peoples' minds, except for families having relatives there. I had noticed this as soon as I arrived in San Francisco. Marge had already faced the downside of Army life—our separation of nearly a year and a half, and the responsibilities of a single parent.

Just before New Year's, we packed up our new 1951 Chevrolet and headed for Fort Benning, making a short visit with Marge's sister, Rosalind, and her husband, Ed Maher, in Upper Darby, Pennsylvania. Ed was an FBI agent in Philadelphia.

At Fort Benning, once again we lived in the Camelia Apartments. However, in the summer of 1952 a Wherry military quarters project called Upatoi Terrace was opened, and with five other fortunate families we moved in. Our second daughter, Rosalind Theresa Mack, was born in September at the Fort Benning hospital.

I was assigned as the executive officer of an officer candidate company in the First Officer Candidate Regiment, which was working at full capacity to provide infantry platoon leaders for Korea. Shortly after I arrived, I was awarded the Silver Star for my actions at Unsan. It was Sgt. First Class Thomas Shea, my platoon sergeant, who had recommended me for the medal.

The officer candidates were drawn from the enlisted ranks of the Army, not civilian life. The selection process was initiated at the unit level. A soldier who

Mack receiving a Silver Star from Maj. Gen. Robert N. Young, commandant of the Infantry School, Fort Benning, Georgia, summer 1952.

met the standards as to education, physical fitness, and past performance evaluations appeared before a local officer candidate board. A high percentage of the candidates were draftees who were college graduates.

The officer candidates pursued a six-month course quite similar to the Basic Officers Course; the attrition rate was in the neighborhood of 33 percent of each company, but there was never a quota. The candidates were organized into platoons, with a commissioned tactical officer assigned to each platoon. Every three days the leadership positions in the platoons and companies were rotated among the candidates. On each training day, the tactical officer accompanied his platoon from breakfast until late at night, rating the candidates' performance and counseling them. Candidates knew that they had at least one pair of eyes on them at all times. In addition, candidates rated each other periodically; their evaluations usually confirmed the tactical officers' assessments.

As the Korean War wound down in 1953 and talks intensified at Panmunjon, fewer officer candidate companies were required, and many tactical officers began looking for other assignments at Fort Benning. Reassignment away from Fort Benning was held to a minimum, because of the costs involved. Initially I was reassigned as the adjutant in the battalion, with the additional duty of deactivating a company.

I looked into assignment to the airborne regiment at Fort Benning, but I had to complete airborne training first. While I was taking parachute training, the regiment was transferred out, and thus I wasn't sure which coal bucket I'd be carrying. When my OC battalion was deactivated, I became the OC Regiment information and education (I&E) officer, a job at which I worked hard but without great inspiration. I was sent to Fort Slocum, New York, for a six-week I&E course, and then I knew which bucket it would be for the next year and a half.

Then I saw a notice in the Fort Benning daily bulletin that the twelve-month Russian course at the Army Language School in Monterey, California, was undersubscribed and that applications for it were being expedited. I applied for the course, and just after Christmas of 1953 Marge, Mary Lou, Rosalind, and I began our drive to Monterey.

The course was rigorous, with the goal of fluency in spoken Russian in one year. I had never studied so hard in my life. I was quite surprised when upon completion of the course I was rated as an interpreter. But then, studying Russian was the only thing I did, day and night, for a year. Years later, after retiring from the Army and becoming an amateur radio operator, I found I could still carry on conversations with Russians.

We were fortunate to find a small house in Pacific Grove, not far from the rocky shore; I memorized my daily dialogue sitting in my car at the rocky shore. While I was at ALS, our third daughter, Elizabeth Marie, was born at nearby Fort Ord, California. After I completed the course, in December 1954, we commenced our six-day drive back to Fort Benning. I had been promoted to captain at ALS and was slated to attend the Infantry Officers Advanced Course, a nine-month program that commenced in August 1955. I was interviewed about becoming the assistant post I&E officer as an interim assignment, but instead I was given command of Company B in the Infantry School Detachment. There I was responsible for 150 soldiers who worked in the communications department at the Infantry School.

Perhaps the most interesting soldier I came to know in Company B was my First Sergeant. He had spent more time at Fort Benning than anyone else there at the time. Other than a year overseas during World War II, he was the "homesteader" of record. It was not unusual for a general visiting Fort Benning to invite him to dinner at the officers' club. He had known many who were now wearing stars when they had been lieutenants.

In August I left Company B and began the Advanced Course, a program dedicated to command, staff, and tactical responsibilities within an infantry regiment. The Army was in the process of reorganizing into the "pentomic" concept, under which the regiment was being replaced by the "battle group," in order to make the Army's field organization compatible with the nuclear battlefield. The course concerned itself with this reorganization, which took effect some time later. The year in the Advanced Course passed quickly; I wrote my monograph on marching fire, using both research on World War II and my own experience in Korea.

In May 1956 I received my reassignment orders, to the Sixth Infantry Regiment in Berlin. In June we boarded a transport at McGuire Air Force Base in New Jersey for our flight to Frankfort, from where we flew in a c-46 to Templehof Aerodrome in West Berlin. Several days later we moved into an apartment on Amhegewinkel Weg, where we would live for three years.

In the summer of 1956 the effects of World War II on Berlin were still clearly visible; there were many gutted buildings in the Western sectors, but nothing like in East Berlin, which, under the control of the USSR, resembled a battlefield more than a city. The city had been divided into U.S., French, British, and Soviet sectors. You could hardly tell the difference between the Western sectors, but there was never any doubt when you entered the Soviet sector.

The Western Allies maintained troops in Berlin, a hundred miles behind the Iron Curtain, to ensure that the city remained accessible by the four principal routes—the autobahn, the air corridors, rail, and the canals—in accordance with the Potsdam Agreement. A great deal of our training and exercises had to do with defending our right of access. The Sixth Infantry was the American contribution to this effort. Being surrounded by twenty-some Soviet divisions, we amounted to a trip-wire defense.

I commanded Company C, at McNair Barracks, a former German electronics manufacturing facility. We had an excellent field training area, the Grunewald, which we shared with the strollers, lovers, and the paramilitary West Berlin Police. There was seldom a training day when we were not in the field. The First Battalion commander was Lt. Col. Tom Cleary (West Point, class of 1941).

We exercised our right to access via the autobahn to Berlin by frequently sending convoys to Helmstedt in West Germany. An infantry company would mount onto trucks, which, with tanks standing by in event the Soviets had closed the checkpoint barrier, would roar through the Soviet gate into East Germany, as the company commander stood watching with a Soviet officer.

Company C, Sixth Infantry Regiment (approaching) during one of the weekly retreat parades in the Ring Strasse in front of the regimental headquarters and MacNair Barracks, Berlin, 1956.

The convoy manifests were bilingual, English and Russian. In addition to an infantry company, the convoys would include a communications van and usually two or three semi trucks with trailers to carry the "atom bombs" we were accused of transporting into and out of Berlin. In actuality, the trailers carried beer into Berlin and carted the empties out.

Every company practiced the procedures they would take if access were denied, but while I was there, only one convoy was ever denied passage into or out of Berlin. On every occasion where the Soviet officer on duty asked or demanded to inspect the cargo in trucks and trailers, he was stonewalled with a *Nyet.* In the one case, however, a two-vehicle convoy with a corporal in charge was prevented from exiting the autobahn into West Germany, at Helmstedt. For three days the corporal denied every request from Soviet officers to inspect the contents of his two vehicles. He and his two drivers camped beside their vehicles, ensuring there would be no inspection. Finally, a high-level State Department official was sent to the scene. He agreed to inspect the vehicles for a Soviet colonel; after peeking into both vehicles, he responded that there were no unauthorized articles aboard. The Soviets were tired of standing in the snow, so they let the Americans pass.

The next day, after the corporal had led his convoy back to Berlin, Maj. Gen. Barksdale Hamlett (West Point, 1930), the U.S. commander in Berlin, called the corporal to his office and promoted him to sergeant. General Hamlet said that for two days the corporal had been, in effect, the chief negotiator on behalf of American rights, and that he was more than deserving of his new stripes for his persistence in defending U.S. foreign policy. A great day for the Army!

Commanders of infantry companies in Berlin had to train their units as integral parts of a combat battalion; this included offensive and defensive operations, communications, weaponry, physical conditioning, transportation, and all the soldierly skills that contribute to unit readiness. Withdrawal and defensive tactics took on special meaning, as the defense of West Berlin would have required a tactical withdrawal to a combined defense line manned by American, British, and French troops.

My family and I often drove into East Berlin on Sundays. There was no wall then, and it was an occupational right under the Potsdam Agreement. We had to face the surly Volkspolizei (East German police) and an almost complete prohibition against buying anything, but we and many visitors from West Berlin visited such places as Treptow Memorial Park, where there were five plots, each containing the graves of a thousand Soviet soldiers killed in the capture of Berlin. For the most part, East Berlin was a drab place, with a facade of new buildings on the main streets blocking the view of old buildings to the rear.

Each of the Sixth Infantry's three battalions went to the Hohenfels Training area in West Germany each year for field training and an annual readiness test. In June 1957, while I was at Hohenfels, another major event took place in the Mack household. Marge gave birth to Richard E. Mack, Jr., in the U.S. Army hospital in Berlin. When our battalion training test was completed, the battalion commander, Colonel Cleary, gave me permission to return to Berlin to see Marge and our first and only boy.

As a result of Company C's excellent performance in the testing at Hohenfels, we were assigned to guard Spandau Prison, where those convicted of war crimes at Nuremberg were incarcerated. One notable among the few remaining prisoners was Rudolph Hess. There was a change of guard ceremony, at which we took over from the Soviets. Following the ceremony, I met the adjutant to the Soviet commander of Berlin, Lt. Col. Igor Medved. I was able to use my Russian, since he claimed to speak no English. A few months later I met him again, at a wedding reception for the U.S. governor of Spandau Prison and his wife. Medved and I spoke Russian once again.

Left to right, Rosalind, Richard E., Jr., Marge, Elizabeth, and Mary Lou, taking a walk in Berlin. Richard, Jr., was born in Berlin in 1957.

After I had commanded Company C for a little over a year, the regimental commander, Col. Glenn D. Walker (later commander of the Fourth Infantry Division in Vietnam), told me that there wasn't much more for me to learn in a rifle company and gave me command of the First Battalion's heavy weapons company. Its previous commander had failed an inspector general's inspection, and I had a month before it was to be inspected again. I found that my predecessor had not used the chain of command but had permitted individual soldiers to come to him when they had problems, bypassing his First Sergeant, platoon leaders, platoon sergeants, and other leaders. He personally designated the employment of individual support weapons, without using his leaders in the platoons. I corrected his errors, and the company passed the next inspection.

A few months after I took command of Heavy Weapons Company, Colonel Walker told me there was a "hot job" in the office of the U.S. Commander of Berlin (USCOB), as the assistant secretary of the General Staff. I interviewed for it and was accepted. This was to be my first opportunity to observe how the

Army was involved in foreign relations during the Cold War, in particular with the USSR. I was responsible for the classified documents, preparing itineraries for important visitors, making arrangements for staff meetings, and preparing correspondence to higher headquarters. Gen. Barksdale Hamlett, as the ranking U.S. officer in Berlin, had a State Department officer as a deputy and was responsible for the many intelligence units operating in Berlin.

There were two items that every visitor wanted on the itinerary: a visit to the mayor's office, a photograph with Mayor Willi Brandt, and a Berlin bear statuette. It was always a big plus if the visitor left with a copy of a West Berlin newspaper containing an article on the visitor and a picture of him. There were also peculiar requests from the visiting VIPs. For example, when the chief executive officer of General Foods visited Berlin, I escorted him and his wife to the Dahlem Art Museum, where the Rembrandt masterpiece "Man in the Golden Helmet" was at the head of the stairwell. I learned after we had been at the museum for only a few minutes that what they really wanted was a premier German after-shave lotion and a new mini–tape recorder. For the remainder of the afternoon, we must have visited every drug store and electronic shop in town, until we had filled the trunk of the staff car with that year's holiday gifts.

Shortly after I was assigned to USCOB, a Soviet captain entered the office, handed me an envelope, and requested my signature. When I opened the letter, I found that the Soviet Commander of East Berlin was notifying General Hamlett that an American soldier had been picked up in East Germany on board the S-Bahn; the Soviets wanted General Hamlett to contact the East German authorities about the man's return. The United States had no diplomatic relations with East Germany, and we refused to meet with its authorities and governmental departments. General Hamlett usually would go directly to the USSR authorities in cases such as this; the Soviets took pleasure in obfuscating matters.

In any event, I wrote an English synopsis of the letter, which was in Russian, at the bottom and passed it in to the general's office. Later in the morning, General Hamlett wanted to know who had written the synopsis. I admitted it, believing I had somehow made a major error in office procedures. Instead, General Hamlett told me that for the past year he had been passing the letters to the State Department translator and had often waited several days for "official translations." He told me in the future just to make a copy of any Soviet letter, give him a synopsis of the contents, and send it for the official translation. He said there had been times when he had worried needlessly over some minor "bitch" from the Soviets, sometimes for days.

Mack conducting an honor guard for Gen. Clyde Eddleman, the USAREUR commander at Templehof Aerodrome in West Berlin in 1957. From left: Gen. Barksdale Hamlett, U.S. commander of Berlin; Captain Mack; General Eddleman.

On Thanksgiving Day of 1958, Nikita Khrushchev, the Soviet premier, gave the Allies six months to get out of Berlin. We received a copy of the State Department message on this matter at 2:00 A.M. The message was conciliatory. General Hamlett told me to get his staff together, and after a meeting, which I did not attend, he came out of his office and handed me a message to be sent to the secretary of state. It said that he had served his country for many years and never thought he would see the day when an official of the U.S. government would give in to a Soviet threat. Later that morning we received a message from the secretary of state rewording the official position to the effect that under no circumstances would we ever consider withdrawing. General Hamlett was definitely the man who was fully qualified to be the U.S. Commander of Berlin.

By early 1959 the Soviet rhetoric had cooled, but there was still a major effort on the part of the East German government to keep the kettle boiling. An example began with invitations received by many in the Allied sectors to visit East Berlin and see a movie based on Dostoyevsky's *The Idiot*. The afternoon before the movie, another captain and I were sent to Treptow Park to test the waters concerning a suspected planned demonstration by the East German communist youth, the Young Pioneers. In fact, we ran into a practice demonstration and had our two staff cars splattered with red paint.

That evening, when Marge and I, with many others from West Berlin, drove to the Soviet theater, there was a Volkspolizei on every corner. There were going to be no incidents. I was surprised to find Lieutenant Colonel Medved, whom I had met earlier, making himself available to interpret for Marge. I agreed with his offer, though I wondered out loud how he would interpret, inasmuch as he had said before that he didn't speak English. This he glossed over, but with a red face.

Marge and I took one leave while we were in Berlin. We went to Chem Zee for a week, making several bicycle trips into the mountainous countryside, as well as a trip to Salzburg, Austria. We were able to take this vacation only because Marge's mother and aunt came to Berlin to stay with our children. We were determined never to leave the children behind the Iron Curtain with a baby-sitter.

Two days before the six-month deadline for the Allies to leave Berlin, Hamlett and his aide went to the Templehof Aerodrome and, with golf clubs over their shoulders, waved farewell to assembled reporters and photographers. They left for a week of golfing in Scotland; Hamlett was a master at thumbing his nose at the Soviets. A few weeks later, the Western Allies still in Berlin, Marge and I, family in tow, boarded the train for an overnight trip to Frankfort. From there we flew to McGuire Air Force Base, New Jersey, and after picking up the Volkswagen bus we had bought in Berlin, we headed west to visit family in Ohio.

I had been assigned to ROTC duty at the University of Scranton, Pennsylvania, an assignment that I had not requested. When I visited the ROTC Department, I found that I was scheduled to attend the ROTC instructors course at Indian Town Gap Military Reservation, near Harrisburg. Luckily, our household goods didn't arrive until after I finished the course that summer.

I picked up Marge on the first of August, and we soon found out that we had moved into a very friendly community. My primary responsibility was to teach U.S. military history to the freshman class, half the first semester, the other half the second semester. The freshmen also had a semester of weapons instruction. The sophomores had a course on national security and communications. In the Advanced Course, juniors had a course in the branches of the Army and preparation for summer camp. The seniors' instruction was a continuation of tactics.

Our production requirement was thirty commissions a year. I was particularly impressed with the dedication of the students to obtaining good educations. Most of them came from the Wyoming Valley part of Pennsylvania. I have always had the impression that it was mostly the home environment that prompts hard work and study. We found that those admitted to the advanced program, completion of which led to a U.S. Army Reserve commission, were academic achievers.

After the second year, in addition to teaching military history, I took over the advanced class. As part of the course we made visits to Tobyhanna Depot, nearby, and to Fort Belvoir and Fort George G. Meade in Virginia, where the students could become acquainted with such Army functions as inspections, discipline, feeding troops, and familiarization on firing ranges. At Tobyhanna we conducted several weekend stays, with bivouacs and squad-level exercises.

In order to emphasize the importance of physical fitness, I was able to get the university to install pull-up bars and a sit-up brace in our classroom; this, together with encouraging the students to jog and engage in other exercise, was the extent of their physical training.

Of the people I met in Scranton, two who left a lasting impression on Marge and me were John and Frances Baldi. John was the chairman of the sociology department and served on the selection board for Advanced Course candidates.

During World War II John had served in Army intelligence on New Caledonia, and he spoke fluent Italian and French. Another was Father Kelley, the Dean of Studies, who, when I was promoted to major in 1961, pinned on my gold oak leaves. I had the feeling that the Jesuits, with their attention to organization and discipline, found the ROTC philosophy quite acceptable.

In 1961, John F. Kennedy visited the city and made a political speech at the National Guard Armory. He may have mentioned the U.S. advisory effort in Vietnam. I remember taking my daughter, Mary Lou, to see and hear the future president for the first time. The crowd was so great that she sat on my shoulders to get a peek at him.

As far as Vietnam was concerned, I remember making a plastic viewgraph from a geography book just to show my ROTC class where Vietnam was. At that time we had advisers with South Vietnamese military units, but it was still "a nice little war," where regular Army officers sought to be posted, a few for career, but most for professional reasons. Careerists began to go there only with the introduction of U.S. forces, as there was little promotion advantage to be gained as an adviser, only an appreciation of the utter complexity of this little

Mack, with Marge, upon being promoted to major, being congratulated by Father Kelley, Dean of Studies, University of Scranton.

war. The stigma that service in Vietnam later accrued had not been conceived; it had an aura of patriotism.

Our Professor of Military Science and Tactics, Lt. Col. John Brady (West Point, 1944), was reassigned to a military assistance role in Turkey in early 1962. Before leaving he sold his old Dodge to me for fifteen dollars; it served me well during ROTC summer camp at Indian Town Gap that summer. We had very little transportation at summer camp, so Brady's old car roamed the trails, hauling ammunition, weapons, rations, and water during the small-unit tactics segment that my team and I presented to each ROTC company at camp.

Following summer camp in 1962, I was assigned to the Command and General Staff College at Fort Leavenworth, Kansas. We moved into the "Bee Hive," a three-story former barracks converted into family quarters. The year at Fort Leavenworth lifted one from company and regimental-level thinking to the lofty arena of division and field army operations. It was conducted almost entirely by the team, seminar, and war-gaming methods of instruction. Every student prepared a staff study and presented it to his section; my study was on how to incorporate counterinsurgency into the advanced ROTC program. We had guest speakers who covered the war in Vietnam, and we had the opportunity to discuss

Mack's picture from the 1963 Command and General Staff College class book.

Vietnam with Southeast Asian officer students, but in the 1962–63 school year there was not a lot of discussion of Vietnam among U.S. officers.

A great deal of the instruction was on staff functions in realistic combat situations; we role-played personnel, operations, intelligence, and logistics staff officers. These map exercises normally required preparation of operation plans or orders. Nuclear warfare was integrated into most scenarios.

In May 1963, I received orders to Vietnam as a regimental adviser, with a preliminary three-month stint at the Defense Language Institute in Monterey to study the Vietnamese language. We rented and moved into a house in Stow, Ohio, for Marge and our family to live in while I was gone, next to her sister Mary Ann. For some of us, Vietnam was to be another adventure in foreign policy execution and military advisory efforts. For many it would become a deadly, open-ended adventure, one that would last for years to come.

# 6 Assassination and Struggle

When in early October 1963 Jerry Brophy, Howie Parks, and I boarded the civilian airliner at Travis Air Force Base in northern California, the temperature was cool. When we landed at Ton Son Nhut Air Base a day later, it was hot and humid, and we began swatting mosquitoes as we left the aircraft. Welcome to Saigon!

Our first stop was at the Majestic Hotel, in what had once been the "Pearl of the Orient" but was now a puritanical, smelly city whose morals were controlled by Ba (Mrs.) Nhu, the sister-in-law of Ngo Dinh Diem, the president of South Vietnam.

The three of us had just completed the Command and General Staff College and a crash course in the Vietnamese language. We sat at the sidewalk cafe outside of the hotel, looking out across the Saigon River; two U.S. Army warrant officer helicopter pilots sat down at the table next to us. We overheard one say he was glad that his last mission in "Nam" was over and that he couldn't wait to get back to Fort Rucker, Alabama. The other one said he would be glad when November came and he could make his trip back to the "Land of the Big PX." Two hours later, they would both be smashed and staggering back to their hotel rooms, one with the barmaid.

After two days of briefings, records processing, and checks, and the issuance of .45-caliber pistols and two clips of ammunition, the three of us departed in different directions. My flight stopped in Pleiku for several hours, and then I flew on to the Da Nang air base; it was already dark when we landed. I threw my duffel bag out on the tarmac and crawled down from the aircraft. I had no sooner picked up the bag than the aircraft began its taxi to the take-off strip. Dust, pebbles, and a sheet of rain driven by the prop wash welcomed me to Advisory Team Two, at the Army of the Republic of Vietnam (ARVN) Second Division, I Corps.

Members of the 1963 Command and General Staff College class as they arrive in Saigon (now Ho Chi Minh City) in October 1963. From left: Maj. Jerry Brophy (later brigadier general), Capt. Roger Demming, Maj. Howard Parks, a Vietnamese child, and Mack.

I could make out a light as I walked toward a hangar. In it there were several Marine Corps H-34 helicopters; two L-19 single-engine, propeller-driven observation aircraft; and a shop-van, from which the light was coming. When I entered the hanger a Marine guard took me to the van, and a lieutenant called Advisory Team Two in Da Nang for transportation. A half-hour later a sergeant picked me up and took me to temporary quarters in Da Nang. (See the map of South Vietnam.)

The temporary quarters building was a two-story motel-like affair. As I went to the second floor, I noticed that the occupants of two rooms below were having a party. I could see several Vietnamese girls in Western mini-dress attire dancing with Americans. In the morning I received a ride to the officers' club and was ready to order breakfast when someone shouted, "Hey Major, if you are assigned to Team Two, you should be seated here at our table, so I can count noses!" I turned toward the voice, and a colonel sitting there said, "Yes, I mean you!"

After I was seated, the colonel explained in a loud voice what everyone else at the table apparently knew, that Advisory Team Two advised the regiments,

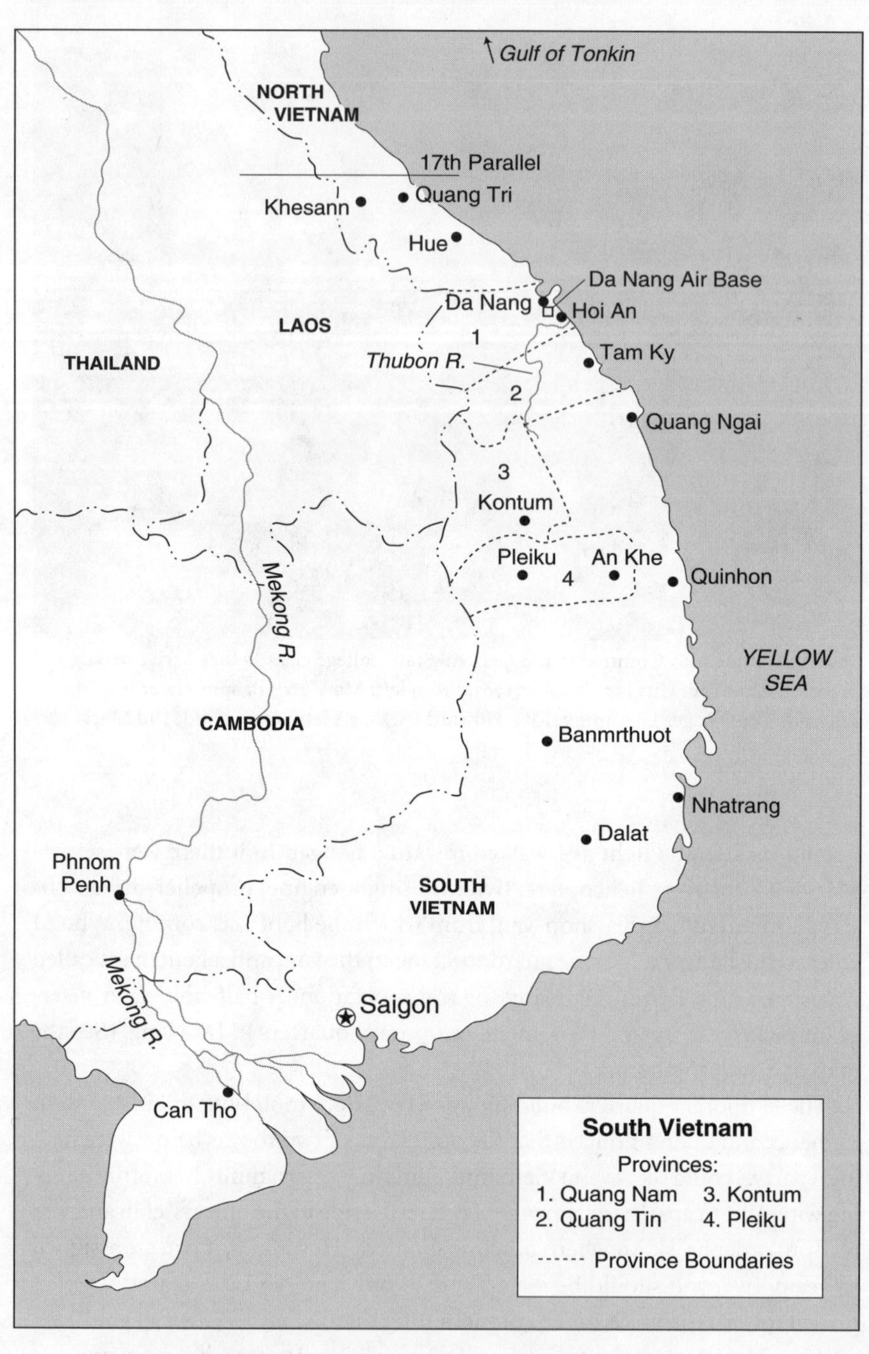

Gulf of Tonkin
NORTH VIETNAM
17th Parallel
Khesann
Quang Tri
Hue
Da Nang Air Base
Da Nang
Hoi An
LAOS
1
Thubon R.
Tam Ky
2
Quang Ngai
THAILAND
3
Kontum
Pleiku
An Khe
4
Quinhon
Mekong R.
YELLOW SEA
CAMBODIA
Banmrthuot
Nhatrang
Dalat
Phnom Penh
SOUTH VIETNAM
Mekong R.
Saigon
Can Tho
South Vietnam
Provinces:
1. Quang Nam    3. Kontum
2. Quang Tin    4. Pleiku
Province Boundaries

provinces, and districts in Quang Nam and Quang Tin Provinces, and units in Da Nang, under the ARVN Second Infantry Division. The colonel then introduced himself as Colonel Pierce (I never did get his actual first name), the senior adviser to the commander of the Second Division. After that there was only subdued conversation between Pierce and an overweight lieutenant colonel next to him. The others—majors, captains, and lieutenants—finished breakfast without introductions, excused themselves, and departed. A PFC then drove me to Team Two headquarters and I went into Pierce's office.

Pierce's first words to me were that he had two vacancies; one was the position of regimental adviser in the ARVN Fourth Regiment, and the other was the province adviser to the Quang Nam Province chief in Hoi An. I told him that I'd prefer the assignment to the regiment. Pierce told me that a major sitting at the breakfast table had arrived two days earlier and had showed a preference for the province adviser position, and so I became a regimental adviser.

Before I left the club, a sergeant brought in a report from a regimental adviser. The report didn't meet Pierce's approval; he called in his deputy, the lieutenant colonel who had sat next to him at breakfast, and told him to inform the offending regimental adviser that he was displeased. The lieutenant colonel obediently did an about-face and departed briskly. I thought this was meant to impress me with the discipline in the team; certainly, I firmly understood who ran Team Two!

Then I met a Maj. Dan Schungel, the G-3 (plans and operations) adviser. He commented that the senior adviser, or SA, held his advisers responsible for everything their counterparts did or failed to do. He told me that Pierce could be very disarming but often struck like a cobra. He said Pierce's peers call him "Bodie." I found out over the next couple of weeks that Pierce had a penchant for overstating the results other advisers achieved, perhaps to improve my efforts—or more likely, those of the regimental commander I advised. The regimental advisers rarely met, but we exchanged views on this matter when we did.

Cpl. William Smith, who was to be my radio operator, picked me up in a jeep at 6:30 at my quarters in Da Nang. I was to use these quarters about ten nights altogether during the year I was in Vietnam. As we passed Da Nang Air Base going south on Route 1 (see the map of Quang Nam and Quang Tin Operational Area), an L-19 aircraft and two helicopters took off and headed south following the same route.

When we reached Thang Binh, we met an American captain waiting for security to go on a medical civic-action visit near Viet An, where we were headed. I decided to wait and take advantage of the security; it was provided by a Regional

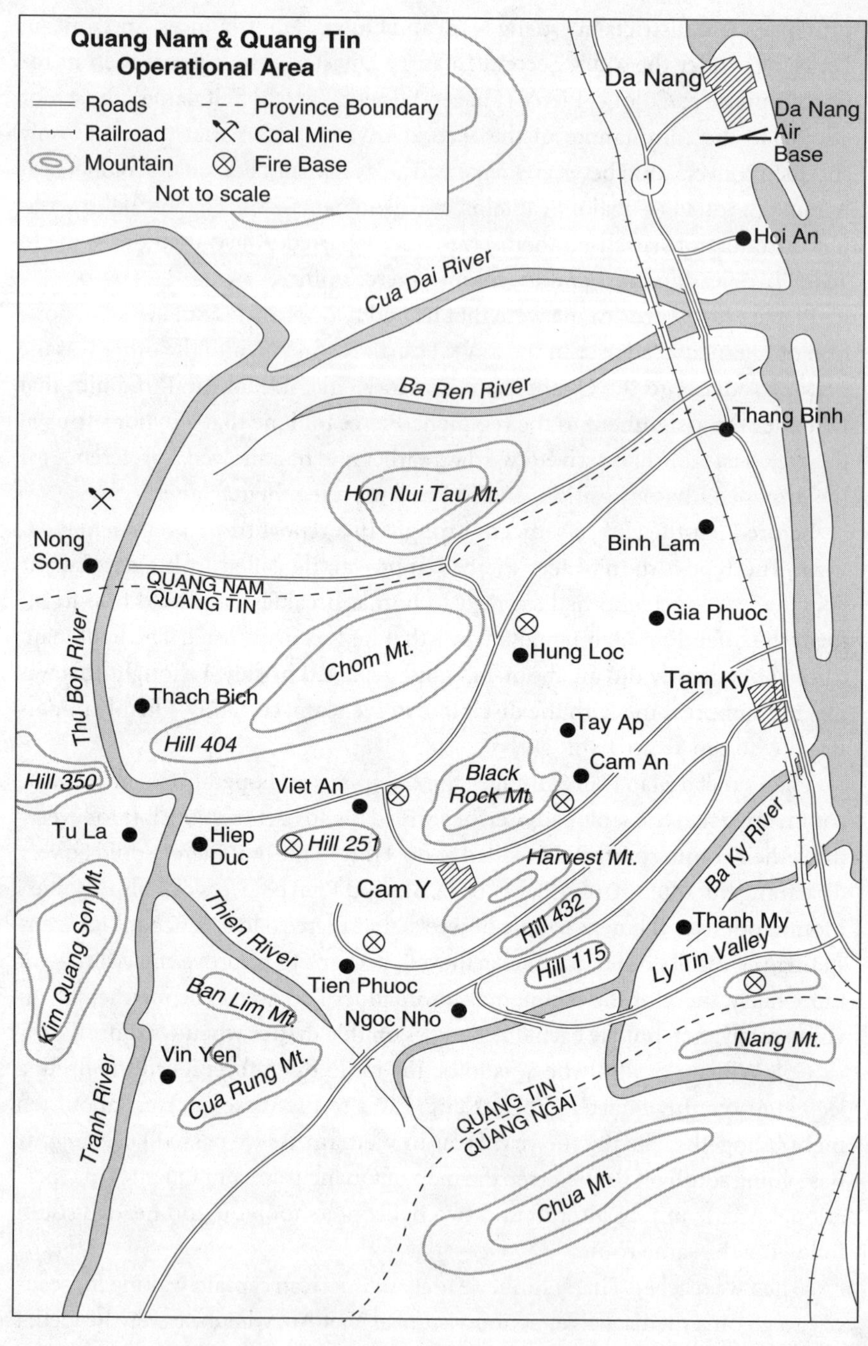

Quang Nam & Quang Tin
Operational Area
Roads
Railroad
Mountain
Province Boundary
Coal Mine
Fire Base
Not to scale
Da Nang
Da Nang Air Base
Hoi An
Cua Dai River
Ba Ren River
Thang Binh
Hon Nui Tau Mt.
Binh Lam
Nong Son
QUANG NAM
QUANG TIN
Gia Phuoc
Hung Loc
Tam Ky
Chom Mt.
Thach Bich
Tay Ap
Cam An
Hill 404
Black Rock Mt.
Thu Bon River
Hill 350
Viet An
Tu La
Hiep Duc
Hill 251
Harvest Mt.
Ba Ky River
Cam Y
Hill 432
Thanh My
Ly Tin Valley
Kim Quang Son Mt.
Thien River
Hill 115
Ban Lim Mt.
Tien Phuoc
Nang Mt.
Vin Yen
Ngoc Nho
Tranh River
Cua Rung Mt.
QUANG TIN
QUANG NGAI
Chua Mt.

Mack surveying a bunker at the ARVN Fourth Infantry Regiment's fire base in Tien Phuoc, Quang Tin Province, in 1963.

Force (RF) squad that eventually arrived in an old truck. (Regional Force units were organized at province level and were similar in organization to ARVN units.) At Viet An I met the Second Battalion adviser, Lt. John W. Hynds, who told me there had been a change in plans and that the regimental CP had moved to a fire base at Tien Phuoc, on the other side of the province.

Smith and I began driving, and after three hours we arrived at Tien Phuoc and the low hill where the Fourth Regiment's CP was located. The guard at the gate waved us into the fire base. Maj. Nguyen Thanh, the regimental commander, came to the jeep and introduced himself in broken but understandable English. (I found out later that he had picked up his English during a six-week stay with a U.S. regiment in Hawaii.) He immediately invited me into his "hooch," where he had a cot set up for me, and next to it a lean-to affair for Smith.

We discussed Major Thanh's artillery, which included a battery of two 105 mm howitzers at the Tien Phuoc fire base. I learned right away that the regiment was "artillery poor" and that its guns required almost constant maintenance visits from Da Nang to keep them operational. He told me that artillery support required his and his operations officer's constant attention. Thanh

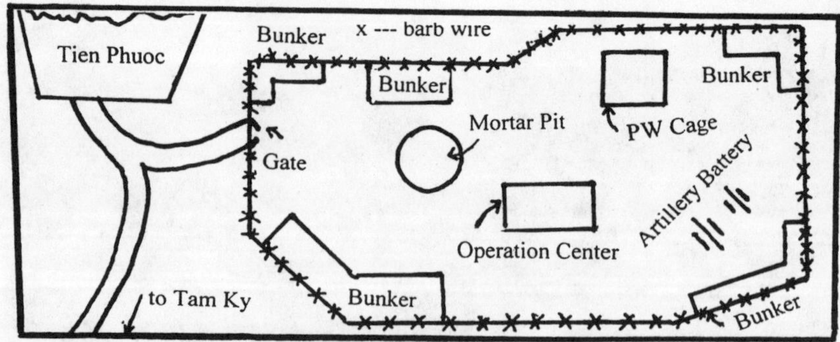


Author's sketch of the firebase at Tien Phuoc.

had his operations officer ensure that all of his units were within the radius of artillery support by constantly checking the guns' effective range.

After we had some tea, Thanh took me around the fire base and showed me his defenses and facilities, to include the artillery battery positioned there, as shown in the sketch. As we checked the 81 mm mortar pit, the artillery battery fired a registration round (to confirm that it was aimed at a preselected point); not expecting it, I was embarrassed by my startled reaction. Thanh smiled and told me that sometimes he reacted poorly when the artillery fired unexpectedly. When we got back to the hooch, he called his sergeant major and asked him to have a cook bring me and my radio operator something to eat. A short time later a cook brought us a bowl of rice, with vegetables and chicken, and a small bowl of *nouc mam,* fermented fish sauce, which added flavor to the food and protein to the body. It was my first sample of a year's worth of Vietnamese food, which, though bland at times, was more than adequate and certainly never caused me to exceed Army weight standards.

During my first night, several artillery missions were fired, but the Vietnamese radio operators put me to sleep as they sent and received Morse code. They used voice communications primarily for administrative purposes. All of my communications with Da Nang were via cw (Morse code), using an old U.S. Army AM radio; my communications with my battalion advisers were through the ARVN's regimental net, also using cw and encoded. My driver/radio operator could transmit and receive forty words a minute. I practiced and eventually reached the high rate of about five words a minute. Smith did all the transmitting; I learned cw just in the event he ever wasn't available.

Major Thanh's home had been in Hanoi, where his father had owned a jewelry store. He was a university graduate who had served in the French colonial forces as a lieutenant. Following the Geneva Conference, he and many colonial

Maj. Nguyen Thanh and Mack. Jeeps and legs were the main mobility in 1963–64, before the U.S. introduction of helicopters in large numbers.

troops had voted with their feet and had come south, becoming charter members of the ARVN Second Infantry Division. I was to learn that Thanh had a deep-seated hate for communists in general and the Viet Cong in particular. He was a strict disciplinarian and extremely loyal to his military superiors. Thanh was Buddhist, as were all of his staff. He was married and had one child.

After breakfast the next morning, the regimental staff briefed Thanh in the same grass-roofed structure where we had eaten and that served as his operation center. The intelligence officer (S-2) reported that the Second Battalion had killed two Viet Cong (VC) and captured one VC, along with a U.S. carbine, a French MAS-36 rifle, a grenade, and two packs with documents, all near Viet An. Thanh became highly emotional when he was informed that the prisoner and documents had been turned over to the Quang Tin Province chief in Tam Ky. "My Second Battalion commander very bad officer; he give prisoner and enemy papers to province chief. I always want first," Thanh told me. "I should put in jail," giving me firsthand evidence of his sense of discipline.

When the operations officer reported that three men had been killed by mines the day before, Thanh told me that mines made for bad morale. I asked him if his company commanders and platoon leaders practiced keeping men dispersed; he appeared to understand and called his sergeant major over and told him to prepare a message to the battalion commanders telling them to emphasize dispersion of their men to reduce casualties from mines. I found out that he always said "Good idea!" when he planned to follow up on advice. Also, if you gave the advice only to him, it became his idea; "face" was all-important in Vietnam, as it is elsewhere.

Late in the morning of the second day, an escort guard brought a North Vietnamese Army (NVA) military adviser, who had provided advice and assistance to local VC, to the regimental fire base. He had been wounded, so Thanh had him patched up and then put in a small prisoner-of-war cage. He was taken into the S-2 bunker that evening, where he was interrogated. The next morning a VNAF H-34 picked him up to take him to Da Nang.

As the helicopter took off, another regimental briefing commenced, and following that Major Thanh and I walked down to Tien Phuoc, below the fire base. I noted that three soldiers followed us. When I mentioned this, Thanh told me, "They protect you! If you get shot I have big trouble." I replied that I would have big trouble also!

We walked through the hamlet and stopped at what Thanh called a "jungle cafe," a structure that was an extension of a house, open on three sides, with a grass roof held up by a series of bamboo poles. We sat at one of the eight small tables; Thanh introduced me to Ong (Mr.) Nguyen Tranh, the café's owner, who spoke no English. He brought us a warm Ba Muoi Ba, a popular beer (33 Beer) in Vietnam.

Although they talked very fast, I understood that the cafe owner was saying that lights at the CP could be seen by the VC at night and that we should shield them. What I wondered was, how did Ong Tranh know the VC could see us? As they talked my thoughts were that the regiment was engaging in Infantry School–type tactics—suspecting VC on every hilltop, circling each as an objective, and attacking the objective conventionally, hoping the VC would remain and fight. I learned early on that the VC (and later the NVA) fought on their own terms, where and when they chose, and this more often than not was where they could do the most damage using ambushes, mines, booby traps, sniping, well planned raids, and a variety of ruses.

The VC aim was to control minds, not hills, and a big part of their goal was to damage Saigon's authority by damaging the capability of Saigon's military forces and of those that supported Saigon. They viewed hilltops as critical terrain at times, but more often they looked for terrain and locations where they could exercise their principal expertise, surprise. To pinpoint enemy units on mountaintops, as U.S. and ARVN intelligence maps often did, had very little correlation with fact.

Momentarily, Co (Miss) Minh brought us bowls of Chinese soup that Ba (Mrs.) Tranh had made. Minh was Tranh's daughter; she wore a colorful Vietnamese dress like city girls wore.

On the way back we passed the district chief's compound. I pointed to a Regional Force company sitting around its cooking fires. Thanh's only remark was that the district chief was a bad officer who collected money from the ARVN officers to give to the Diem family.

When we returned to the fire base, Thanh called his executive officer, Captain Vinh, and told him to turn on only lights that were shielded from view. After Vinh left I asked Thanh if he thought there were VC living in the hamlet. He didn't respond.

Two days after our visit to Tien Phuoc, Major Thanh awakened me at about 4 A.M. with "We must go." By 5:00 we were riding down to Tien Phuoc, a three-quarter-ton machine-gun vehicle in the lead, followed by Thanh's jeep and another three-quarter-ton truck. The gate to the hamlet was open, to let the peasants enter for market day; many were already assembled at the flagpole, with their produce, chickens, dried fish, rice, and other food for sale. We stopped in front of the house that belonged to the hamlet chief, not far from the flagpole. The hamlet chief came out of his house, and almost immediately two men lifted something rolled in a *nepa* mat from the second three-quarter-ton truck and placed it at the flagpole. Toes were sticking out one end of the mat and hair at the other end.

Thanh bowed briefly before the hamlet chief and then in a loud, clear voice commended him for providing information that permitted them to kill the VC lying near the flag pole. He pinned a medal on the hamlet chief, smiled, and got back in his jeep. The body was returned to the three-quarter-ton truck, and we drove to the gate. When we got there, the hamlet chief caught up with us and pleaded with Thanh to take him to the fire base on the hill. Thanh agreed, if the hamlet chief would provide additional information on the VC in the hamlet. The hamlet chief got into the jeep and came to the fire base with us.

Two days later, Major Thanh sent a platoon from his First Battalion to Tien Phuoc and apprehended two VC and an NVA cadreman, the latter with a satchel charge and a description of the VC organization in Quang Tin Province. Three weapons were also captured. The prisoners were flown to division headquarters in Da Nang, after the regimental S-2 milked them for information most of the night. Later the First Battalion searched several hamlets and captured additional VC and weapons.

On the last day of October 1963, the Fourth Regiment was recalled to its base camp in Da Nang. For the officers and men of the regiment, it meant they would see their families. For the VC and any NVA, it meant that control of the province was returned to them.

Early on November 1, 1963, advisers in the Da Nang area and elsewhere in Vietnam were notified to remain in their quarters until further notice. In Saigon, Generals Tran Van Don and Duong Von Minh, in collusion with a few key

Mack accompanying a South Vietnamese platoon on the Cua Rung Mountain in Quang Tin Province, during an operation in 1964.

Americans, had decided that President Ngo Dinh Diem and his brother should be deposed on that day. A Buddhist uprising against him was tearing the country apart, and relations with the United States were festering. Diem refused U.S. offers of asylum and tried to escape. He and his brother were captured on November 2 and were summarily executed in an armored vehicle. The playing of martial music over the radio stations gave notice of the transfer of power.

On November 4, Gen. Nguyen Khanh, commanding I Corps, with the ARVN First and Second Divisions and responsibility for the northern four provinces, authorized a massive parade in Da Nang as General Minh took over the government in Saigon. Unfortunately, the parades and celebrations were but a prelude to the instability that went with the change in national leadership. I imagine that Ho Chi Minh and Gen. Vo Nguyen Giap proposed a toast!

My instructions were to return to what I had been doing before the coup. I believed that we were now entering a phase where military solutions would be sought for the political problems that faced South Vietnam, the main one being the maintenance of South Vietnam as an independent state. Ho Chi Minh was a nationalist first and a communist of convenience; he sought unification of Vietnam and probably had the support of most of the population. The chance to get Ho Chi Minh to emulate Tito had passed when our strategists decided that the U.S. interest in Vietnam was in containing communism and accordingly had supported the French colonial venture.[1]

Mack at the Thien River in 1964, near Tien Phuoc.

The Fourth Regiment was soon deployed to Phuoc Binh in Quang Nam Province, near the boundary with Quang Tin, to conduct operations along the Thu Bon River. (See the Quang Tin and Quang Nam Operational Area map.) An entry onto the Ho Chi Minh Trail was located south of the Nong Son coal mine, believed to be in the vicinity of Thach Bich. Flying in an L-19, almost at water level, along the river between Hills 350 and 404, I clearly saw under the rocky ledges of Hill 350 sampans that appeared to be loaded with supplies. The heavy rains had flooded the Thu Bon River; the only practical entry for the regiment's two battalions (one battalion had remained in Da Nang on popula-tion-control duty) was by helicopter, and supply and evacuation would re-quire river craft. Major Thanh and I crossed the Thu Bon in a sampan and visited the manager of the Nong Son coal mine, who lent us two of his motor-ized barges and a small speedboat. Colonel Pierce had visited us earlier in the day and told us not to expect any division assault boats—although in fact we would receive two.

(Pierce had also brought mail with him. I received a letter from Marge in-forming me she had purchased a piano and that the girls were taking piano lessons. Elizabeth wrote that she had a calendar to remind her how many days I had left in Vietnam.)

The regimental CP was relocated from Phuoc Binh to the soggy banks of the Thu Bon, across from Nong Son. U.S. Marine Corps H-34 helicopters lifted the Third Battalion to the northwest of Hill 350. Because of heavy rain, the

First Battalion, less one company, crossed the river on coal barges near Nong Son. It attacked toward the Third Battalion. The First Battalion company on the east side of the river attacked south toward Thach Bich and Hill 404. The bottom of one barge had been reinforced with lumber and jeep shock mats; two 81 mm mortars had been placed in it to provide close support.

By the fourth day, the First Battalion was knee deep in mud on the west side of the river, but it had compressed an estimated vc company between itself and the Third Battalion. The company on the east side of the river commenced receiving fire from the vicinity of Thach Bich. The Third Battalion further squeezed the vc company on the east slope of Hill 305, hard up against the river. Major Thanh ordered the First Battalion back to the east side of the river, from where it was to attack toward Thach Bich and Hill 404. The fifth and final day of the riverine operation began with a battalion on each side of the river. Major Thanh and I started our fifth trip up the river in the speedboat to ensure that the First Battalion promptly commenced its attack on the east side of the river.

As we cruised around one bend in the river, we heard the crack of several small-arms rounds over our heads. The boat driver accelerated too rapidly, and the engine died, as several more rounds cracked overhead. Then one round hit the boat, and the three of us jumped in the water. The boat was carried down the river by the current. We all hung on to the boat, until I crawled back into it and managed to get the engine started. Major Thanh crawled aboard, and we pulled in the operator. I drove the boat the rest of the way to the First Battalion crossing area, where Thanh and I went ashore. We never saw the speedboat or its operator again.

The First Battalion was being supplied from a barge when we arrived, and several wounded were being placed in an assault boat for evacuation. Thanh and I went forward with the battalion commander to get a better view of Thach Bich and Hill 404. The mortar barge was firing on Hill 350. While we watched, a vc machine gun opened fire from low on the slope of Hill 350; the battalion commander's radio operator was wounded. The mortars on the barge placed several rounds on the machine gun. Two vc could be seen running toward the river.

Thanh ordered the Third Battalion, less one company, to cross to the east side of the river on the supply barge to assist the First Battalion attack on Hill 405, leaving one company to block the vc on the river side of Hill 350. Part of the vc company on Hill 404 began withdrawing to the southeast, while another part attempted to cross the river to Hill 350. The latter group ran into the concentrated fire of the two 81 mm mortars on the barge, and shortly human and sampan remains were floating down the flooded Thu Bon River. The First and Third Battalions then continued the attack up Hill 404, but the VC had dispersed toward the southeast.

The company remaining on Hill 350 captured two wounded VC and found a large cache of weapons and ammunition under ledges at the river's edge, where I had seen sampans from an aircraft. The wounded VC and weapons were placed on the supply barge. Floating VC bodies were also loaded onto the barge, and several men boarded the barge to guard the prisoners. The barge then returned to the Fourth Regiment's CP, where the weapons cache, prisoners, and dead VC were off-loaded. The First and Third Battalions, with a company on the west side of the Thu Bon, continued to search toward Hiep Duc, to the south.

When Major Thanh and I returned to the CP, on the banks of the Thu Bon, we received word that the senior adviser and division commander would arrive the next morning. A mass grave was dug on the side of a small hill, and the VC dead were placed in it, but they were not fully covered with dirt. Not far away the captured weapons were assembled. Thanh wanted to show the results of the "riverine operation."

Next morning Pierce's helicopter made a pass over us, looking for the CP, then landed on the muddy banks of the river. By the time the officers got to the CP, they appeared irritated by the mud that clung to their boots and clean, bloused trousers. The division commander immediately took Major Thanh aside, and I went with Colonel Pierce to the VC burial site. Colonel Pierce began by saying he had never heard of anyone being so dumb as to base the success of an operation on two coal barges. He was very upset over the mortars' being fired from the barge, telling me it was against regulations to fire a mortar from a less than stable base.

I took him to the assembled VC dead and then to the assembled weapon cache, and as he looked I suggested that the two waterlogged Fourth Regiment battalions had done a good job, and I added that without the barges they would still be out there slogging through mud up to their knees. Then I told him that I thought that Major Thanh should be commended rather than reprimanded. After seeing the operation's results, Pierce acknowledged that his rebuke had been premature. He told me he would speak to the division commander in favorable terms concerning the operation.

The division commander returned to the helicopter after his session with Thanh, without seeing the VC weapons and bodies. Regardless, he had already told Thanh that he wanted a battalion to sweep both sides of the river in search of weapons—what, in effect, the Third Battalion was already doing. It found more weapons and several dead VC.

Although the U.S. Ninth Division would conduct riverine operations in the Mekong Delta later in the 1960s, this was probably the first such operation in I Corps. I would later write an article on it, published in the Infantry School's book *A Distant Challenge,* in 1970.[2]

The First and Third battalions swept as far as Hiep Duc, where the Third Battalion company crossed the river at a ferry. The First Battalion ran into a vc platoon near Binh Kieu; a vc mine wounded one man, and two others were wounded by small arms fire. Major Thanh then ordered the Third Battalion to search the valley to the east of Hiep Duc as far as Viet An. The regiment's Second Battalion was relieved of its security mission in Da Nang and was directed to set up its command post on the high rise at Phu Vinh Dong, south of Viet An. The regiment would later move its cp from the Thu Bon River banks to Viet An; its operational area consisted of the easternmost part of Quang Tin Province.

At about six o'clock on a damp, misty morning, I was shaving, looking into a scratched metal mirror that swung back and forth in the light breeze blowing down the Thu Bon river. We were planning to move the cp to Viet An, as soon as the river began to recede after a week's heavy rain. I heard the Vietnamese words *bee zhett* (killed) coming from Thanh's radio and the name "Kennedy" being repeated often. Then Thanh came running from his tent yelling, "*Tee-uta* [Major] Mack, President Kennedy dead!" We went back to the tent and listened as the Vietnamese announcer said that Kennedy had been assassinated in Dallas while riding in a motorcade. Vice President Johnson had already been sworn in as president. Major Thanh remarked that the government and the people in Vietnam would be very fearful that this would affect the U.S. support of the war.

I had Smith send a message to the senior adviser for confirmation of the radio report. Fifteen minutes later, I received a short message from Da Nang confirming that President Kennedy had been assassinated and that President Johnson had been sworn in. I had already prepared a message for the battalion advisers, which I sent via the ARVN net:

DATE-TIME GROUP: 230730 NOV 63
TO: WATERMELON 36, 31, 53
PRESIDENT KENNEDY WAS ASSASSINATED ON 22 NOV IN DALLAS, TEXAS; THE PRESIDENT WAS KILLED BY AN UNKNOWN ASSASSIN WHILE RIDING IN A MOTORCADE ON A MAIN STREET. VICE PRESIDENT JOHNSON HAS BEEN SWORN IN AS PRESIDENT OF THE UNITED STATES. AS SENIOR US REPRESENTATIVE IN YOUR AREA, YOU SHOULD REFLECT THE FEELING OF THE PEOPLE OF THE US FOR A GREAT MAN WHO DIED FOR HIS COUNTRY.

Do not speculate on any of the effects this may have on US policies, which will without doubt remain the same under President Johnson. . . . Watermelon 46

("Watermelon" was the current code name for advisers in the Second ARVN Division.)

There was a noticeable amount of anxiety within the Fourth Regiment's staff. Major Thanh displayed considerable concern; he asked several times whether I thought President Johnson would continue to support the war as Kennedy had done. With the caveat "I'm just a major," I told him I thought the support would not change. A few years later, many would have disagreed with the "no change" aspect of my response, after the entry of U.S. ground forces and the escalation of military support of the war.

The Fourth Regiment's CP moved to Viet An on November 24. The First and Third Battalions now swept and searched astride the road from Hiep Duc to Thang Binh, near Highway 1. I suggested to Major Thanh that we visit the Second Battalion CP, on the pinnacle of land near Phu Vinh Dong. We departed on foot from the regiment's CP at Viet An, with a rifle platoon as security. As we turned east toward Phu Vinh Dong, we received sniper fire from the direction of the hamlet Cam Y. Major Thanh contacted the Second Battalion commander and told him to send a unit to investigate.

It was the division's policy to not react against snipers firing on vehicles but to continue to the destination. I had told Thanh that this policy encouraged snipers to move in closer and thus improve their accuracy. I informed the advisers at division level, who were the ones who had set this "don't react" rule, that the Fourth Regiment would respond to sniper fire on a case-by-case basis. We succeeded in capturing several snipers.

It took us a half hour to climb to the Second Battalion CP. Normally a local Popular Force platoon (locally trained village defense) occupied this peak, overlooking the Phu Vinh Dong area. We spent the night at the battalion CP. At about 2 A.M. the dogs began barking to the east of Cam Y. Shortly thereafter we heard firing; the VC were attacking Cam Y. By the time a battalion reaction force got to the hamlet, the VC had broken off contact; artillery was fired on their route of withdrawal. Luckily the VC hadn't set an ambush along the reaction force's route, as often happened.

It is important to remember that for command visits during the advisory era, we seldom had the convenience of a helicopter. We relied on vehicles or went by foot, except at division level. The risk of mines and ambush on roads and trails reduced the frequency of command visits. Early the next morning we started back to the regimental CP at Viet An, arriving after an engineer platoon arrived there with orders to improve the road from Viet An to Cam Y and Cam An.

The regimental operations officer, Captain Loi, had provided the engineers with a small rifle platoon, organized from the mortar company, for security. The rifle platoon and engineer platoon were to organize their security en route. By the time we returned to the CP, the engineer platoon and its security had departed. About noon, a large volume of gunfire and several explosions were heard southwest of the CP, and a column of black smoke appeared in the direction of the gunfire. Major Thanh ordered the remainder of his mortar company, less two mortar crews, to investigate.

Thanh and I accompanied the mortar company as it moved cautiously toward the column of smoke. We had been moving for over an hour when three men came running toward us down the road. Two had been wounded. As they approached, I heard one of the men yell *"Cuoc phuc-kich!"* (ambush) and we knew the engineer detail had been ambushed. The three told us that everyone had been killed except them. When the engineers had arrived at a point where heavy rains had washed out the road, they had unloaded their bulldozer and front-end loader; the engineer platoon leader had told the engineers and the infantry to eat while he devised a plan to fix the road.

Everyone had moved into the washed-out area and begun eating their rice balls, when suddenly they were hit on all sides. Several VC had thrown satchel charges at the vehicles (two dump trucks, one bulldozer, one front-end loader, and two smaller trucks). Asked if the infantry had set up any security outside the washed-out area, the man who was not wounded (he had been one of the infantrymen) said it had not, that the platoon leader had said he would put out security after they had eaten.

Upon looking over the devastation, including at least forty dead ARVN soldiers—stripped of their weapons, ammunition, foot gear, web belts, and equipment—and the smoldering vehicles and equipment, my first doubt arose as to how long losses such as these, were they American, would be accepted in the United States. Major Thanh went into a rage.

A month earlier, at the Tien Phuoc fire base, a Marine brigadier general had asked Thanh what motivated the VC to continue to fight against significant odds. The general remarked that if Thanh could answer that question, he might foresee a positive outcome for South Vietnam. The South Vietnamese leaders should have been asked the same question, since success depended upon loyalty to the Saigon government. It was my personal hope that we would avoid this never-ending sinkhole of human despair, but in a very short time our solution would be to apply battlefield dynamics, so important in conventional warfare but of little value in an insurgency involving a major political goal. I hadn't the foggiest notion then that the other side had the advantage of time. In fact, however, each day was a day closer to the enemy's achievement of his goal, unification of Vietnam under Hanoi, and one less day available to us to deny him that goal.

The ARVN dead were loaded on a truck and returned to the dry rice paddy next to the CP; before sunset the bodies, covered with *nepa* mats, ponchos, and tenting, had attracted thousands of buzzing flies. The burned-out equipment at the ambush site served now as a memorial to the soldiers who had died and as a trophy for a VC victory. The road was never repaired while I was on this tour of duty in Vietnam; it remained a warning to those who thought American troops could prevail where the South Vietnamese could not. It would be well over a year before former president Dwight D. Eisenhower told President Johnson that the South Vietnamese government could not be kept in place "with bayonets" and that the "consent of the people" was crucial.[3]

The morning after the ambush, the senior adviser flew the division commander to Thanh's CP, the helicopter scattering the covers placed over the bodies as it landed. Fifteen minutes later, we sat in the sweltering mid-morning heat under canvas as Thanh briefed the two senior officers on the ill-fated road repair mission. I had been helping him with his English, so he would frequently summarize in English for the division adviser.

When it appeared the division commander was about to ask questions, Colonel Pierce beckoned to me to come outside with him. He told me that he wanted a full, detailed report on the ambush, from the time the engineers arrived at Viet An until the bodies were returned. He knew that within a day he would be sending a report to the Commander, U.S. Military Assistance Command, Vietnam (COMUSMACV) and that shortly thereafter he could be briefing the "front office" there. He did not hold me responsible for the ambush, but he said it did show the need for improving the battlefield awareness and skills of the junior officers and soldiers. He also remarked that Thanh wouldn't be relieved, because the division commander had no one whom he could trust to replace him.

The Fourth Regiment was ordered to move its CP to Hung Loc, on the road to Thang Binh, and was given the mission of sweeping the area within the Hiep Duc–Tien Phuoc–Tam Ky–Thang Binh area; the division G-2 had claimed there were two or three VC companies in that area.

Major Thanh was told that the American advisers were coming up with a new plan, which they called the "saturation concept." This would require the regiments to remain in the field for long periods of time. Each battalion and company was to have specific operational areas. Platoons were to operate by random patrolling of company-designated areas. Periodically the company areas of responsibility, as well as the battalion areas, would be relocated.

The purpose was to increase contacts with the vc to the point that they would be put on the defensive, as the ARVN and Regional Forces increased their familiarity with the terrain and vc operations, and thereby took the initiative. There was to be a short training period before the saturation concept was initiated. The Vietnamese described this concept as "the plan to soak the battle area with troops," that I described in detail in the *Military Review,* November 1967.[4]

The regiment's first contact after it established its CP at Hung Loc was in the northeastern part of its operational area of responsibility, at Xuan My, not far from Highway 1. Fifteen vc had walked into the Xuan My hamlet at night and assassinated the hamlet chief, disarmed its Popular Force defenders, destroyed a *pungi*-stake moat and barbed-wire fence, and carried off the telephone and radio provided by Quang Tin Province.[5] The report that there was no radio contact with Xuan My came at 6:00 A.M. the next morning, and within an hour the province chief, district chief, the First Battalion commander, Major Thanh, and I were there.

The hamlet chief, who had been appointed by the province chief, was laid out on a straw mat in his house, surrounded by candles; his wife was being consoled by the province chief. None of the hamlet residents was at the scene, which was uncharacteristic of such events in Vietnam. The district chief told Major Thanh that there had been ill will between the local people and the hamlet chief and his family, because he had been appointed by the province chief; ill will also existed between the province chief and Major Thanh, because of the province chief's attempts to interfere with the regiment's operations, as Thanh saw it.

The province chief arrested the hamlet's Popular Force defenders and sent a squad from the Thang Binh Regional Force company to defend the hamlet. He then appointed a member of the hamlet as acting chief. He took the slain hamlet chief's wife and children with him to province headquarters.

Thanh and I went to Tam Ky, to brief Lieutenant Colonel Nhan, the assistant division commander, on the Fourth Regiment's dispositions. After the briefing, Thanh and I, with a convoy of three trucks, began our return to the CP at Hung Loc. As we turned on to the Viet An road, we saw off at a distance to the south a large column of smoke rising from Binh Lam; using field glasses we could see several houses burning. Thanh notified his First Battalion, operating in the Black Rock Mountain area, that he was going to investigate the fires and ordered a company patrol in the direction of Binh Lam.

Upon reaching Binh Lam, we discovered that the vc had entered the hamlet in broad daylight, rounded up the defenders, seized their weapons, and burned their homes. The hamlet chief had been assassinated. His wife stood in front of her destroyed home with her children, as many people consoled her. One of the hamlet's defenders pointed to the hamlet of Gia Phuoc and said the vc had headed in that direction. Major Thanh had the infantry platoon dismount from the truck, and we moved toward Gia Phuoc, after Thanh warned the platoon to be alert for an ambush. Within twenty minutes we received several rounds of small arms fire from Gia Phuoc, as smoke began rising from that hamlet.

Next we saw about ten figures running from Gia Phuoc toward Black Rock Mountain. These vc came under intense fire from a First Battalion unit; three vc were killed, and two were wounded and captured. In Gia Phuoc also, the hamlet chief had been assassinated, and his home was among those burned. There was a large gathering of tearful peasants, some comforting the hamlet chief's wife. Major Thanh consoled her also and gave her money. I assisted the platoon in putting out the fire, throwing buckets of well water on the burning homes.

These three incidents, two during daytime, displayed a heightened vc confidence, remarkable in an area where ARVN reinforcements were available. But Major Thanh's rapid response to the attacks on Binh Lam and Gia Phuoc had led to the capture of two vc, who under interrogation identified the general location of a vc company in Black Rock Mountain. Major Thanh's response turned into an opportunity to go after a vc company.

As a principle of war, surprise entails confronting the enemy when, where, or by means to which he is unprepared to react effectively. It is not always necessary that the enemy be taken totally unawares, only that he become aware of the action against him too late to react with an effective force or counteraction. As the weaker of forces, the vc maximized the advantage of surprise to make up for the lack of conventional tools of war, which their adversaries had in abundance. This is not to say that they disregarded other principles of war—offensive, objective, simplicity, and so forth—only that the principle of surprise was the focal point at which their military capabilities aimed. The People's Army of Vietnam (PAVN), usually called the North Vietnamese Army (NVA) by Americans, respected the principle of surprise as well.

The interrogation of the two prisoners involved in the assassination of the hamlet chiefs and burning of the hamlets of Xuan My, Binh Lam, and Gia Phuoc revealed that at times the vc would risk operating in an area that was within the supporting distance of ARVN and province-level reaction forces. In this case they had extended the element of risk too far and had lost the advantage of surprise.

It was determined from the interrogation that the vc in this operation had not been from Quang Tin province but were a specially trained team that was used for assassinations. The most important information was the vc company operating on Black Rock Mountain; it became a prime objective of the Fourth Regiment.

Before an operation against the vc company could commence, I received a message from an attached Sixth Regiment battalion that their adviser, Captain Payne, had been wounded by a sniper as he was shaving early that morning. When I notified Colonel Pierce, his outraged response was that if the Fourth Regiment had provided better security for Captain Payne, he would not have been a casualty.

Neither I nor Major Thanh had met either Captain Payne or the battalion commander. They were operating in and about Harvest Mountain (Nui Vu), just south of Black Rock Mountain (Nui Da Den). It might have been a simple task to visit that battalion had a helicopter been available, but none was. The battalion commander told us that Payne had lathered up and then walked to a clearing where the early morning light was better. The battalion commander was furious because no one had stopped Payne from going into the clearing. He knew that as battalion commander he would be blamed for the adviser being wounded. Counterinsurgency was dangerous business. I spent many hours responding to Colonel Pierce's questions.

All of the advisers with the ARVN Second Division had been notified that they would return to Da Nang for three days' and two nights' rest and recuperation over Christmas. Early on December 24, Smith and I started out for Da Nang, but not before Major Thanh warned us several times that we should have Colonel Pierce send his helicopter to pick us up. "vc know you go to Da Nang and they will mine road or set up ambush," Thanh must have said a dozen times. The fact of the matter was that the battalion advisers were even deeper in the "boonies" and needed helicopter transportation to Da Nang more than we did.

We "hot-rodded it" to Highway 1, and from there to Da Nang was a piece of cake. After taking a shower and putting on a clean uniform, I went to the officers' club and sat at the bar with the G-3 adviser, Maj. Dan Schungel. We discussed the saturation concept as it was to be presented to the Second Division commander and his staff—how the battalions' would be given operational areas that would change every two weeks, and the companies similar areas, within which they would conduct random platoon-sized patrols, how eventually the ARVN could become as familiar with the region as the vc were currently. Eventually this could reduce the vc capability to exploit the principle of surprise, by restricting their knowledge of where the arvn were operating. At the same time, the vc would be uncovered.

Schungel mentioned that the division staff was not behind the plan 100 percent, since it had learned that the American leadership in Saigon was opposed to the concept, even though it was an American idea developed by Team Two in Da Nang. The Americans opposed the concept because it did not offer the dynamics of major search-and-destroy operations. comusmacv permitted the concept to be exercised but did not visit or send representatives to analyze it. Notwithstanding the lack of American interest in Saigon, the arvn Second Division would find that the new concept held promise, and it was adopted for a period of time. Granted, it was not dynamic, but it did get results.

We also discussed the arvn's use of artillery. In general, the number of "tubes" (guns) available to a regiment was never commensurate with the area to be covered. For example, the Fourth Regiment had a battery of four pieces (105 mm) in direct support at two fire bases, one of which was its cp. In addition, the regiment had four mortars from its mortar company set up at the fire base. The mortar company was trained for, and used in, a rifle-company role.

It didn't take a rocket scientist to figure out the radius of lethality of the direct-support artillery (sixteen thousand yards) and the safe lanes within the regiment's area of responsibility. We knew that the vc avoided coming within range of the artillery and that when they did they used stealth to the maximum to avoid detection. The regiment's mortars were employed primarily for base defense, seldom to support battalions.

An announcement on the club bulletin board on Christmas Day suggested that the vc must be celebrating Christmas as well, because during the past twenty-four hours there had been no incidents in I Corps. There was also a notice that all regimental and battalion advisers were to report to the Second Division briefing room on the last Thursday and Friday of January 1964 to attend a combined American and Vietnamese orientation on the saturation concept.

The high point of Christmas in Da Nang was the five letters I received from Marge. Her description of the presents for the children and of the family Christmas party, held two weeks earlier, were food for homesickness.

The three days in Da Nang were a time for reflection. It was becoming obvious to me that what we were involved in was a problem that only the Vietnamese could solve. I had become convinced that the United States should never think of committing ground forces to preserve a military dictatorship that had only limited popular support. I would become even more convinced of this in January, when the I Corps commander, Gen. Nguyen Khanh, toppled the officers who had ousted Diem.[6]

It was 6:00 A.M., December 27, as Smith and I sped down Highway 1 past Da Nang air base, now with an increased number of Air Force planes, without normal U.S. markings. The traffic was sparse as we turned right at Thang Binh and headed for the Fourth Regiment's CP on Hill 251, east of Hiep Duc. The Second and Third Battalions were starting a search operation in the Hiep Duc area, while the First Battalion continued to operate near Black Rock Mountain, with its CP at Cam An. An artillery battery was left on the high fortification at Viet An, so that it could support all three battalions.

Before Christmas, I had suggested to Thanh that we put the CP on Hill 251 to have better observation over the areas in which the Second and Third Battalions were to operate. He arranged to have several peasants from Trung Ai prepare two shelters and four bunkers on the hill. Within two days the work was complete, with a *pungi*-stake moat around the CP.

At times I would get the feeling that the Fourth Regiment's leaders were attaining a better appreciation of how to combat the insurgency, but then I would see an ARVN company moving into the jungle to conduct a search operation in single file, rather than deploying its three platoons on parallel routes to increase the search area. Still, there was never a doubt in my mind that Thanh, with his twenty years of conducting counterinsurgency operations, had vastly more experience than I did. While this did not limit my advice to him, it sure as hell made me ensure that I avoided harebrained suggestions.

The Vietnamese Air Force (VNAF) had only a minimal mobility capability, and so we relied on the Marine H-34 squadron at Da Nang. There was no effective Vietnamese air-ground system, either liaison or communications. Generally, the Fourth Regiment was a 2.5-mile-an-hour unit, without air; in the jungle it was slower.

During December and January, we placed renewed emphasis on the conduct of ambush operations, sniper training, and mine/booby trap awareness. The regiment trained sniper teams for each of the battalions and had good results. The battalions provided closer supervision of the preparation and execution of ambush patrols. Some improvement was attained, but the successful ARVN ambush remained rare. (For that matter, U.S. forces weren't successful at ambushes either, when they were introduced.) The Second Division advisers hoped that the VC capability would be diminished as the ARVN's presence in the battle area took effect and a new awareness was generated, where once it had rushed back and forth between fort and jungle.

An American who "roamed" about Quang Tin as an "agronomy specialist" arrived from nowhere at the CP on Hill 251. He supposedly was helping to increase rice production, with a new strain of rice. The agronomist arranged with Major Thanh to get operational information, so he could avoid "combat areas" in his travels. In exchange, Thanh received contributions to his "consoling fund," which he distributed to grieving families upon the death of a relative from VC or friendly fire. Rumor had it that the "agronomist" was in fact a member of a major U.S. agency, namely the CIA.

The major activity in the Fourth Regiment's area took place in the two independent, unrelated operations conducted by the Second and Third Battalions around Hiep Duc, while the First Battalion patrolled the Black Rock Mountain complex.

The Second Battalion crossed the Thien River and swept the Cua Rung and Binh Nim Mountains and jungles south of Hiep Duc. The battalion had little contact with another estimated VC company until it descended the Cua Rung Mountain complex into the rice fields near Vinh Yen; there its lead elements received sniper fire from three directions. About the same time, the battalion adviser pointed to thirty VC moving from Vinh Yen toward the Tranh River. Then the lead platoon of the battalion ran into an ambush. The two platoons following it placed fire on the enemy. The company commander then ordered an attack on the enemy ambush positions, and the VC withdrew, running toward Vinh Yen. As the company pursued, the road erupted in five places as electrically controlled mines exploded. Two men were wounded.

Reaching the Tranh River, the Second Battalion found four dead and five wounded on the east bank of the river, and on the far bank there were several wounded VC being helped along. An artillery mission was placed on the VC, and they dispersed. The lead elements of the battalion commenced crossing the Tranh River on local sampans; Major Thanh had already dispatched two assault boats to the crossing site. The whole battalion then crossed the river; the battalion's losses were seven dead and twenty-one wounded by the time it was across the river. The VC lost sixteen killed and thirteen prisoners, all wounded, plus a considerable store of weapons and ammunition. The battalion patrolled the west side of the Tranh River as far north as Tu La, experiencing only sporadic sniping during the remainder of the operation.

North of Hiep Duc, the Third Battalion spent two days searching the valley where the Chom and Hon Nui Tau Mountains met. The peasants in the area stated there had been no VC in the area for almost a year. The Third Battalion commander then met with the district chief of Dai Phong to coordinate its patrols on Hon Nui Tau Mountain with the chief's Regional Force company.

The mountain was within Quang Nam Province, so the district chief went to his province chief to get approval for the joint operation. Permission was not granted. It was another case of political-military disagreement in the field, with insufficient influence applied at division and corps level.

Major Thanh redirected the Third Battalion to sweep through the Chom Mountains, which were completely within Quang Tin Province. With three companies abreast, the battalion patrolled and set up patrol bases on the mountain, without contact. En route it passed a Regional Force compound; in it could be seen the RF men in their hammocks, on an extended siesta. It doesn't get much worse than this at squad level in any army. There were different standards among military units—and the ARVN commanders wondered why they had a high desertion rate.

Early in the morning on the third day, three rounds of 82 mm mortar fell on the northernmost company on Chom Mountain; there were no casualties, even though two rounds went off overhead, detonated by tree branches. The enemy mortar was thought to be on the high ground above Thach Bich, an area searched by the battalion a month and a half earlier—substantiating that in Vietnam you controlled only what you occupied. (This point somehow never played a major role in American planning and strategy. Presence was, and will continue to be, of influence once the military option is exercised.)

The first evidence that there were VC in the Chom Mountain came when a platoon of the center company sustained two killed and three wounded from an electrically activated mine. Patrolling by the company was curtailed until the casualties could be evacuated. The next day another man was killed and two were wounded by an electrically controlled mine. Moments after the mine incident, the platoon was ambushed, at a cost of another killed and three wounded. There were no known VC casualties. The VC had effectively slowed the battalion's sweep toward the Thu Bon River, a wearing-down process that depleted the battalion's military and political stamina, although it reached Hill 404 with little additional contact.

As the Second and Third Battalions operated in western Quang Tin Province, the First Battalion continued searching Black Rock Mountain and expanded its patrols to Harvest Mountain, with only minimal contact. Near the end of January 1964, the regiment was ordered to close out its operation and to move to Da Nang for the announced briefings and training on the saturation concept.

At the beginning, there was less than full acceptance of the saturation concept by many Second Division officers. Perhaps the main issue had to do with requiring platoons to conduct random patrolling. Many of the platoons in the regiment did not have good enough leadership or experience for semi-independent operations. Some of the leadership deficiency was solved by "cleaning house" in the division's staffs and rear area, as well as by brief training while the regiments were in Da Nang.

There was also some naiveté at the advisory level, in that the senior adviser and his staff had failed to get input from the field during the conceptual stage, other than making sure that the ARVN officers and men had the word "saturation" in their vocabulary. Many of us knew that our counterparts were concerned about the inexperienced NCOs and lieutenants who led platoons.

Thanh and I had already discussed the problem of small-unit leadership. I told my battalion advisers that they should get to know all nine platoon leaders in the battalions they advised, and I suggested that officers sitting at administrative and logistical desks in Da Nang be screened for platoon leadership duties. I had my logistical staff adviser, a combat-arms captain, screen the rear to get the hard-chargers moved forward.

Following the briefings and training in Da Nang, the Fourth Regiment was given its initial battalion operational areas (BOAS), and each battalion commander established company operational areas (COAS), where the rifle platoons would conduct random patrols. I remember telling Major Thanh that he was about to become a real authority in Quang Tin Province, much like the county sheriff in our country, but with a lot more clout. I advised him not to mention this to the province chief, a politically appointed military officer, designated directly by the "leadership" in Saigon.

The BOAS were oriented about battalion CPs, which were located as follows: First Battalion at Viet An, Second Battalion at Thanh My in Ly Tin Valley, and the Third Battalion at Tien Phuoc, with the regimental CP at Cam An, all in Quang Tin, to the west of the Highway 1 and the railroad. The men were to be given leave to visit their families, since they would not be returning to Da Nang after operations, as in the past. Tactically, platoons were to report hourly while on patrol, and all contacts with the enemy would be forwarded to the regiment hourly.

It didn't take long before daily contact increased significantly as the units filled in the gaps of their knowledge about VC operations. As an example, a Third Battalion platoon patrolled down Black Rock Mountain and, after setting up a defense for the night, retraced its tracks in the morning until it heard voices nearby. The platoon launched an attack on what turned out to be a VC base camp; it killed three and captured four in the assault. The vc prisoners said they had seen the platoon go down the hill and had remained silent because of its combat power. They had then lowered their guard, not expecting the platoon to return, and had been surprised.

It was also learned during the interrogation that the hamlet of Cam An, at the foot of the regiment's cp, was to be attacked soon. The regiment had an rf company attached, and part of it was used to reinforce this hamlet's defenses. At about 1 A.M. two nights later, dogs in Cam An began barking. An estimated vc platoon assaulted the hamlet but found itself in an area that had been laced with *pungi* stakes. The *pungi*s, plus the Regional Force reinforcements, halted the initial assault. A few vc did manage to get inside the hamlet, but an ARVN platoon from the mortar company attacked, and they withdrew. I had accompanied the platoon, with Thanh's reluctant approval, because there had not seemed to be an immediate response to the initial vc attack.

When the vc renewed their attack, to get immediate response I fixed my .45-caliber pistol loaded with tracer ammunition and after a few shouts of "*Ban di, Ban di,*" (fire, fire) I got the defenders to return fire. The vc then withdrew, passing through 81 mm mortar rounds fired from the regimental cp, and they did not return. I learned a lot that night about why vc assaults often were successful; slow response from defenders headed the list.

In the morning we counted twelve vc dead outside the hamlet, some impaled on the *pungi* stakes, and four dead inside. In addition, two wounded vc were captured, along with a large quantity of weapons. One seriously wounded vc, who later died, told the regimental intelligence officer that his platoon had been on Harvest Mountain for several days planning the attack on the hamlet. There were no regimental casualties, but two of the rf defenders were wounded.

There were indications that the saturation concept might be disturbing vc plans. Ten nights after the attack on Cam An, the regimental cp, at the end of a finger of land extending from Black Rock Mountain, was attacked at 2 A.M. by an estimated vc company. The artillery and mortars were dug in, a trench connected the four bunkers of the cp, barbed wire and *pungi* stakes were in place outside normal grenade range, and a four-man outpost was higher up the finger of land toward Black Rock Mountain.

There were minor attacks from the south and east and then a major assault from the northwest, on the uphill side; the vc hurled satchel charges into the artillery and mortar positions. Luckily there had been a 50 percent alert on the defense line, and the outpost reported and responded to the attack on them. The artillery and mortar crews fought from their positions as infantrymen;

their main weapons couldn't be fired. The vc got into the cp, and the s-2 and his five men were killed. Major Thanh and I rounded up three cooks and two lieutenants and commenced firing and throwing grenades until we saw three vc withdraw from the position. The vc then withdrew, under heavy fire. The regiment lost two officers and eight men killed and nine men wounded. Two of the men killed were at the outpost that had alerted the cp. In addition, one 105 mm howitzer and two 81 mm mortars received significant damage.

The enemy losses were thirteen killed and three wounded, who were captured. In addition an assortment of rifles, 9 mm burp guns, and two U.S. carbines were left behind, as well as several potato-masher grenades, packs, and a sizable amount of ammunition. One captured vc informed Major Thanh that many members of his company were living in nearby hamlets; he was "encouraged" to identify which hamlets, but he refused. He also said the company had been operating from both Harvest and Black Rock Mountains and that they called upon the local hamlets to provide them with food.

The division commander and the senior adviser arrived late in the morning of the day after. The cp had been cleaned up, and our casualties had been placed at the foot of the hill, awaiting evacuation. The vc dead had been collected outside of the cp, and a detail was digging a mass grave for them halfway down the hill. I suggested that the nearby hamlets be notified so the population could screen them for relatives and thereby give us some idea how pacified the area was. Thanh told me that division policy was that vc dead would be buried immediately in a mass grave. Major Thanh informed the division commander of the friendly and vc casualties and then led him to the enemy dead and the captured vc arms and equipment.

When Major Thanh told about how the outpost had given the alert and added that two of the men had been killed, the division commander repeated several times that the outpost had not been large enough. Each time his voice got louder. Major Thanh tried to tell him that the outpost had accomplished its mission of alerting the cp. While the division commander was taking Thanh to task, I was showing Colonel Pierce the weapons and equipment that the vc had left behind. I told him that I believed we had won the battle, expanding on the many blood trails along the withdrawal route. He said he was going to talk to the division commander about battle casualties.

Prior to departing from the cp, Colonel Pierce told Major Thanh that he was very impressed with his defense against a very determined vc assault. It was obvious the division commander heard Pierce's remarks; prior to entering the helicopter he shook hands with me and then shook Thanh's hand and told him to keep up the good work. As a parting gesture, Colonel Pierce said, "It looks like we got the VC angry about our saturation tactics!"

A Second Battalion company providing security for an engineer company repairing a road from Ly Tin Valley to Ngoc Nho had already had a significant success, setting up an ambush near the abandoned hamlet of An Xoan. As a prelude to the ambush, a platoon had made several searches of the old hamlet and found a substantial quantity of *lua* (unhusked rice). The platoon also noticed that on the banks of the shallow stream there were many tracks leading to An Xoan. The platoon had deployed a stay-behind force in an ambush position along the trail to the old hamlet. That night the VC entered the killing zone, and the ambush patrol had placed a high volume of fire on them. There was very little fire returned, and the VC had run hastily from the area, leaving three dead and one wounded. I made it a point to let Colonel Pierce know about the successful ambush. He said he would pass it on personally to the division commander.

Then on June 4, the successful ambush in the Second battalion wilted with the death of 1st Lt. Ralph Redmond, an adviser in the First Battalion. He had been at his post for less than two months and was killed instantly in a land mine incident, shortly after he returned from two days rest in Da Nang.

It would have taken a thousand more successful ambushes to make an impact on the insurgency in Vietnam. I had spent nearly eight months in Vietnam, and if you but looked at the thousands of approach routes the VC had, you could see what a mistake it would be to commit U.S. troops here. Even so, as time went on we found that we were having better results with the saturation concept, in the increased number of contacts, but with the obvious indifference of MACV, it was becoming questionable whether the approach would survive.

Early in July, I was assigned as the division G-3 adviser, when Major Schungel rotated back to the United States. My new counterpart, Lieutenant Colonel Nhan, was the assistant division commander and had his CP in Tam Ky on Highway 1. The G-3 advisory concept changed when Nhan was given command of the task force, which included both the Fourth and the Sixth Regiments, in Tam Ky, in Quang Tin Province. My duties were oriented to task force operations rather than advising the G-3 in Da Nang.

I was sitting in a folding chair in front of the task force CP, still thinking of the successful ambush that had occurred at the end of my duty as adviser to Major Thanh, when off on the horizon a column of black smoke rose and an occasional flame licked up. Looking at my map I could see that it was in the direction of Ngoc Nho, which was about ten miles west of Tam Ky. As the black smoke increased in volume, I ran into the CP looking for Colonel Nhan. His batman said he was still taking his siesta; I told him to wake him up, because I had something important for him.

Major Thanh had just arrived with his new adviser, Maj. Richard Hipler, to meet with Nhan. They were there to discuss the pending visit by a representative from MACV to check on the increased contacts reported by the Fourth Regiment as a result of the saturation concept. When Nhan joined us I pointed out the black smoke, which appeared to be coming from burning oil and gasoline. I recommended that we immediately investigate and suggested that we use a platoon from the armored reconnaissance troop. Fifteen minutes later, Colonel Nhan and I were in the lead M-114 track, a full-tracked reconnaissance vehicle, often used as an armored personnel carrier. The recon vehicle kicked up dust as we sped toward the source of the smoke.

Arriving where the road ran between Hills 432 and 115, we saw the complete ruin of the engineer company that had been sent to repair the road from Thanh My to Ngoc Nho. Every vehicle in the convoy was burning fiercely; lying on the ground and in vehicles were the men of the company, all dead, many having been given the coup de grace. On the north side of Hill 115 were many camouflaged "spider holes," which the VC had used to surprise the engineers. Nhan had the platoon leader place his tracks on line and attack up Hill 115, as if there was a VC unit dug in there. There was no one on the hill, or anywhere else in the area. The VC were versed in not extracting defeat from the jaws of victory.

It appeared there had been two fatal mistakes: the infantry company charged with the security of the engineer company had not provided that security; the engineers had placed at the head of their column the slow-moving grader and dozer, neither on its lowboy trailer, and at the end of the column had been a large dump truck. All three had been disabled by explosives and set on fire, then the stalled convoy had been destroyed, men and equipment.

We assumed that VC, acting as wood cutters, had concealed their weapons, ammunition, and explosives in firewood packs and had gone directly to spider holes prepared earlier; this explained the firewood beside each spider hole. Nhan told Major Thanh that as soon as possible he wanted to know why the Second Battalion hadn't provided the engineer company with a security unit. Nhan knew that he would have to report this ambush to the division commander within the hour. Major Thanh informed the Second Battalion Commander about the ambush and asked why he hadn't provided security for the engineer company.

Thanh had a response within fifteen minutes. The battalion commander had already informed the regimental CP at Cam An that the engineer company had departed without notifying anyone. A full company from his battalion had been in a night position around the road project, but the engineers had withdrawn on their own after finishing the work.

This was probably one of the worst ambushes to date in the Second Division, on the basis of the personnel and equipment losses. I was surprised when Nhan asked what I thought he should report to division. I advised him to say that his account was based on initial information and that he planned to investigate personally and provide a report within a day. I then told him we should immediately question the battalion commander and company commander charged with the engineers' security. Nhan's initial report was, "The Engineers departed on their own." He accepted my advice, and within fifteen minutes we were heading south on Highway 1 to the Second Battalion. By the time we had returned to our CP, Nhan had finished his report, and it confirmed his initial one. I sent a similar message to the senior adviser.

The next morning, around 8:00, the senior adviser's helicopter came in low over the CP, with Colonel Pierce, the division commander, and Pierce's replacement, Col. Henry Koepcke, Jr. They flew on to survey the ambush site from the air and then returned to the task force helicopter pad. Colonel Koepcke was introduced to Nhan and the others present, and then Nhan briefed the group on how the VC had set up the ambush site and waited for the engineers. He said that they had probably had someone watching the engineer company work; when it withdrew the VC had either sent a messenger or used radio communications. It was obvious to all that the engineer company commander had departed without notifying his security and had compounded this error by not mounting his heavy equipment on lowboys.

The saturation concept was now marred by a disaster, which in turn might be the basis for its curtailment by Saigon. Colonel Koepcke probably had been briefed about MACV's feelings about the saturation concept. MACV representatives now arrived to observe the Second Division's saturation operations. Less than a week later, Koepcke and the I Corps adviser proposed that the Fourth and Sixth Regiments conduct an operation in southern Quang Tin Province. During the planning period, I was notified that I was to report to Da Nang to fly to Hong Kong for my week of R&R. When I returned nine days later, the two-regiment operation was over, with negative results.

On his first visit to the task force after I returned from R&R, Colonel Koepcke said that saturation tactics were behind us and that he wanted more attention paid to VC mining operations. As I recall, he wanted all roads and trails that the ARVN used to be swept in advance. Nhan knew he would have to agree with the new emphasis on mine clearance, but he told me that it would affect response time adversely, unless we could get more helicopter support. I don't believe he ever placed any emphasis on mine clearance in the two regiments he controlled.

In the early morning of August 9, 1964, the VC staged a major attack on the Second Battalion CP at Thanh My, in the Ly Tinh Valley, in southern Quang Tin Province. Thanh, alerting Nhan of the attack, said there had been high casualties on both sides, including an ARVN company commander, who had been killed. At 4 A.M. I awoke in my shack to the loud voices in the CP. Although I didn't understand every thing he was saying, I understood enough to know that Nhan had ordered Major Thanh to have a company at Chien Dang on Highway 1 in an hour, to be picked up by the armored reconnaissance troop. Nhan added that he would command the reaction force going to assist the Second Battalion. Joining them, I looked at the map and recommended that a platoon of the reconnaissance troop move ahead and secure the bridges at Tra Ly Tay and Vinh Dai. Colonel Nhan approved the recommendation; I told him I would accompany the advance guard.

The first section of two M-114 reconnaissance tracks reached Tra Ly Tay, made a cursory check of the bridge, and continued toward the bridge at Vinh Dai. After it had gone about a mile, there was a loud detonation at the first bridge. I was with the second section of three tracks, and when we reached the bridge, I found wires running to an empty sampan, from which the bridge had been detonated electrically. Fortunately, the bridge had been reinforced with steel beams and would still support the tracks. We contacted the platoon leader, who was with the first section of M-114s, and alerted him to possible mines on the road at the bridge. He found that the second bridge had not been prepared for detonation, so I recommended to Colonel Nhan that a small security detail be left at each bridge.

A squad from the Second Battalion met us at the turnoff to Ly Tin Valley and led us to the base of Hill 405, where the battalion fire base was. It was 7:45 A.M. when Nhan, the reconnaissance troop commander, and I climbed the hill to the Second Battalion CP. Near the road a row of fifteen ARVN dead had been laid out, covered with pieces of plastic. Nearby was a group of twenty VC dead, assembled for burial in a mass grave.

I met Lt. John Boss, the new battalion adviser; he had received a gunshot wound in the arm during the battle but was still helping in the reorganization after the attack. As we reached the CP, several mortar rounds landed near the two artillery pieces on the hill. Down below on the road, several rounds from a VC recoilless rifle were fired at the M-114s. But unlike the South Vietnamese leaders at Ap Bac in January 1963, whose lack of courage and hesitation had permitted three companies of vc to escape, Colonel Nhan responded with a coordinated infantry and m-114 attack, with the M-114s used as tanks.[7]

Attacking into a small valley, bowl shaped and closed at one end, two Second Battalion companies cleared the vc from behind dikes in dry rice paddies. The m-114 that Nhan and I used moved with the other tracks on the right flank until we reached a level plain. Nhan directed artillery and mortar fire on the sides of the bowl. At one point we stopped; I jumped out and carried a wounded arvn soldier into the m-114.

Upon reaching the plain, all of the m-114s moved in echelon across the plain and placed .50-caliber fire to the front and lower portions of the valley walls, as the infantry fell in behind us. Suddenly there was a shattering recoilless-rifle hit on our m-114, killing the driver and spraying the inside of the track with blood and fragments; the vehicle went into reverse and stalled. Nhan, the reconnaissance troop commander, and I ran to a nearby paddy dike.

Remembering the wounded man in the m-114, I returned and found him still alive. The vc were now peppering the m-114 with small arms fire; it sounded as if I were in a fifty-gallon drum and someone was beating on the side with a hammer. I returned the fire with the vehicle's .50-caliber machine gun, along with the other tracks, which were near the far end of the bowl, until I ran out of ammunition. Artillery and mortar fire was now falling on the flanks and far end of the bowl.

I placed the wounded soldier over my shoulder and started for the nearest dike. By now helicopter gunships had come in and were rocketing the flanks and far end of the bowl. As I jogged along, what I believe was a recoilless round exploded to one side of me, but I was outside of its bursting radius. I found Colonel Nhan at the dike directing artillery fire on what was now an inferno of burning tall grass. I placed the injured man behind the dike with a medic who was attending another wounded arvn soldier. The troop commander saw us and backed up his m-114 to the rice dike where we stood; Nhan and I got aboard. We saw a mass exodus of the surviving vc into the open plain to escape the burning grass and withdraw to the west. Nhan told the troop commander to get back in line with his advancing line of m-114s.

By this time the reconnaissance troop commander was having a field day, directing his m-114 gunners to fire on the vc in the open as they ran for the road the engineer company had recently repaired. You could see several streams of .50-caliber tracers converging on the bunched-up, retreating vc. After the battle seventy-four vc dead were counted, most of them as a result of the arvn infantry and M-114 attack. Documents and prisoner interrogations indicated that two VC battalions had attacked the Second Battalion, the first such coordinated attack in I Corps.

It was a stroke of luck that the gunships' rockets arrived when they did and started the grass burning, and that the wind from the South China Sea had spread it across the VC positions. Who says luck doesn't assist in battle? More important, Nhan had ordered an attack!

I prepared a detailed report on this battle in Ly Tinh Valley. It was forwarded to MACV in Saigon, but only after the I Corps nonbelievers changed it from a two-battalion VC attack and attempted ambush to a one-battalion VC event. The Bronze Star for valor that I later received cited the enemy as the VC Ninetieth Battalion.

Unknown to me and the advisers in Team Two, the U.S. Navy was becoming involved in a Gulf of Tonkin situation that would provide the Johnson administration with a blank check for future involvement in Southeast Asia. The North Vietnamese were accused of attacking the destroyers *Maddox* and *Turner Joy*. It is questionable whether an attack on the destroyers took place, but the report that went up to the White House spoke of an attack on U.S. vessels "on the high seas." Shortly thereafter, Congress gave Johnson the authority to commit U.S. Forces in Vietnam and take all necessary actions to repress enemy attacks, prevent further aggression, enhance security, and determine when peace and security had returned.[8]

As for me, my radio operator and I now sat in the old one-story building we called "the shack" for about two weeks. It was obvious from the daily reports that came in from the regiments that very little VC contact was taking place in Quang Tin Province. Colonel Nhan said that he thought there was going to be a change of command in the Second Division and that when this word got out, there would be a tendency for operations to slow down. Nhan was disappointed that the saturation concept, which had been just starting to reap rewards of more contact with the VC, was no longer emphasized in the division. Representatives from MACV, most of them colonels, were now making inspection trips to the Tam Ky CP, but they seldom went forward into the province to visit the regiments and battalions.

By early September 1964, personnel reassignments had pretty much purged the saturation concept from the divisional and advisory memory. Only a handful of the adviser class of 1963 and '64 was still around. I don't know if MACV was concerned that there would be any continuity in the saturation-concept efforts; in any case, the one-year tours that the advisers had at division and province level would certainly assure its demise. The limiting of field-grade officers (major, lieutenant colonel, colonel) to one-year assignments in Vietnam ensured tactical and technical discontinuity. The policy deterred any professional approach to solving the advisory and the later military challenges of the war.

As I sat in my shack one afternoon early in September, Colonel Nhan walked in and told me that he had just brought his wife and children to Tam Ky. I had the feeling that he had been fearful about their being so far away, in Dalat. He then told me that the division was about to seal the saturation concept's coffin, by conducting another two-regiment operation in the Ly Tinh Valley, where the two vc battalions had attacked in August.

Colonel Nhan was, in my opinion, an above-average professional, and I could see that he was not happy with this operation in an area where there were no current indications of a vc concentration. With the division and corps changes in command and the newly arrived advisers at those levels, it looked like we were starting all over again rather than improving on successes in counterinsurgency efforts. I had to agree with him, and I even thought of giving him my own feelings—that the U.S. Army sought commonality in its efforts, one size fits all, based on its recent experience. Unfortunately, our tactics in Vietnam had very little to do with what was needed there. But I copped out, and I didn't tell him.

A week later, Nhan's task force CP was set up on Hill 405, in Ly Tin Valley. The Fourth Regiment was to attack west in the valley, and the Sixth Regiment was in position, several miles to the west, to attack east. There were several large tents placed near the CP to accommodate the "guests," some from MACV, who would observe this dynamic, probably MACV-orchestrated, operation. The operation lasted for three days. Some of the guests stayed overnight, but by noon on the second day all of them were gone. The only contacts were with vc mines, which killed and wounded several ARVN. When the operation ended on the third day, the saturation concept ended with it; the regiments resorted to shorter-term, attack-and-withdrawal operations.

At the end of September 1964, as I began counting down the days until I would rotate to the United States, I visited the Fourth Regiment CP near where the engineer company had been ambushed and destroyed. The regiment's Third Battalion was conducting a sweep operation to the south of Hill 115. We could see two companies of the battalion moving south toward Trung Cuu, and at a greater distance we saw a long column of vc moving south of Trung Cuu. It appeared the vc were well armed. The ARVN companies were an hour from the

VC column, but the artillery-fire direction center on Hill 432 thought that the VC were too close to Trung Cuu hamlet to fire on them safely.

Circling above were three VNAF T-4 fighter-bombers, which we attempted to contact; then we tried to get gunship support through Team Two in Da Nang. We failed, and the VC escaped unharmed. This was a sour note upon which to end my first "one-year tour" in Vietnam. When I returned to the CP, a message was waiting for me to return to Da Nang by October 3 for transportation to Saigon and rotation to the United States.

As if in farewell, that night a typhoon blew in from the South China Sea and destroyed many buildings in Tam Ky. As Smith and I sat in our shack, we saw the building supports start to sway. We quickly decided to load our radio, maps, and weapons into the jeep trailer in preparation to move up the road to the province adviser's compound. Smith backed the trailer up a small rise behind the shack so we would pass the equipment out through the window. With a fierce blast of wind from the sea, I saw one end of the building collapse; I made a quick dive through the window and landed in a rice paddy.

Several days later I was in Saigon, staying at the Continental Hotel while I waited for a flight home. It was there, on the hotel's long covered porch, that I learned that a friend of mine, Maj. Reed Jensen (West Point, 1949), had been killed in an ambush on July 28, 1964.

During my trip to the States, I heard over and over from a major I sat with how Gen. William Westmoreland was going to win the war in Vietnam. The major had visited him at MACV and had at one time been his aide. The major never gave me any details on how the war was to be won; he only impressed me that he was loyal. But that's another story.

# 7 The Holding Pattern

Our commercial flight landed at Travis Air Force Base, California, early on October 9, 1964. From there I flew south to visit my parents and sister in San Diego for a couple of days. My bland diet in Vietnam had made it difficult to eat rich food in the States, but a prescription from the San Diego Naval Hospital alleviated this problem.

Flying toward Ohio, I reflected on my third such trip in this direction after participating in a war, although Vietnam was still thought of as a "military advisory effort." This wouldn't be my last trip to Vietnam. The war was the issue in the 1964 presidential election. If there was a national preference, it was for the incumbent, Lyndon Johnson, because of the belief in the president's promise that Asian boys should fight Asian wars. I must admit that I bought his position and voted for him.

Six months later, in the late spring of 1965, American boys would be given that responsibility, and I was kicking myself for voting as I had. In my political naiveté, I had not considered the impact that the closest advisers to a president have on him. Johnson's three warhorses—Robert McNamara, secretary of defense; Dean Rusk, secretary of state; and McGeorge Bundy—probably could have done without a Vietnam, except for the positive footnote they thought it might give them in history. At the same time, President Johnson was in a position to restrain his warhorses, as a result of his landslide election victory. Instead, he chose to use the Tonkin Gulf Resolution as an excuse for war rather than consider any diplomatic approach. It was truly unfortunate for the country, considering the substantial international support he would have attained through diplomacy and restraint.

After I arrived home, Marge and I went to New York City, attended the World's Fair, saw "Fiddler on the Roof," and visited her Aunt Louise. On our return to Stow, we planned a get-together with her brothers and sisters and their families. Vietnam was on American minds; I found that people were asking about more than where Vietnam was located, as they had a year before. I put together a photo story of my time in Vietnam, containing pictures most representative of that year. The last picture was me boarding the plane for the United States, with the caption, "I hope we never make the mistake of deploying U.S. ground forces here."

My new assignment was in the Intelligence and Communications Department of the Naval Amphibious School (NAMS), at Little Creek Naval Amphibious Base, near Norfolk, Virginia. We still had the Volkswagen bus we had bought in 1959, but since we would be separated while the children finished the first semester, I bought an older Chevrolet to drive to Little Creek; I drove the car for the next three years. I found a three-bedroom house in Norfolk and spent two months building a bedroom at one end of the large family room for my oldest daughter, Mary Lou.

After moving our household goods into our new home, I flew back to Ohio for Christmas and brought my family to Norfolk. There can be no doubt that when children have to sever relationships with friends, wonder who their new friends will be, and face a new school situation, they feel great anxiety; "military brats" have to repeat the experience every two or three years. On the other hand, there is a tendency for these children to adjust more readily to change in later life. I suppose it depends on the child, each being of a different makeup.

The first morning in the house on Doumar Drive in Norfolk, Rick told me there was no one to play with. I saw a boy across the street throwing snowballs; I told Rick that if he threw a snowball across the street, he'd soon have someone to play with. Rick did that, and a half-hour later he and his new friend Allan Jasper were throwing snowballs at a telephone pole. Rick and Allan were good friends for the next three years.

My assignment to the Navy gave me a broadened view of the U.S. military, but this was particularly the case when it came to the Navy–Marine Corps team. During a series of classes that I gave on the amphibious concept, I never failed to point out that my purpose in being at NAMS was not to contest a very successful team but to do my small part to maintain the state of the amphibious art in the Army. I mentioned that the Navy-Army team had landed the largest number of troops on hostile shores; I can remember the reactions to that sacrilegious statement. When I provided the documentation, I got the attention of the class.

My tour at NAMS ended when I was promoted to lieutenant colonel in September 1965. I opted for the Army Representative position on the staff of the

Adm. Frank W. Vanoy, COMPHIBTRALANT, presents Mack with the Vietnamese Gallantry Cross with palm in 1966 at the Naval Amphibious Base, Little Creek, Virginia.

Commander, Amphibious Training Command, Atlantic (COMPHIBTRALANT), also at Little Creek. Inasmuch as my family was now adjusted to the Norfolk scene, I was happy to be able to complete a normal three-year tour in the area.

During my first year with the Navy, I found that I was called upon quite often to speak before Navy organizations as well as local civic groups on my experiences as an adviser in Vietnam. As time went on I detected an increase in skepticism in the questions being asked, particularly since my presentation dealt with the lower-level military advisory effort I had experienced, whereas our country now had a more strategic involvement, with a less than stable government.

The war in Vietnam continued, but events had already taken place—though they were not made public—that were directly affecting the course of the war and the future escalation of U.S. forces in Vietnam. For one, a disavowal had been made by the secretary of defense about his visits to Saigon in October and December 1963. After his October visit, McNamara had assured President Kennedy that "the military campaign had made great progress and continued to progress." After his December visit, he admitted to President Johnson that the statistics he had used earlier had been greatly in error and that the current situation was "very disturbing." The lack of leadership in the U.S. government and the "indecisive and drifting" McNamara cited the South Vietnamese junta as central to the problem. Also, in 1964 Gen. Paul Harkins had been replaced by Gen. William Westmoreland, and although there was very little progress that year, by 1965 Lyndon Johnson was an elected president, with a mandate, he thought, to do as he felt necessary in Vietnam. Add to that the untenable security situation and guerrilla activities that prompted Westmoreland to recommend that two Marine Corps battalions be landed for the defense of the Da Nang Air Base. His request was honored by the president, and on March 8, 1965, the marines became the first ground forces committed to Vietnam. By the end of 1965, there were two hundred thousand U.S. troops in Vietnam.[1]

I obviously had little influence over the politics of the Vietnam War; I didn't even know the details of what was going on. Still, after spending my duty hours giving my best, in my free time I became involved in a way with Vietnam, by writing articles that highlighted the military environment there. I had several articles published in the *Marine Corps Gazette, Infantry, Army Aviation, Military Review,* and others. The subjects ranged from sniper training, ambushes, and combat photography to helicopter-borne assaults, mines and booby traps, and reducing the soldier's load.[2]

On the local scene, Marge joined the Amphibious Wives' Club and was the treasurer of the Little Creek thrift shop. Mary and Rolly went to Norfolk Catholic High School, and Elizabeth and Rick went to public schools. Mary and I spent many Friday nights at the "issues of the day" movies at Old Dominion College. Rolly was involved in cheerleading in high school and spent weekends volunteering at a Norfolk orphanage. Rick finally got a BB gun, and we set up a range in the garage.

In the fall of 1966, my boss, a Navy captain, was given a command at sea. The chief of staff told me that I was the next senior officer in the Plans, Operations, and Training (POT) department, and Adm. Woodrow W. McCrory, the training command commander, had decided that I was to head the POT staff until a Navy captain was assigned. It didn't take long to hear the "buzz" that a Navy commander (the equivalent naval rank to lieutenant colonel) also on the POT staff was only five days junior to me. Although it was an interim assignment, running the department would have looked good on his record. Regardless, I took over POT and was involved immediately in the staff's activities, whether or not my background suited the assignment.

Vice Adm. John Sidney McCain, the Commander, Amphibious Forces, Atlantic (his son John, a naval aviator, was to be a prisoner of war, a senator from Arizona, and a candidate for the Republican presidential nomination) tasked our command to determine the best and worst of the thirteen tank landing ships (LSTs) in the Atlantic Fleet. I was to have an answer by Monday morning!

It was Friday! That in mind, I presented "our" problem to my staff but received only blank stares. Luckily, I had spent time at NAMS and knew that most ships had refresher training annually, so I called the officer who headed the Ship-to-Shore Department at NAMS and found where the records were. By closing time, I had all the records needed to compare the LSTs. After determining what areas were examined in the refresher training, we constructed a matrix board and gave a weighting to each area, as determined by the Navy members of the staff. I then told the staff to be back at 8:00 A.M. on Saturday, to analyze the records. I also told them that we would select the best two LSTs and the worst two, and then list the remaining ships in three groups of three, each in descending order.

On Monday morning, I briefed Admiral McCrory on the results. He agreed with our methodology, accepted the top and bottom LSTs, and asked me to leave my charts. Later in the day he briefed the force commander. On Tuesday morning the chief of staff called me in and asked me how I had arrived at the USS *De Soto County*'s being the thirteenth (worst) LST; the night before, it had run into the Chesapeake Bay Bridge, temporarily blocking one of the bridge's two lanes. Admiral McCain had contacted Admiral McCrory to tell him that the worst LST had been confirmed. My stock rose, even if the results of our analysis had been misinterpreted, slightly.

After a couple of months solving amphibious training problems, Capt. James S. Spillman (USN) was assigned to take over the department. His first instruction to me was to set up the coming summer's Naval Academy and Naval Reserve Officer Training Corps (NROTC) amphibious training at Little Creek. I reviewed the previous year's midshipmen training and noted that over half of it had been more academic than "hands on." At about the same time, Admiral McCrory retired, and in the interim the Marine Corps brigadier general commanding the Landing Force Training Unit (LFTU) became the acting commander of the training command.

With this in mind, I organized a training program oriented more toward the Marine Corps mission in amphibious operations, with midshipman participation as squad leaders and boat coxswains in seizures of landing sites, demonstrations of casting and pickups of frogmen by a SEAL team, helicopter combat assault training, and firing the M-16 rifle. The interim commander approved the training plan, and the Marine Corps placed a battalion landing team on temporary duty at Little Creek for demonstration and instruction purposes. Each midshipman was to lead a squad ashore to seize an objective, and have the experience of bringing a "mike boat" (LCM, a large landing craft) ashore at an appointed place, taking care not to broach the craft sideways to the surf.

My assignment ended, and I was assigned to the staff of U.S. Army Europe (USAREUR) in Heidelberg. We departed from McGuire Air Force Base for Frankfurt on November 30. Since I would not receive quarters immediately, we arranged to stay at the Frizia Garni pension on Rohrbacher Strasse in Heidelberg. The pension provided the children with a continental breakfast, they ate lunch in the school cafeterias, and we all went out to dinner at night.

I was assigned as the chief of plans in the office of the Deputy Chief of Staff, Intelligence (DCSINTEL). Most of my time was spent as the DCSINTEL member of a command, control, and logistics study, known as "CCLS-70," aimed at streamlining USAREUR, which was competing for resources needed by the U.S. Army in Vietnam. The position was a daily grind involving coordinating CCLS-70 matters and running the plans branch.

Maj. Gen. Richard Whitney, the DCSINTEL, was a great person. He knew how to command with consideration for others, an attribute many general officers lack. On the second Sunday of my tour, I was in the office, and I received a call to come to his office. He asked, "Are you Lt. Col. Richard E. Mack, 058492?" (citing my Army serial number). I answered affirmatively, and he said, "How dare you let yourself be assigned to DCSINTEL and then permit yourself to be picked up for the U.S. Army War College class of 1969?" All in jest, of course. To say the least, I was a bit amazed, since I had visited Career Management in the Pentagon three weeks earlier, and no mention had been made of attendance at the War College, in Carlisle, Pennsylvania. I can't recall my response, other than that I would do the best job possible in the six or seven months that I'd be with DCSINTEL.

While we were in Heidelberg, Rolly attended her first prom, as well as all of the high school dances. Mary met some German students, and the high point of her stay was the Fasching festivities before Lent. Elizabeth stayed close to the Frizia Garni, and normally she and Rick accompanied Marge and me on short trips to such places as Mannheim. Fortunately, an officer loaned us his 1950 Chevrolet, the same year as the one we had left in Berlin in 1959, so we had a means of getting around while waiting for our own automobile to arrive. This gave Marge the opportunity to visit the interesting places near Heidelberg. Unfortunately, she fell on the ice and broke a bone in her foot, which put her in a cast for most of the winter. She never complained, even while we continued to live in the pension, with its several flights of steps.

An embarrassing event for DCSINTEL occurred when Radio Luxembourg announced that Czechoslovakia was tearing down the reinforced-concrete, electrified fence between it and West Germany in several places. For some reason this had gone unnoticed by our armored cavalry border patrols and the West German border guards, both of which had responsibility for border surveillance. The Czechs followed up by reinstalling the fences. Throughout the cold war, the U.S. focus had been on critical routes into West Germany, a most important one being the Fulda Gap. When the Tet Offensive took place in Vietnam, German students protested against our involvement there, which added to the complexity of our position in Europe.

During my tour in Heidelberg, President Johnson announced that he would not run for reelection in 1968. The heightened protest against the Vietnam War and associated U.S. policies had prompted him to make this decision. The assassination of Martin Luther King on April 4, 1968, followed by the assassination of Sen. Robert F. Kennedy two months later, created in turn heightened racial tension, turmoil, and finally destabilization on a national scale, adversely affecting the president's "Great Society" programs. In sum, the year 1968 was not a time of clear-cut goals in the United States.

Three months before we were scheduled to leave Germany, we were assigned a set of quarters at Patrick Henry Village; in fact, we received half of the maid's quarters on the fourth floor of an apartment-type building, with the equivalent of eight bedrooms, a living room, dining room, kitchen, and two bathrooms. It was rags to riches! Mary Lou's high school graduation was conducted in the Heidelberg Schloss (castle), after which our short time in Germany came to an end. We boarded the train for the port of Le Havre, France, where we boarded the liner SS *United States* for our return trip. The three-day voyage was a pleasure for us all.

Shortly after docking in the New York, we knew we were home when we entered the long lines for passport checks and customs declarations. My only thought was, "What a first image of the United States, particularly in the case of foreign visitors." After picking up our 1965 Nash Rambler, we headed west to Marge's mother's home in Stow.

In early July, Elizabeth and I drove to Carlisle and made arrangements for housing. I was assigned a separate, four-bedroom house. While there, I visited Col. Tom Cleary, who had been my battalion commander in Berlin. Before the War College classes began, Marge and I had time to become acquainted with the Cumberland Valley, where Carlisle is located. Our daughter Mary Lou departed for California to attend San Diego University. Rosalind and Elizabeth attended the Catholic school in Shirmanstown, and Rick went to Saint Patrick's School in Carlisle.

During the year I spent at the War College, we met many people we had served with before, even a few from the Officers Basic Course and the Eighth Cavalry Regiment in 1950–51. The school was described by some as a "gentlemen's course," probably because there were no examinations. The two facilities that were highest in student participation were the golf course and the officers' club. Neither Marge nor I played golf, and we seldom went to the officers' club. We weren't alone in this, though.

The course was conducted in seminar sessions. One student was selected as the seminar leader, with the task of organizing the members to research, analyze, and derive conclusions on selected issues. The course began with an attempt to rewrite the Constitution and ended with a recommendation of a U.S. national strategy and a military program to support it. In addition to research in the college library, there were also guest speakers, who normally discussed current issues. The individual student projects involved research on subjects approved by the college, and they were presented both in writing and orally. My project was to write two essays, one on nation building and the other on a current issue, "Black Power." I had a mentor for each essay, with whom I met weekly to show my progress.

Shortly after Richard Nixon was elected president, his national security adviser, Henry Kissinger, came to Carlisle as a guest speaker. This prompted the students as well as faculty to ask him about changes that might be expected in foreign policy. Vietnam was the prime area of interest, and there was an intense desire to learn of changes that might come about in national strategy and military programs. Kissinger's responses, as I recall, could best be described as "Stay tuned."

Vietnam stayed on the front burner, especially among officers for whom it had been their first combat experience, and most of all for those who had commanded battalions there. Battalion command is the goal for most lieutenant colonels in the combat arms and logistics services, some perhaps considering it a rite of manhood. Of the thirty colonels and 152 lieutenant colonels in the class of 1969, 132 had commanded battalions, the majority in Vietnam. Among this group of 182 officers, the following decorations had been awarded: Medal of Honor, one; Distinguished Service Cross, eight; Silver Star, sixty-two; and Distinguished Flying Cross, twenty-one.[3]

Although there are more factors than battalion command and decorations, it was quite evident that chances of assignment to the Army War College were enhanced by having commanded a battalion. Inasmuch as I had not, I asked myself, "How did I get here?" My answer was that it must have been the articles I had published in service magazines. My advisory experience may also have contributed indirectly to my assignment.

I entered Vietnam as my first choice when I submitted my preference for my next assignment, and hoped I would receive orders to Vietnam and be placed on the battalion-command list.

At the end of the academic year, the annual National Strategy Seminar was conducted, during which dignitaries from all walks of life were integrated into the student seminars. In our seminar group we had the chief of research and development of General Electric, the managing editor of *Forbes,* and the under secretary of labor. As I recall, when we discussed our recommended national strategy, the under secretary thought the goal we had established to reduce unemployment to 4.5 percent wasn't low enough. The GE representative also took issue with the 4.5 percent figure, saying it was too low for productivity purposes, and for the rest of the day we listened to a real-world discussion.

It was a year after the Tet Offensive, and I noted an increased optimism at the War College, quite out of line with the actual situation in Vietnam. The new policy was Vietnamization of the war, turning the burden over to the South Vietnamese government and its military forces. In my own mind I questioned whether I had done the right thing in volunteering for a second tour in Vietnam. My father had told me that he believed it was a stupid thing to do, to return to a losing war. Regardless, the die had been cast, and duty called; I could no longer afford any ambivalence.

I have little doubt that during my year at Carlisle, the War College's requirement that issues be thoroughly researched gave me a much deeper understanding of the complexities of devising a military strategy that supports national policy. While a few students discussed their contributions on the Vietnam battlefield, particularly those for whom it had been their sole combat experience, there was a general reluctance to engage in what I would call the "war-story syndrome." I found that the faculty preached no party line with respect to the Vietnam War.

Then I departed on my second tour to Vietnam and left the holding pattern.

# 8 America's War

I landed at Cam Ranh Bay on August 7, 1969, just as the sun was setting on a hot, sultry evening. As I walked across the tarmac from the air-conditioned aircraft, I wondered how long it would take me to adjust to the heat, let alone the mosquitoes. Twenty minutes later I was sitting in an air-conditioned building, listening to a briefing with other officers on how to be successful in Vietnam. I heard one officer say, "You'll be successful if a year from now you are boarding an aircraft for CONUS [the continental United States], sans body bag." During the briefing the terms "Vietnamization" and "drawdown of U.S. forces" were used several times.

I was assigned to the Fourth Infantry Division in the Highlands, outside of Pleiku. The division commander was Maj. Gen. Donn Pepke. I arrived at the division base, Camp Enari, on August 9, via a C-130 aircraft, helicopter, and jeep; by 11 A.M. the division G-1 (adjutant, or administrative officer) was looking at my records, from which he noted that I was on the battalion command list; he printed my name on a smudged piece of acetate with several other names. He had no idea, however, when I would take over a battalion.[1] Finally he told me I was assigned to the Third Brigade, as the deputy to Col. Volney Warner (West Point, 1950), the brigade commander. The meeting concluded with the afterthought that Col. Gordon J. Duquemin, the chief of staff, wanted to see me. I ate lunch in the officers' mess, tablecloths and all, prior to seeing the chief of staff. I was unimpressed with the comfortable living and working conditions I saw at Camp Enari.

Duquemin welcomed me to the division with the usual praise of its distinguished past and then told me I would like working for Colonel Warner, a real hard-charger. Out of the blue, he said he had a surprise for me: he congratulated me upon being on the colonels list—that is, I had been selected for promotion and awaited only a vacancy among the Army's authorized number of colonels. He told me that I might be promoted before I commanded a battalion. This concerned me; the G-1 hadn't known when I'd get a battalion. I spent my first night in the comfort of an air-conditioned van at Camp Enari. I was to go to the Third Brigade's Fire Base Oasis by helicopter the next morning.

That night I walked around the base and saw, among other things, a swimming pool, unused; prefab barracks, mostly empty; and an electrical power-generation facility that could provide for the needs of a small city. I had already noted the modern office furniture in the division headquarters and the neat tablecloths and napkins in the officers' mess. All the roads were paved, and flowers and shrubbery had been planted at the entrance to each building. It all seemed alien to the mission of the dirty-socks infantrymen who were more than likely "humping" the mountains and trails about Camp Enari.

I could see one reason why we were not winning the war. This was an infantry division headquarters out of touch with its combat elements. These were harsh words after only a brief observation, but the commanding general and his staff had established a center of luxury and comfort that required at least the equivalent of an infantry battalion, nearly 10 percent of the division's combat strength, to defend.

Colonel Warner met me at the chopper pad, and within a few hours I was impressed with his manner and his grasp of the brigade's operational area. Warner had commanded the brigade for about six weeks and had showed that he was a dedicated combat commander.

He gave me a rundown on Fire Base Oasis's defenses and facilities, and then we walked the line. In addition to defensive positions and considerable artillery, there were logistics units, a forward air control (FAC) detachment, and a landing strip to support FAC aircraft. Warner pointed out that one of my duties would be to ensure for him that the defense positions were manned properly, primarily by the logistics units. Fire Base Oasis had a barbershop, a small post exchange and tailor shop, and a bare-bones mess facility. Warner pointed out that I would have a van just like his for my quarters. Both vans had been dug in, since the fire base had recently sustained a determined NVA attack and frequently received mortar fire.

After lunch in the mess hall (no doilies, tablecloths, or napkins here), we went to the brigade tactical operations center (TOC), and Warner briefed me on his general area of operations (AO), as is shown on the map of the Central Highlands. He wanted me to keep myself fully knowledgeable on brigade operations, but he made it clear that he would make the decisions on operations

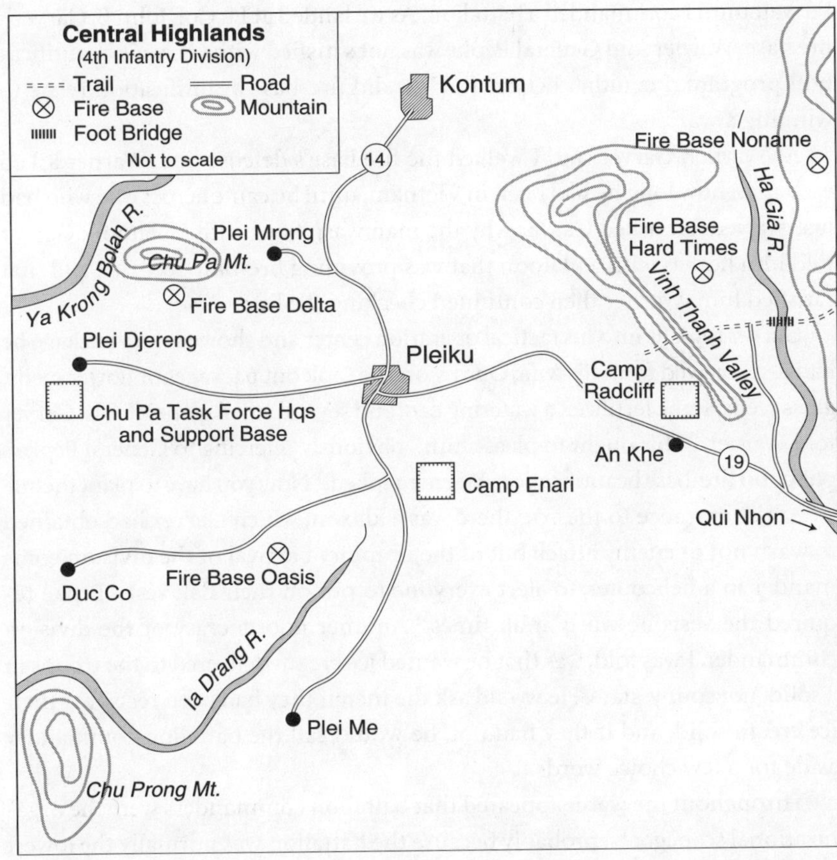


and policy. From time to time I would be designated as a task force commander for ad hoc brigade operations, and I also needed to be knowledgeable about the Vietnamese Regional Forces (RF). Finally, he said I would be called upon to write up citations and recommendations for decorations. He then had me join him on a helicopter visit to each battalion fire base.

As we flew to the first battalion, he told me that he wanted me to visit the battalions and check on whether they were enforcing the division commander's policy that all replacements were to be integrated into rifle platoons immediately upon assignment. I could see that this was an item where we might disagree, because I firmly believed that replacements should be given time to acclimate themselves, by being assigned to on-the-job training at a fire base for a week before joining a platoon. This was not the time to pester him with this;

I'd wait until I commanded a battalion. As we landed at Lt. Col. John B. Garver's fire base, Warner said General Pepke was not satisfied with Garver's beautification program. I couldn't believe it. How did fire-base beautification relate to winning a war?

As Warner, Garver, and I walked the fire base's defense line, Warner asked each man how long he had been in Vietnam, until he came across one who had just arrived. He asked Garver why the man wasn't out with a platoon; Garver told him he was with a platoon that was providing fire-base security, and that satisfied him. Warner then continued checking the line.

Garver took us into his tactical operation center and showed me a package he had just received from his wife. One by one he took out packages of flower seeds, grass seeds, some fertilizer, a watering can, and several small garden tools. Garver told Warner, "This ought to please him," obviously referring to General Pepke's policy on fire-base beautification. Warner replied, "Now you have to plant them!"

At the entrance to the TOC there was a klaxon, which Garver had obtained to warn not of enemy attack but of the imminent arrival of the division commander in a helicopter, to alert everyone to put on their flak vests. Pepke required the vests be worn at all times.[2] Another idiosyncrasy of the division commander, I was told, was that he wanted ice cream delivered to the troops in a solid, not soupy, state. He would ask the men if they had been receiving their ice cream solid, and if they had not, he would call the battalion commander aside for a few choice words.

Throughout the war it appeared that battalion commanders were the organizational scapegoats, probably because the battalion was normally the lowest level that division or corps commanders ever visited on the battlefield. It was almost as if every battlefield problem could be solved by relieving the battalion commander. And I wanted to be a battalion commander? So be it!

By the end of the day, I had visited two more battalions and had a good idea what my duties were. Like any deputy, I would be doing what Colonel Warner had responsibility for but didn't want to do himself. I soon found that Warner departed in his command helicopter first thing in the morning and returned in the evening after a day of supervising his battalions.

The next day, I toured the Fire Base Oasis defense line and found there were several sectors that provided attackers with excellent approaches, not covered properly with either automatic weapons or mortar fire. I contacted the officers who had responsibility for the sectors, and they promised to make the necessary corrections. Two days later I found the corrections had not been made; I told the officers concerned (they were members of a maintenance unit) that I would be inspecting them again that night. When I inspected the line, I found the corrections had finally been made. I inspected the line at night because the men defending it had worked all day and thus were likely to fall asleep at night.

I inspected bunker positions daily for drugs—bunkers were a favorite hiding place—but found none. In Vietnam, drugs were least common within the combat battalions, because of isolation from the larger cities, where the major drug traffic took place. Individuals going on R&R, for example, could visit major cities in the Pacific area, where drugs were available, but on their return they could be searched.

Two weeks after I arrived, Warner instructed me to accompany a Regional Force battalion making a sweep southeast of Fire Base Oasis in the Ia Drang Valley. As far as I could determine, my only purpose was to learn something about their operations; I didn't have a radio, so I couldn't request any support. When we moved out in the morning, I wasn't surprised to find the battalion moving in column, searching on a front one man wide. They were searching in the same area where the First Cavalry Division had fought a major battle in October and November 1965, southwest of Plei Me.[3]

By noon the battalion had made no contact, so it halted while the men prepared their rice. Shortly, there was an explosion. A mine had been activated; one man had been killed, and five others were wounded. A few minutes later a helicopter hovered over an opening in the jungle. The helicopter landed, and in it was Warner. I gave him a report on the operation, and he told me to hop in. Warner said in passing that if anyone was going on a combat mission, it would be him. He was smiling, but I had the feeling that this was a technique he used in leading; by staying in the front line, he'd always set the example. The brigade operations officer told me the reason for picking me up was that the province chief and his adviser had been upset that I was "advising" the battalion commander. Whatever!

A few days later Warner told me that he had been informed that I was on the colonel's list. Then he told me that I wouldn't need a battalion command, now that I had been selected. Knowing that Warner and the division chief of staff talked on the secure microwave telephone nightly, and assuming that Warner was telling me that my getting a battalion was in question, I reiterated that I still wanted one.

One morning Warner dropped me off at Garver's battalion so that I could encourage Garver to get his fire-base beautification started. When Warner picked me up again, I told him that there had been a vast improvement, with rock-lined walks, flowers, and a grassy plot in front of the TOC: "It is now an excellent reference point for NVA mortars." I don't believe Warner appreciated my bit of levity. (Shortly thereafter Colonel Garver completed his battalion command assignment and later returned to West Point, to be a professor of geography. He would become a cartographer with *National Geographic* magazine; I was impressed by him.)

In October 1969, Colonel Warner maneuvered a battalion into a position in the Chu Pa Mountain complex (see the Central Higlands map) where there had been indications of a sizable NVA force. The evidence of enemy presence was sufficiently credible that he had convinced the division commander to attach two additional battalions to the Third Brigade. A successful operation had been conducted there in the past. About the same time, Warner told me that if I could arrange for a regiment of ARVN troops from Kontum Province to join with Third Brigade units in a Chu Pa operation, he would let me head up the task force. Accordingly, I went to the province headquarters in Kontum City.

Upon landing at an improvised landing pad near the province headquarters, three of us—myself and a newly assigned major and a captain—commenced walking along a trail to a jeep, three hundred yards away. There was an arrow made of bamboo strips lying on the trail. Suspecting the arrow pointed toward a mine, I stopped our group, and we made a roundabout path to the jeep. When we reached the meeting, I voiced my suspicion of a mine on the trail from the helicopter.

The ARVN regimental commander, the province chief, and his U.S. adviser were present. The province chief told us that the regiment in question was under his operational control and that he could approve its operation with the Third Brigade. We agreed that the ARVN regiment would coordinate its operations with the Third Brigade's Chu Pa task force. The ARVN regiment's AO would be from the Chu Pa Mountain proper to a certain unnamed river to the south. The Third Brigade task force units, two battalions, would operate to the south of the same river.

Upon returning to the helicopter, I learned that an ARVN engineer team had probed the path to the helicopter and found a U.S. "bouncing betty" mine.[4] The ARVN lieutenant returned the small woven bamboo arrow to me; I have kept it, as a sign of very good luck.

I commenced working on the Chu Pa task force plan as soon as I returned to Fire Base Oasis. Colonel Warner provided me with a small staff and some support personnel. We selected the Civilian Irregular Defense Group (CIDG) camp at Plei Djereng as the task force CP and as an advanced logistics base for fuel and ammunition support of the helicopter units and general support of the two

U.S. battalions.[5] The plan became operational on October 9, when the logistics base and CP were opened and artillery was deployed to the Plei Djereng area. The artillery—two batteries of 105 mm howitzers, a battery of 155 mm howitzers, a section of 8-inch artillery, and a section of 175 mm guns—began harassing-and-interdiction fire on October 12. General Pepke spent most of the day at the artillery site at Old Plei Djereng, on the Ia Grai River.

On October 17, I flew with our FAC over the area of operations and picked out six landing zones, LZS, to be cleared by dropping two-thousand-pound bombs. The two-thousand-pounders, used often when entry into thick jungle was planned, would topple large trees and produce LZS at the bottom of funnels formed in the triple-canopy, hardwood jungle. Some helicopter approaches had to be cleared further by engineer teams, which rappelled into the LZS from helicopters.

The First Battalion of the Thirty-fifth Regiment (1/35th, for short) and the Third Battalion of the Twelfth Regiment (3/12th) were flown into Plei Djereng on C-130s, and their companies conducted helicopter assaults into the LZS beginning on October 19. After a ten-day artillery preparation of the AO, plus the dropping of the bombs, however, the NVA had had every reason to leave the Chu Pa complex. Any hope of surprise had been lost. The question might be asked, were there other ways of doing this? Certainly there were, but that was moot when the how was decided from outside the task force headquarters, with the mode of implementation imposed on the task force commander. Hey, we grew up in Vietnam exercising "dynamic operations"! Success? That was another matter!

The operation continued until the first week of November 1969. One company of the 3/12th Battalion was ambushed and sustained several casualties. There were several minor contacts with small NVA units. The 3/12th brought its mess (cooking) section into its fire base at LZ Delta and subsequently sustained a number of casualties and damage to its artillery from an NVA mortar attack. I had questioned the battalion commander's judgment in bringing the mess section into the fire base, principally because the smoke from ranges could give the NVA a targeting reference and unnecessarily put the CP and its occupants in harm's way. The welfare of the troops has its place, but not placing them unnecessarily in danger is of higher importance.

The ARVN regiment reported that it had had no contact with the enemy during the operation. Both of the U.S. battalions were ordered to sweep east to Highway 14. The 3/12th Battalion withdrew its security from Hill 1019, overlooking Fire Base Delta, believing that a CIDG platoon from Plei Djereng would provide the security. However the CIDG platoon refused to land there, believing it was occupied by NVA. I volunteered to land on Hill 1019 with my radio operator to show the CIDG platoon that the hill was not occupied. We landed, found no NVA, and so reported; the CIDG platoon landed, and my radio operator and I were withdrawn. The 3/12th then commenced its sweep to the east. Had there been NVA on the hill, I hoped the battalion commander, Lt. Col. John Foss, would have assisted me.

As the Chu Pa operation ended, I remembered having told myself in my first tour, when I had been an adviser, "If only these were U.S. units, the results would have been better." In fact, however, aside from the bells and whistles, mostly mobility assets, that we had imported into the Vietnam War, we were pretty much doing what the French and South Vietnamese had done before us.

I had the definite feeling that I had been the task force commander in name only, and that the job had been offered to me in compensation for not getting a battalion. There was no doubt that with the current command arrangement in the division, I had no chance of commanding one. I was unable to detect among the Third Brigade's battalion commanders any particular gift of command that I didn't have, except that they were academy graduates. I was now of the opinion that the division chief of staff had found it convenient to fill my battalion command space with other people more to his liking. Being "on the command list" was wishful thinking!

Lieutenant colonels served only six months in battalion command, which voided any continuity in purpose and strategy, had there been a purpose or strategy to start with. There was nothing magic about six months. It had everything to do with not winning the war—the idea was to let as many as possible of the preferred officers get their command "tickets punched" while the war lasted. There was little continuity at the fighting edge, only multiple short-term attempts to please the chain of command. There were no tactical or strategic thinkers being produced.

When I returned to Fire Base Oasis, Colonel Warner told me to continue with the task force in the Plei Mrong area, with the same two battalions. He also suggested that I check with the chief of staff on the battalion command regarding my prospects before it was too late. Right or wrong, I wondered if Warner was the sounding board for Colonel Duquemin; I thought he probably knew that there was no battalion command on my horizon.

Toward the middle of November, I took my staff, now reduced, to Plei Mrong, west of the Chu Pa complex, and reestablished the task force. We built a bunker on the flat plain where Plei Mrong was located. It was evident to me that both battalions were in a "resting" mode. After a day at Plei Mrong, I received a message instructing me to report to the division chief of staff at Camp Enari. At our meeting the chief of staff told me that I was not going to get a battalion; I could go to another division to see if a battalion was available. My response was that I thought all lieutenant colonels needed a battalion but that I wasn't going out to look for one! I didn't go into details but returned to Plei Mrong.

A week later there was a change of command, and Maj. Gen. Glenn D. Walker took over the division from General Pepke. Walker had been my regimental commander when I had been in the Sixth Infantry Regiment in Berlin. He had held every leadership position in the Fourth Infantry Division, from platoon leader to, now, division commander. I returned to Oasis for Walker's visit. When he asked me what I had been doing, I replied that I was waiting to command a battalion. Four days later I received another message instructing me to report to Camp Enari, this time to the commanding general. As I walked past the chief of staff's desk, he remarked that he thought I was going to get a battalion. It was the 1/8th Infantry Battalion, nicknamed "The Bullets." So go politics in the U.S. Army.

The battalion's change of command took place during the first week of December at Camp Radcliffe, another monster-sized base with an extremely large perimeter, near An Khe, to the east of Pleiku. Occasional battalion-sized sweeps were needed to search for enemy *within* this camp. Another Fourth Division white elephant!

During most of December my battalion CP was within Camp Radcliffe, where we augmented the logistic units on the perimeter at night, patrolled outside the camp, and conducted training. A search through a least-accessible part of the camp revealed that unknowns, probably VC, had been living there; the camp's security needs equaled or were greater than those of Camp Enari. No wonder we had needed over five hundred thousand troops in Vietnam! But now forces were being drawn down, and we'd find out exactly how much rear-area real estate we really needed.

My battalion was scheduled to conduct a search-and-destroy operation centered on the hamlet of Plei Ko Jena, about twenty-seven miles northwest of Camp Radcliffe. We had already made a reconnaissance of the objective area, selected four LZs, and scheduled the combat assault for January 2, 1970.

On New Year's Eve all was quiet until midnight, when the battalion and other units on the perimeter fired a "mad minute." The Army aviators were having a party at the airfield, and at midnight they began firing hand-held flares, one of which struck and destroyed a helicopter. A private first class from my battalion had been on security guard at the airfield; charges were to be preferred against him for not stopping the pilots from firing the flares. I wrote a letter to the division commander telling him I thought the charges were unfair, in that the PFC could not reasonably have been expected to stop a group of carousing officers bent on mischief. The charges were dropped. Later, after we had deployed from the camp, the NVA conducted a surprise raid on the airfield, and several more helicopters were destroyed.

During the night of 1–2 January, 1970, the NVA attacked the Special Forces and CIDG camp at Vinh Thanh district headquarters, about fifteen miles north east of An Khe. (See the Central Highlands map.) The attack resulted in two Americans being killed and three wounded, as well as a large number of CIDG casualties. My mission in the Plei Ko Jena Valley was scrubbed, and I was ordered instead to conduct a combat assault into the Vinh Thanh Valley. I made a reconnaissance of the valley by helicopter while my company commanders organized their helicopter loads, and an hour and a half later I deployed the companies north, east, and west of the valley.

During my reconnaissance I had decided to try the saturation concept we had used in 1964, by placing my companies in operational areas to conduct patrols and ambushes. I would rotate them periodically through the fire base to provide security for the CP and the artillery; this would give them some relief from the constant patrolling routine. As the helicopters dropped off their cargo of men and equipment in the jungle edges of Vinh Thanh Valley, lumbering Chinook helicopters came up the valley with a mini-bulldozer, artillery pieces, and cargo nets hanging below, loaded with ammo and supplies. Conex-container staff facilities would be placed in the dugouts prepared by the minidozer.[6] One after the other the loads were dropped off at Fire Base Hard Times. (Rather than using the name of a wife or a girlfriend, as often done, "Hard Times" had been chosen as a sign of the times.) The companies made no enemy contact upon insertion into the periphery of the Vinh Thanh Valley; the NVA had withdrawn.

The valley included several hamlets on both sides of the Ha Gia River, which ran through the center of the valley, with a wide expanse of rice fields on both sides of the river and one dusty road on the west side. About a mile south of the fire base, there was a rice mill that served the valley, primarily the west side. The district chief told me there was a "good side" of the valley and a "bad side." The west side, where the fire base, CIDG camp, rice mill, and the district headquarters were, was the good side. The bad side always had a bountiful harvest, but to cross the river to take the rice to the mill meant paying for a ferry ride.

It was well known that the peasants on the bad side sold their unhusked rice (*lua*) to the NVA, who wanted it because unhusked rice contained a natural preservative, as opposed to milled rice, which was difficult to store. The ferry fare was a sore point with the peasants.

I found out about the selling of *lua* to the NVA from my civic-action officer, a lieutenant who conducted small projects for the people on both sides of the river. He spent more time on the bad side, using a squad to build school desks from ammunition boxes, and passing out vitamins to the peasants.

The battalion had been in Vinh Thanh Valley for over a week—three companies humping up and down the trails in the surrounding jungle, and one company providing fire-base security and conducting ambush patrols in the valley—then the district chief notified me that he had a group of entertainers coming to the district headquarters. He invited men from my battalion, as if we were here on vacation. I declined the offer.

Two days later a major from the South Korean Tiger Division arrived at our CP and requested permission to place an artillery unit within our perimeter to support Korean operations. I told him he would have to provide his own defense for his artillery, as it would take at least two rifle platoons to extend the defense from our positions. He didn't like my response, but two days later he was back with a battery of 105 mm howitzers and two platoons of infantry. He also brought bundles of brochures that he wanted to distribute to my battalion, to encourage our soldiers to take R&R in Korea. I told him it wouldn't be appropriate for me to encourage my men to go to Korea on R&R, but I let the brochures be passed out. From then on, the Koreans took over an unused rice field early each morning to do tae kwon do. I invited the major to attend our briefing each morning so he would be aware of operations in the area.

A pet peeve infantrymen had with senior officers flitting about in helicopters was their demands that LZs be prepared so they could land and inspect units. This was a time-consuming and difficult exercise just so a neatly dressed colonel or general could observe an operation that was already oversupervised.

After about a month at Hard Times, with daily contacts with the NVA picking up, the battalion reconnaissance platoon ran into a bunker complex deep in the jungle at the north end of Vinh Thanh Valley. The platoon sergeant saw the bunkers at a distance, halted his platoon, and crawled closer to get a better view. He saw two NVA soldiers sitting on a bunker, unaware they were being observed. Crawling closer, he finally shouted, "*Chua hoy,* you motherf———s!" (referring to a program encouraging VC and NVA to defect). The two NVA reached for their AK-47s. That was their last move, as the sergeant cut them down with his M-16. Then a high volume of fire erupted from the other bunkers. The sergeant requested that artillery fire be placed on the bunkers and backed away as 155 mm howitzers began firing. After the fire mission was completed, the sergeant moved forward again and saw several NVA running up the mountain through the foliage. The sergeant had his platoon fire on the retreating NVA and saw two fall to the ground.

I had already sent B Company to reinforce the reconnaissance platoon. It pursued the NVA up the mountain, but the NVA had already dispersed. It found five killed and two wounded at the bunker and along the trail up the mountain. One of the dead was an officer. I told the B Company commander to be alert for an ambush and told the reconnaissance platoon sergeant to hold in place at the bunkers. I had already requested cargo nets and helicopter support to retrieve a good-sized ammunition cache and notified the reconnaissance platoon sergeant that we would evacuate the ammunition.

Company B continued up the ridge, reporting many blood trails, which indicated more NVA casualties. The company halted at the highest point and set up a defense for the night. Early the next morning, as it continued along the ridge into a rocky open area, the lead platoon received automatic-weapons fire from the far end of the ridge. Two men were wounded, and a request for artillery support was made. Because of the proximity of the troops to the target, the fire request was denied.

In the meantime, an Air Force mission had been redirected to support the 1/8th Battalion, but the forward air controller was having trouble identifying the target. When I got to the scene in a helicopter, I was able to hover over B Company and get the company commander to make visible from the air the forward edge of his lead platoon, and then to withdraw a safe distance. The FAC marked the target with rockets, as jets circled above awaiting confirmation of the target. The next thing I heard was that the FAC had aborted the support mission. I shouted into the mike, wanting to know who had aborted the air strike, and found it was Brig. Gen. John G. Wheelock III, an assistant division commander, in a helicopter above me; he responded he couldn't see the target that the FAC and I saw, adding, "Rank has its privileges." Minutes later, after the company withdrew a bit, I directed artillery onto the target. Following the fire mission, Company B advanced and found two more NVA dead and three NVA wounded. A medical evacuation helicopter removed both the U.S. and NVA wounded. Later a Chinook helicopter retrieved three cargo nets of ammunition.

When I got back to Hard Times, I found several pieces of mail from home, one being my monthly bank statement—oh, happy day! Marge wrote about the Christmas holidays and what she had bought for the children. She mentioned that when I received this letter I would probably be near the halfway point of my tour in Vietnam.

A few days later, Company A found another large cache of weapons and ammunition in the jungle north of Vinh Thanh Valley. Chinook helicopters hauled five cargo nets full to Camp Radcliffe. Several of the NVA who had been guarding the cache were casualties.

My civic-action officer was always searching for ways to get more people on the "bad side" to bring their rice to the mill on the "good side." He mentioned at a morning briefing that if there were a bridge across the river, he could get most of the peasants to bring their rice to the mill. I had to agree that it would reduce the availability of rice to the enemy. Two days later, an engineer platoon and its security reached Fire Base Hard Times after grading and repairing the valley road, damaged earlier by a typhoon. The platoon loaded the grader on a lowboy, but the dozer wouldn't start, so the engineers left it on the road a half-mile from our CP and said they'd send a mechanic to get it started. With that the engineer platoon departed for Camp Radcliffe.

In the middle of the night, the dozer's engine started, its growl heard distinctly at the CP. It dug a deep trench and then drove into it; the trench was then camouflaged and the trail obliterated. The next morning the mechanic arrived by helicopter, and a search was made of the nearby area, but to no avail. The mechanic returned to Camp Radcliffe. At about the time I was notified about the missing dozer, one of my officers told me that the civic-action officer had a degree in civil engineering and also a hobby of tweaking hot-rod engines. I "disregarded" his comment, but I didn't forget it entirely.

For the next few nights, the groan of the dozer could be heard as it moved rock and soil out into the Ha Gia River, just south of the CP. On the other side, a group of peasants was busy day and night piling rocks from the river bank to form a bridge abutment. Just before dawn the dozer would be returned to its camouflaged position. Finally I queried the civic-action officer; he admitted that he had commandeered the dozer but assured me that he planned to retain it for only a couple of days more. Then he told me the officer in charge of the engineer platoon was in on the plan, which was to build abutments on both sides for a footbridge to span the river. I saw no reason to check further.

The division engineer, a Lieutenant Colonel Brinkerhoff, reportedly flew the length of the road from Route 19 to Fire Base Hard Times but was unable to find the dozer. Then I received word that sections of footbridge and floats that had been ordered by my battalion would be available in two days. I had my executive officer, who was at Camp Enari, make arrangements for their delivery. The footbridge arrived, and the dozer was found, just as mysteriously as it had disappeared, on its lowboy in a hamlet just south of Hard Times. When the engineers returned to pick up the dozer they very kindly helped span the gap between the revetments and then took their dozer back to Camp Radcliffe.

My civic-action officer was right; the peasants on the bad side soon began carrying their rice across the bridge to the mill on the other side of the river. I found out later that if the bridge hadn't been used to span the Ha Gia River, it would still be on the ground at Camp Enari, collecting dust. It wasn't long before a trail was formed from the jungle on one side of the Vinh Thanh Valley to the jungle on the other, via the footbridge. We called it the Oregon Trail and set up ambushes on it. As a result five NVA were killed, and six were wounded and captured. One of the dead had a sizable amount of gold leaf in his pack, perhaps intended to pay for the *lua,* which was getting to be in short supply! A major source of rice for the NVA had dried up.

While our footbridge escapade was taking place, we were continuing to saturate the mountainous jungle adjoining the valley with random company patrols, normally at platoon level. Company A ran into an estimated platoon of NVA in prepared bunker positions northeast of Vinh Thanh Valley. The NVA had prepared, on a comparatively bare knoll, a 360-degree position that was visible from the air but not from the ground. Two men in the company were wounded by fire from one of the camouflaged bunkers. I had the company withdraw a safe distance and surround the bunker. Fifteen minutes later my artillery liaison officer (ALNO) and I were circling the area in a helicopter. The company popped smoke to mark its position, and I had it withdraw farther. About then we began taking fire from the enemy position, as the ALNO commenced registering artillery on the bunker position. The first round was on target; after it struck we took more fire, two rounds striking the helicopter.

I told the ALNO to have the artillery fire for effect, and we moved out of range, turning control of the artillery over to the company commander and his forward observer. Following several fire missions, which caved in two of the bunkers, the company attacked and seized the complex. NVA casualties were five killed and four wounded; the bunkers had a light machine gun and lots of ammunition. The prisoners confirmed that they had been involved in the attack on the CIDG and Special Forces camp in Vinh Thanh Valley.

The division commander told me several times to refrain from conducting search-and-destroy operations in the jungle; this was not unlike the distaste for friendly casualties shown by ARVN leadership during the adviser period. Ironically, my battalion would later participate in a multibattalion operation in deep jungle terrain.

It came to my attention that Company A had an all-black platoon and that the previous battalion commander had known about it. I took it upon myself to question the company commander as to how he was going to desegregate the platoon. When he stated he had no plan, I instituted one for him. I was not totally surprised about the situation, since I felt that regardless of the Army's lead in desegregation, there still was an element in the Army that was not fully supportive of it.

I told the company commander that in addition to assuring that combat awards were actually awarded, he was to replace wounded and transferred black soldiers with Caucasians, effective right away. I then had the black platoon assembled at Hard Times and told them about the changes taking place and the reason, which was to conform to U.S. Army policy. I was amazed when the platoon sergeant, who was black, told me he appreciated the straightforward way I approached what could have been an explosive situation. I made sure that when he rotated back to the States, he was awarded the two Bronze Stars for valor that he had earned. Several other black members of the platoon were also awarded the decorations they earned prior to departing for home.

An item that I still considered very important to the efficiency of the battalion was how new soldiers were received and prepared for combat. I let my officers and the sergeant major know that it was necessary to let new men get used to the climate, the tactical environment (foxhole preparation, mines and booby traps, alertness, weapon maintenance), sanitation requirements, and health dangers. I set the acclimatization period at one week and had the battalion sergeant major oversee the process. I could think of nothing more inefficient than a soldier who had been immediately sent out with a unit, overwhelmed by the heat, sweating profusely, swatting mosquitoes, and wandering around on his own. I found that a week to adjust placed the soldier physically and mentally in a more productive state.

I was making a reconnaissance for a new fire base north of Hard Times when I received a warning order that my battalion would participate in a two-brigade, compression-type operation of a type that had been executed several times by the Korean division. In simple terms, the concept called for the brigades to form up their battalions in a gigantic circle and then decrease its circumference, searching, patrolling, and attacking toward the center.

Meanwhile, in mid-March 1970, General Walker told me that the 1/8th was scheduled to be deactivated by the end of April and that I was to be the only one in the battalion who knew it. At the same time, he told me my battalion would have to move its fire base from Hard Times to where it could support

Mack with his artillery liaison officer, left, and the Company B commander, Captain Herron, at a battalion observation post in April 1970, "awaiting visitors."

the two-brigade operation in April. Within a week I had moved the fire base to Hill 3166, fifteen miles north of Hard Times. We deployed the 105 mm howitzer battery to the new fire base, which we called "Noname," but left the 155 mm battery at Hard Times.

I planned to take a light CP with me and accompany my units on the compression operation, inasmuch as I had never seen my brigade commander since I had taken over the battalion. I informed General Walker of this. On the day the operation commenced, I had my companies lined up on the rice fields near Hard Times. General Walker flew in and watched the loading of the first unit. He saw one machine-gun-squad leader busily checking out his men. Pointing to the sergeant, Walker said, "That man is doing a good job supervising his men; it's too bad he has that pigtail and feather in his helmet." I explained to the general that the man was a full-blooded American Indian on his second tour to Vietnam and that on his first tour he had earned a Silver Star. As I recall, Walker responded, "Perhaps it would be best not to mention the pigtail and feather to the sergeant; leadership begets leadership!" That's what made General Walker a great leader and commander.

I accompanied B Company on the combat assault, taking three radio operators, an operations captain, an intelligence lieutenant, and an operations sergeant. I found that with this mobile CP I was able to control operations as well as from a CP on a fire base. There is no substitute for supervising by presence.

Before the compression operation, the division G-3 had briefed the overall concept of the operation in such a manner that I felt he had never operated in thick jungle, where this operation was to take place. His presentation visualized the two brigades of soldiers as if they would be holding hands, like a group of children playing "ring around the rosie," all moving inward toward the center of the gigantic circle. If this had been what was expected, we'd still be out there, cutting through the jungle. I had learned in 1963–64 that infantry units don't move very far, for very long, hacking through the jungle; individual men move even slower. In thick jungle, you can normally expect the best results from platoons in columns advancing on line, providing there is a trail system. While concepts can be pictured on map boards, in actuality the troops face the uncooperative demands of the terrain.

I maintained good communications with my S-3, Maj. Sam Ebbeson (later a lieutenant general), at Fire Base Noname, and throughout the operation I received excellent response from the artillery. On the first day we had no contact, but we did find what appeared to be an NVA base camp, with huts, a medical treatment lean-to, still-warm cooking fires, handmade tables and chairs, and a crudely marked cemetery. I planned to move to A Company during the day, so I arranged a contact point and departed from B Company.

That night, A Company commander Captain Hess and I moved onto a knoll after crossing a rushing mountain stream. On top of the knoll we found further evidence of the NVA, in the form of cooking fires, still smoldering, and several ammunition boxes with Cyrillic markings. During the day the division G-3 attempted to obtain a more precise location of units down to company level. The units popped smoke to mark their locations from overhead, but unfortunately the triple-canopy jungle obscured most of the smoke.

During the night we heard firing a number of times; however, we never found out whether it was friendly or enemy. Early the next day, I had each company send patrols in random directions for an hour and a half to see if we were by-passing NVA. We had no contacts, but I assumed some small enemy units watched us as we humped by them.

At about 3:00 P.M., I was with the lead platoon of A Company as we started up a steep trail. Suddenly a hefty seven-pound, steel-tipped arrow flew down the trail, hitting no one but causing everyone to seek cover off the trail. I quickly stepped back and to the side and immediately was impaled by three *pungi*

Mack commanding the First Battalion of the Eighth Infantry in a Vinh Thanh Valley assault. A barbed *pungi* stake is embedded in his left arm, April 1970.

stakes—in my arm, my side, and my butt. The jungle on either side of the trail had been laced with *pungi* stakes, the points of which had been treated with buffalo dung (the *pungi* stake wound in my butt later became infected).

Three of the worst cases, out of a total of ten, were evacuated by helicopter. A company medic removed two of the *pungi*s from me but left the one in my arm, after shortening it. From my CP position with Company A, I could see across a wide valley to my fire base. As it got dark I could see the muzzle flashes produced by the fire requests I had sent. At about 2:30 A.M. the next day, heavy firing was heard in Capt. Robert E. Chadwick's Company C. He reported that a small NVA unit had attacked one of his platoons' positions and that two of his men had been wounded. Chadwick's FO had requested a fire mission; when it was fired, C Company heard a lot of screaming. In the morning its men found three NVA dead and one wounded.

After two days of trying to get the lines straightened, all battalions were instructed to send contact patrols to their left flanks, as a means of aligning the forward edges of the battalion positions. A medical evacuation helicopter approached but was fired on from the position where we had been the night before. We waved the helicopter off and placed artillery on the source of the firing. No further fire was received by the helicopter, so it landed and evacuated the wounded.

Moments later, another helicopter hovered over my CP and then set down where the "dust off" (helicopter medical-evacuation) had just taken off. General Wheelock exited the helicopter; when I met him he remarked that it would have made life easier for him if I had stayed at my fire base. I responded that maybe that's why we weren't winning; most of the information and guidance was being generated at the fire bases and not from the front line. There was too much attention given to the convenience of commanders. His response was something like this: "You might have something there, but I'm afraid it's a little late to change minds to a winning mood. Besides, as you know, we are on our way out of Vietnam."

Shortly after the general left, I received a message from the brigade that the operation would end at noon the next day. No reason was given, but I had to assume that we had hit a dry hole. I later received a message that I should close down Fire Base Noname and assemble the battalion at Hard Times for return to Camp Enari. When we arrived at Camp Enari, after a three-hour ride on Highway 19, we found that many changes were taking place, in connection with the drawdown of U.S. forces. For one, the Fourth Division command post and its administrative and logistics units had been transferred to Camp Radcliffe. Camp Enari was being turned over to the ARVN. For another, Fire Base Oasis was now a company position, soon to be closed.

It was sad to be required to disband the Bullets Battalion and send the men to other units as if they were objects being used to plug holes, rather than soldiers who had already undergone a trying military experience. It became a symbol of America's misadventure in Vietnam, and it struck at the very core of human nature from which morale and esprit are developed. Our civilian and higher-level military leaders completely failed to understand that the warrior sacrifices not for country, flag, or political persuasion but for his comrades. There was little morale remaining in the battalion and equally little time to rebuild the spirit needed to prepare these soldiers for their assignments to other units. It would have been better had the Army sent the men home with the unit's flags, particularly the draftees and lower-ranking NCOs. The Army failed in this respect.

My main responsibility was to hold this shrinking force together until only I, with my pistol, remained to be reassigned. I had told my executive officer to use the unit nonappropriated fund to purchase a memento for every man in the battalion. He found a vendor who could make bayonet-like letter openers with the battalion seal on them. As the men were reassigned, they were given letter openers. We made sure that every man eligible for the Combat Infantry-man Badge received orders for the badge.

When there was one platoon remaining, we held the deactivation ceremony and encased the colors. My last official act was to ensure that the battalion's unused silver punchbowl and goblets were packed and returned to the United States, with other "heraldry" items. My last personal act was to complete writing letters to the parents or closest relative of each man who had been killed, assuring them that it had not all been in vain. I sincerely believed that!

I had four months remaining on my tour. General Walker recommended me to be the deputy commander and chief of staff for the U.S. Army Head-quarters Area Command (USAHAC) in Saigon. The command was responsible for the administrative, logistical, and security support for the twenty thou-sand–plus members of all U.S. services and foreign services who served in the U.S. Military Assistance Command, Vietnam (USMACV).

I got the job, and my first concern after meeting my boss, Col. Bob Young, was to go to the hospital to have an abcess on my butt drained, the result of the *pungi* stake puncture I had received. After that I interviewed each of the principal staff officers who would work for me, and two days later I had a list of twenty-one major actions that awaited solution and needed my attention. Among these actions were the transfer of bachelor officer and enlisted quarters security to the occupants, an emergency electrical-power plan for a threatened power-facility strike, and tighter fiscal controls over the club system in Saigon.

About two days later, my telephone rang at noon, and a highly irritated Marine colonel informed me he had just returned from BOQ One (the quarters for senior colonels), where he had been unable to float in the pool during the noon hour because his inner tube was missing. After visiting BOQ One and seeing the NCO in charge, I found that the pool rules prohibited placing objects in the pool. We found the inner tube; I told the sergeant to deflate it, and that I'd take it from there. That afternoon, I called the colonel and told him I had found the tube, adding that using it in the pool had been a violation of a standing order of the commanding general, USAHAC. I told him I would arrange to have the tube delivered to him at his desk. He declined my offer, and I never heard from him again.

A week before I was to go on R&R to Hawaii to meet Marge, a maid strike erupted in BOQ One. This was serious—it could result in senior officers show-ing up at MACV without pressed uniforms and shined shoes! A Navy captain came to my office and demanded that I negotiate with the maids and make them an offer. I told him I'd look into it. It turned out that the maids were not under contract with the U.S. government; instead, they made verbal contracts with individual officers. I sent MPS to BOQ One, armed only with blankets, and had them carry the maids out of the BOQ. Then I had a notice in Vietnamese put up at the gate that maids had only verbal contracts with individual officers and that they would be permitted to contact their respective officers to make arrangements about wages. The maids were issued ID cards that permitted them to be in the BOQ from 6:30 A.M. to 5:30 P.M. daily. I had noted that several of the prettier maids lived in the senior officers quarters.

When I arrived in Hawaii on R&R, I found that Marge had not arrived. I went to the hotel, cleaned up, and put on civilian clothes to go to the reception center and wait for her. I opened the door to leave and—*surprise!*—Marge was standing there. We rented an automobile and spent the week traveling to every corner of the island. The week went by very fast, and when it ended I boarded an aircraft for Saigon, as Marge awaited her flight home. I had about two months remaining in my tour in Vietnam.

There was an area in Saigon called "the Plantation." It consisted of bars, tea houses, go-go girls, bordellos, cheap shops, run-down sidewalk cafes, narcotic dealers, and any number of places where AWOLS and deserters could hide out. There even may have been men there who had been reported missing in action, who had now set up permanent residence. Periodically, a military police battalion would conduct a sweep, searching the area for stray U.S. military personnel, apprehending them, and bringing them back under military control. The day I returned to Saigon, the MPS and Vietnamese police initiated a sweep of the Plantation; it turned into a pursuit up and down stairs and across rooftops. The first day they rounded up several men suspected of being AWOL, absent without leave.

The second day of the sweep, they chased what they believed to be another errant soldier; when he refused to stop, an MP shot him in the leg. It turned out, however, that the soldier was assigned to the Twenty-fifth Infantry Division and had been on a legal pass to Saigon at the time. As a result of an investigation, future sweeps were governed by new rules concerning the when and where of the use of deadly force. The drawdown of U.S. forces in Vietnam reduced the number of military police available to sweep the Plantation, until finally the sweeps were discontinued.

While I was in Hawaii, U.S. and South Vietnamese ground forces had invaded Cambodia, in an attempt to hobble the NVA by capturing or destroying its forces, arms, and ammunition being kept there for a major offensive. The theory had been that such an NVA offensive could severely jeopardize the U.S. forces remaining in Vietnam after the next large U.S. withdrawal, when 150,000

Mack being congratulated by Brig. Gen. Verne Bowers (later major general) upon promotion to colonel in Saigon, July 1970.

troops were to leave. President Richard Nixon revealed the incursion via a television address to the nation on April 30, 1970. The captured NVA arms, equipment, and ammunition were put on display, ostensibly to demonstrate the success of Nixon's Cambodian adventure. I visited this display and noted that three of the items were ammunition in cargo nets that had been captured by us in the Vinh Thanh Valley two months earlier. Whatever the NVA lost by the incursion was rapidly replenished.[7]

As the drawdown continued, it became necessary to restructure the security of troop quarters, which were U.S.-subsidized hotels, for both officers and enlisted personnel. This required that each troop housing facility develop a defense plan using the occupants of the facility, with the senior occupant designated as responsible. All these security plans had to be inspected.

It was less than thirty days before I would depart from Vietnam when I received orders promoting me to colonel. This was made official when Colonel Young held a promotion and awards session after a staff meeting. I had a promotion party at the Four Seasons Club in Saigon, issuing a blanket invitation to everyone, officer and enlisted, in USAHAC.

The night before I left Saigon, I received a call that a bomb had gone off at an enlisted housing facility. I went to the facility and found two dead, several wounded, and much confusion. One ambulance now arrived; I called our operations center and told the duty officer to get at least three ambulances. Then

Mack, shown in this autographed photo, receiving the Legion of Merit medal from Col. Robert Young, commander, U.S. Army Area Support Command in Saigon, August 1970.

I collected several sergeants, and we tended to the wounded. After the casualties were evacuated, the senior sergeant reorganized the security of the facility, and I departed for my quarters.

The next morning I had breakfast with Colonel Young at BOQ One. He told me that my replacement had told him the night before that I had made a mistake by going to the scene of the bomb incident. Young had told him that if there was another bombing, he wanted him to do the same as Colonel Mack had! I thanked Colonel Young for the comment, and two hours later I departed from Saigon.

When the plane arrived at Travis Air Force Base, all the officer passengers were taken to the officers' club to await their baggage. While we were at the bar, an Air Force major came in and announced that a demonstration was anticipated at the gate that we would pass through in a bus, heading for the civilian airport. He then said the base commander had suggested we change from uniform to civvies. I told the other returnees, "I am wearing my uniform, and I'm proud of it." We all wore our uniforms as we went out the gate. There were about twenty-five jeering people across the street from the gate. Welcome home!

A month later, I received a letter from Young. He said my replacement had gone home on emergency leave and wouldn't be returning. He asked me jokingly if I'd consider returning to USAHAC. In my reply I wrote, "I wouldn't mind, but Marge said No!!!"

# 9 The Cold War Continues

By the time I returned to the States, Marge had already moved the family from the rented house to a duplex on Marshall Ridge at Carlisle Barracks, where I was assigned to the Strategic Studies Institute (ssi).[1] Our youngest daughter, Elizabeth, was attending Carlisle High School and had become proficient in clothing design. Rick was still going to St. Patrick's School and now had a paper route. Marge was a volunteer at the Carlisle Barracks Thrift Shop, and Rosalind was preparing to attend Bowling Green State University in Ohio. Our oldest daughter, Mary, was in her third year at San Diego State.

After meeting the family in Stow, we went to Carlisle, reaching there as the move-in of the 1971 class at the War College was commencing. Scads of kids roamed the small post, and the streets filled with moving vans, their drivers carrying furniture into the neat rows of white Cape Cods. Once again, students with thoughts of promotion and higher-level command and staff positions prepared for a year at the Army's premier gentlemen's course.

Two years earlier Marge and I had gone through the same thing; we were happy that that experience was history. I was now an iconoclast, concerned about the Army's institutional well-being—worried that the integrity of its leadership was being lost, that the Army was fast becoming an institution whose leaders sought more to preserve their own prestige than to instill and reflect the esprit so necessary for successful military forces. In any event, to some of us in the military it was clear that by 1970 America had lost its first war and that the civilian and military leadership then in the Pentagon was the residue of that lost war. The sad results should have brought about a complete overhaul of the leadership of the Army, not rewards to failed generals and colonels. The first requirement for leadership was the selection of leaders who understood and projected honesty and integrity to their civilian bosses, not empire builders and ticket punchers.

The only victors were those officers who had steadfastly supported administration programs with respect to Vietnam and had bowed ignobly to an unthinking chain of command that stretched from the Pentagon to COMUSMACV. They would fill high leadership posts for the next twenty years. I hoped they would learn how to inspire greatness, but I am not convinced they ever did.

By November, at SSI we were completing a study on the redeployment of a division from Korea to Europe in the event the "balloon went up" there. As I recall, we found that we could get the troops to Europe but that equipment for them would have to be prepositioned there, because it was probable that the Republic of Korea would not permit us to take our equipment with us.

Our research required frequent visits to the Deputy Chief of Staff for Operations (DCSOPS), in the Pentagon. Normally we would fly down in a helicopter in the morning, give our presentation on the progress of a study, and then visit offices associated with the study, seeking information and obtaining consensus. Consensus was a very valuable part of the study procedure, especially when we were stretching the envelope of acceptability with a proposal.

For example, during one trip we met with Air Force officers who were associated with the mobility staff, to discuss the transport of personnel and equipment from Korea to Europe. One very bright Air Force major gave us an excellent rundown on the capabilities of the C-5A transport, which was being considered as the means of transporting equipment from the United States to Europe and elsewhere, along with a small number of personnel. One point that seemed particularly cogent was that if there was a possibility that we wouldn't be transporting equipment, which was in fact the case, the requirements for the Air Force's aircraft would be limited. His suggestion was to bring into the scenario the Civilian Reserve Air Fleet (CRAF), which ostensibly provided for redeploying personnel via civilian airlines. He told us also that the C-5A was not intended for external lines of communications—that is, for movements between points outside the continental United States—but for internal lines, between the United States and a foreign destination. This was because of the aircraft's high air-crew demands and material-handling requirements. This gave us a fresh point to consider in future deployment studies.

Two items that continuously kept our brains active were the Nixon Doctrine and the high-level planning, to which we were not privy, going on at the level of the Joint Chiefs of Staff (JCS). We visited many offices to gain insight into the latter type of information; most of it was highly classified, and often, it had been determined that we had no need to know. However, after only a few visits to the Pentagon, we found that there were many high-level documents floating about, including JCS planning documents, that were available for review.

For example, the president's national security adviser would periodically circulate a National Security Defense Memorandum (NSDM). On occasion, when asking a member of the Army operations staff about a specific aspect of foreign policy, I would be shown an NSDM and be permitted to read it in its entirety. "Need to know" aside, this was helpful in researching our study issues. I personally questioned the easy availability of such high-level national policy; the copying machine made distribution between friends and associates a "piece of cake."

The Nixon Doctrine led to government's announcement in 1969 that the United States would no longer take the lead in counterinsurgency or regional wars, but that the affected nations themselves would have to do so; this had escaped many of us. A current application of the doctrine at the time in the form of operative mechanics, "Vietnamization" and the gradual draw-down of U.S. forces in Vietnam, had not crystallized—and there were still almost as many versions of the Nixon Doctrine as there were people describing it. Invariably, the question of how proposals in our studies affected the Nixon Doctrine would come up at briefings in the Pentagon, and the briefer would have to respond in the "best-guess mode."

I was on a notification list for seminars on foreign policy issues, a program sponsored by the State Department, perhaps as an educational or public-relations endeavor. I attended several of these seminars, and at one the guest speaker was Maj. Gen. Alexander Haig, a presidential national security adviser. During the question-and-answer period, which was attended by many high-level managers and vice presidents in industry as well as educators, I asked the speaker if he could give us a thumbnail description of what the Nixon Doctrine covered. The response from the general was quite simple: he couldn't recall that the president had ever told anyone exactly what the Nixon Doctrine covered. This was said in a serious vein. When I returned to SSI, I included Haig's comments in my "after-action" report, but I couldn't find anyone who would believe them. In any event, I never again wrestled with the Nixon Doctrine syndrome at briefings. One man's guess was as good as anyone else's.

During my last year at SSI, I accompanied the 1973 War College class to the Panama Canal Zone. While I was there I found that the position of the Deputy Chief of Staff for Operations, U.S. Army South (USARSO), calling for a colonel, would be available in June of that year. I had never been assigned to Central or

South America, and as there was a brigade in the Canal Zone, the posting opened an opportunity for brigade command.

The unified (multiservice) Southern Command was commanded by a four-star general known officially as the Commander in Chief, Southern Command (CINCSO). He commanded the Army component and two smaller Air Force and Navy contingents, to which augmentation forces could be attached. CINCSO had wide security responsibilities throughout Central and South America, responsibilities that included military assistance and training, as well as disaster relief and diplomatic support. The Army component was responsible for the readiness and support of an infantry brigade, for executing military assistance programs, providing security for the Canal Zone, conducting jungle training, and for the general logistics responsibilities including, housing, recreation, and health. I became USARSO's Deputy Chief of Staff for Operations, Plans, and Training, also referred to as G-3.

The Canal Zone was in fact America's only attempt at socialism, inasmuch as it had a controlled economy, and only those who worked on the canal or for a direct-support activity could live there. This is a cynical view, perhaps, but it is more fact than fiction.

During my assignment, we lived at Fort Amador, at the entry to the Canal on the Pacific side. Elizabeth attended the Canal Zone College (a junior college), and Rick attended Balboa High School. We lived in one of several concrete-block homes that formed a semicircle facing Panama City and the Bay of Panama. The homes were of sufficiently substantial construction that they could serve as forts, should an answer ever emerge to the question, "Who is the enemy?"

My principal responsibilities as the G-3 involved maintaining and updating plans for the security of the canal, budgeting for the operations and maintenance of the assigned Army units and other U.S. agencies, maintaining and staffing the Army operations center, planning and conducting security and evacuation training, and for acting as the point of contact for command reorganization activities (about which, more below).

One of my first visits was to the office of the G-2 (intelligence), Col. Jerry Sills, where I was briefed. Two items of note came up, one being the periodic visits of the Panamanian intelligence officer, Guardia Nacional lieutenant colonel Manuel Noriega. The second anomaly was the small refurbished building, behind USARSO headquarters that was used for Noriega's visits. The building was equipped with a bar, overstuffed furniture, television, a refrigerator, and a stereo sound system. Sills assured me that Noriega always came prepared with current information, especially after he had been to Cuba and had visited with Fidel Castro.

Sills explained that the Panamanian dictator, Gen. Omar Torrejos Herrera, had never set foot in the Canal Zone. Torrejos considered the Canal Zone an imperialist scheme that physically divided his country. He had seized power in August 1968 (and he would retain control until he died in a suspicious aircraft accident in August 1981).[2] Sills also reminded me that in 1964 the Panamanians had made serious attacks on the Canal Zone because the Americans had refused to fly the Panamanian flag at Balboa High School. Presidents Eisenhower and Kennedy had made concessions to the Panamanians by permitting the flying of the flag of Panama, but local authorities had not applied this concession to schools. As a result, when Canal Zone students raised the U.S. flag and an estimated two hundred Panamanians entered the Canal Zone to fly their flag beside it, rioting ensued. The Panamanian flag was torn to pieces, the U.S. Marines were called out, and over the next three days eighteen Panamanians were killed.[3]

The deputy USARSO commander in 1964 was now, in 1973, the USARSO commander (Maj. Gen. George L. Mabry, Jr., holder of the Medal of Honor). Relations with Panamanians were tense. Every Panamanian child wandering into the zone was considered a potential bomb thrower or at the least someone attempting to steal from the "rich" Americans.

I noted on the wall beside Sills's desk a large signed photo of Gen. Augusto Pinochet of Chile. Sills told me Pinochet was his personal friend from his own days as the military attaché in Chile. Pinochet had been staying in Sills's quarters, two houses from mine, in the spring of 1973, and then had returned to Chile. I found that Sills's associations were significantly different from the normal ones of a command G-2. (A couple of months later, Pinochet spearheaded the bloody coup that overthrew and executed the socialist president of Chile, Salvador Allende.)

In addition to the resignation of Vice President Spiro Agnew in the fall of 1973 and the appointment of Cong. Gerald Ford as the vice president, the United States faced an oil shortage as a result of the Yom Kippur War. The Department of Defense directed reduction in fuel consumption; we were required to submit a plan within a very few days (over a weekend) to conserve fuel in the Canal Zone. As G-3, I was responsible for preparing the plan. My plan gave priority to vehicles and aircraft being used for training purposes, and it placed stringent controls over their use for administrative reasons. All use of helicopters had to be approved by the G-3 office. The plan was approved and forwarded by General Mabry to Washington.

Then the "fun in the sun" side of the Canal Zone life surfaced. The deputy commander, Col. John Sadler, and another colonel had a helicopter land in front of the headquarters building to pick them up and transport them to Rio

Hato for a game of golf. I brought this to the attention of the commanding general, the deputy's boss, and received the "boys will be boys" response. That was the beginning of the end of our fuel conservation program.

A couple of weeks later, the ambassador to Panama had a cocktail party at which both the unified command commander and General Torrejos were present. Torrejos mentioned that he had offered an infantry battalion to the United Nations as a peacekeeping force to be used in the Golan Heights following the Yom Kippur War. At that time, Panama had only regional Guardia Nacional companies, which were primarily paramilitary units, used for police and internal security purposes. Torrejos obviously knew that a report of his offer would be made through military and ambassadorial channels to Washington and that, what with the U.S. sensitivity to security in the Middle East, a plan for training and equipping a Panamanian battalion would be forthcoming—and it was.

I had the "honor" of briefing Omar Torrejos on the plan, which he accepted without comment. (What's that about looking a gift horse in the mouth?) Within four months, U.S. Air Force transports were loading a Panamanian battalion for its flight to Israel and the Golan Heights. It wasn't long before a second battalion was being trained and equipped. Panama now had a battalion capability, which was a considerable upgrading from a regional Guardia Nacional posture.

Gracias, Estados Unidos! You now have an enemy!

During 1973 and 1974 the U.S. Army Forces Command, in Atlanta, conducted a reorganization plan that affected the bases in Hawaii, Alaska, and Panama. The purpose was to standardize them. Later, we might have called the reorganization a "one size fits all plan," especially with respect to Canal Zone basing. I chaired the reorganization planning committee—not unlike the committee that designed the camel—as a G-3 activity.

I can recall two incidents that defined the character of this reorganization process. One had to do with a Maj. Gen. Jeffrey Smith, Deputy Chief of Staff, Operations for the U.S. Army Forces Command, during a visit to Panama. I remember telling him that the U.S. bases in the Canal Zone differed from the others being reorganized, in that you had to pass through a foreign country when going by land between the Pacific bases and the Atlantic ones, quite different from bases in Alaska or Hawaii. There was no road that directly linked the Atlantic side with the Pacific side within the Canal Zone. The response was, "Ho hum."

I accompanied General Smith on a helicopter flight from the Pacific side to the Atlantic to see Atlantic activities at first hand. The weather turned foul in the afternoon, grounding the helicopter and requiring our return to the Pacific side by automobile. It took us over three hours; at several places the road was nearly impassable, and at one point we were stopped by the Guardia Nacional because of poor conditions ahead. When I again pointed out the dissimilarity of the Panama Canal Zone from Alaska and Hawaii, I again received the ho-hum response.

A couple of weeks later, I was at Forces Command (FORSCOM) in Atlanta for the final briefing on the reorganization plan. One sensitive item had not been resolved: the rank of the commanding general (CG), USARSO; the incumbent was a major general. FORSCOM had determined that all three bases would be renamed with brigade designations, which went unquestioned by the USARSO commanding general and his deputy, Col. John Sadler. General Smith asked me at the final briefing what the normal rank was of an officer who commanded a separate brigade. I told him: brigadier general. He took my answer as a recommendation, and the rank for the commander of the Army element in Panama became brigadier general. The CG, USARSO and his deputy "went ballistic" when I called to notify them.

Several weeks later, Omar Torrejos offered to the commander in chief of Southern Command to give airborne (that is, parachute) training to U.S. personnel. As G-3, I was called upon to get approval from the Department of the Army and then to seek volunteers for the training. It took several weeks to obtain approval, but once it was received, many volunteers came forward. The Special Forces in the Canal Zone organized the volunteers, gave them language classes on the Spanish technical vocabulary of airborne training, and prepared them with a physical training program.

When the volunteers arrived at the Panamanian La Chorreo training base, they found that in addition to Americans and Panamanians there were Costa Rican and El Salvadorean trainees; all of the trainees were organized into a company, and the senior trainee, a U.S. Army captain, was designated the company commander. I went to see the training several times and was very impressed with the Americans, who received "special" treatment from the Panamanian trainers. For every mistake the instructors assigned push-ups, and it could be seen that the Americans, to a man, beamed broad smiles as they did their push-ups, their punishment. The smile response was picked up by the non-American trainees, until it was standard that all trainees smiled doing push-ups. Every American completed the airborne course, but a number of other trainees failed. The American trainee company commander organized a graduation party, which was attended by all of the graduates. It was a great day for the Americans.

Our daughter Rosalind came to the Canal Zone for Christmas in 1973. There seemed to be a student party every evening at Fort Amador, and at one of the parties Rosalind met a 1st Lt. B. Hudson Berrey (West Point, 1972), who was now a student at Texas University's Medical Branch in Galveston. This was the start of a lifelong association between "Hud" and "Rolly."

The illegal entry of the Democratic Party national headquarters in the Watergate apartments in Washington, D.C., and the investigation that followed were top cocktail party subjects in 1974. I recall that the hope that President Nixon would escape impeachment was toasted during command functions.

One of my responsibilities was to approve the manifest for parachute jumps made to qualify for "jump pay." Colonel Sadler, as the commander of an embassy rescue-and-evacuation contingency force, made practice jumps periodically. In an actual rescue operation, the obvious way of inserting a rescue team would be to have it jump onto and secure an airfield. However, Colonel Sadler as a matter of practice made solo jumps into Lake Gatun; reportedly, he had a bad back. One of the members of the rescue team was a medical officer, who also had to make practice jumps. On one occasion, I placed the medical officer, a colonel, on the same manifest as the deputy commander, not realizing that a soft, solo jump into Lake Gatun was a "deputy commander perk." In a show of pettiness, Colonel Sadler had me take the medical officer off the manifest. I often wondered what he'd do if he actually had to jump on the terra firma of an airfield.

This incident remains clear to me because on the evening following the manifest incident, I had a cocktail party in my quarters. Sadler entered flushed red with anger; he came straight for me and vented his displeasure in a loud, abusive voice, obviously heard by all in attendance. It appeared that he was under the influence of something; eventually his wife led him to a far corner of the room. This was a standard behavior of this individual, who loved to expound on "his rise above the crowd" without having been a "ring knocker" (an academy graduate).

Marge attended Rolly's graduation from Bowling Green State University in June 1974 and returned to the Canal Zone in July. I was at the final reorganization meeting in Washington, D.C., so I was unable to attend. When I returned to the Canal Zone, I was sincerely pleased with my first year in the DCSOPS position and fully expected to get the command of the infantry brigade. But it was not to be. It was a one-two punch. First, I received an efficiency report in which the rater was the chief of staff and the endorser was the deputy commander; the chief of staff was fair, but the deputy commander scalped me. His numerical ratings and written remarks would obviously eliminate any possibility of brigade command. On top of that, I was notified that the deputy commander's golfing buddy would take over the brigade when the present commander departed.

At first I thought those were the breaks. Then I remembered that the deputy commander had never counseled me or remarked on my performance, as he was required to do, except on the downgrading of CG, USARSO from major general to brigadier general, which had been determined by Forces Command, not me. I also remembered how he had berated me at the cocktail party. Without mentioning the above, I met with the commanding general and voiced my objection to the deputy's low efficiency rating. The CG, having already reviewed the efficiency report, took my concern lightly and dismissed the matter as unworthy of reconsideration. His response—and my unspoken objection to my efficiency report's having been both written and endorsed by officers of my own grade who, though senior to me, had been passed over for promotion—told me that it was time to take action. I wrote a letter to Career Management, requesting a reassignment. The CG sped up my reassignment, but at the same time he gave me a letter of commendation.

There was one blessing in leaving the Canal Zone. I had never thought that it was a very good environment for a teenager, and I was happy to get Rick out of it. I could see that the goals of many of the teenagers there were no higher than to get jobs with the Canal Company and to live lives in the sun. I could see that this was already becoming appealing to Rick; I knew he could muster higher goals. A secondary consideration was the obvious abrogation of our position in the Canal Zone; there was no question but that we were giving up once again, as in Vietnam.

Lt. Hud Berrey returned to the Canal Zone on leave shortly before Marge, Elizabeth, Rick, and I departed for the United States. My deputy, Lt. Col. Armando Carillo, and his wife invited Rolly to remain in the Canal Zone with them until she returned to Bowling Green to work on her master's. Until then she could renew her relationship with the officer who was to become her husband in 1975. She also had a job in the Canal Zone, with the Army Mapping Agency, which gave her another reason to remain.

The day we departed from Howard Air Force Base, August 9, 1974, was the same day Richard M. Nixon lifted off from the White House lawn after resigning the presidency of the United States. In effect, I was doing something quite similar, but with nobler reasons.

We arrived at Charleston, South Carolina, in the early afternoon of August 9 and arrived in Colmar, Pennsylvania, twenty miles north of Philadelphia the next day. My final assignment with the Army was as senior adviser to the commander of the seventy-ninth Army Reserve Command (ARCOM). The commander, Maj. Gen. Frederick Welsh, (USAR) had his headquarters in a large building in an industrial park in Colmar. My office was in the same building. The commander of Readiness Region II, Maj. Gen. Francis Powers, based in Fort Dix New Jersey, was my boss and also was Gen. Welsh's rating officer. The commanding general of the First Army was Power's boss. The ARCOM in 1974 consisted of all the U.S. Army Reserve units (National Guard not included) that were located east of the Susquehanna River in Pennsylvania and all those located in New Jersey. I had forty-five active duty Army officers and noncommissioned officers who advised ARCOM staff sections and units.

After finding a house in Lansdale, Pennsylvania, and taking my daughter Elizabeth to Syracuse University, where she registered. I contacted General Power's office at Fort Dix and then met with him. I could see right away that his responsibilities required the patience of Job, which he had. His success relied greatly upon influencing part-time senior officers to improve their units' readiness, and he was amply equipped with the requisite leadership abilities. The guidance he gave me was to devote the maximum possible amount of time to training and recruiting. I informed General Powers that within the next two years I planned to retire but that I would give the training and recruiting programs my best effort. General Powers told me that Brig. Gen. John Eisenhower was the deputy commander of the ARCOM where I would be advising; I was to take every opportunity to get his views on the status of training and personnel readiness. Powers left me with the feeling that Eisenhower sensed lethargy among the ARCOM's officers, particularly at the lieutenant colonel and colonel level, and was not happy about it.

As I left his office, Powers reminded me that he had a senior-advisers meeting the last Friday of every month. As I started down the stairs, Col. Mike Frischette, the chief of staff's deputy, called to me, and we went to lunch at the officers' club. At lunch, Frischette reiterated what Powers had implied, that there was a lack of dedication among the senior officers of the Seventy-ninth ARCOM. He also said that Powers had put this in writing to the ARCOM commander at least three times in the last six months, but to no avail.

It appeared as if my predecessor had been buddy-buddy with the senior ARCOM officers; he had even sought civilian employment from one of them upon retirement. Frischette told me to not fall for the citizen-soldier business with which the ARCOM commander explained away reserve units' and officers' shortcomings. He said also that General Welsh was running for president of the Reserve Officers Association, another distraction that impinged on the readiness of the ARCOM's units. The ARCOM at the time had about 135 Army Reserve units under its wing. The ARCOM commander could be loosely likened to a division commander; he was responsible for the training, staffing, and logistical support of the diverse units under his command.

The senior adviser, unit advisers, and staff advisers were in many ways augmentees; they took over normal command and staff actions during the week, when their counterparts were pursuing their civilian careers, and advised, inspected training, and assisted their counterparts during drill days. During the week I acted in the capacity of the ARCOM chief of staff, calling upon General Welsh at his place of business when an ARCOM command decision was necessary. There was also a civilian staff, which conducted staff functions during the week. There was plenty of room to ruffle any number of feathers, since my advisory chain of command to the Readiness Region commander paralleled the ARCOM chain of command.

In short, I learned to do what I believed was right, rather than second-guess my reserve counterpart. To be sure, there was no end of discussion among the reserves about the regulars preempting them, in even stronger language. In my first meeting with General Welsh and his chief of staff, Col. Richard Smith, I remarked that during the week that I had been there I had met with the civilian staff, and that it appeared to me that from records and reports that the two major areas that needed attention were recruitment and training. As I halfway expected, Welsh quickly responded that he realized certain weaknesses existed in the two areas mentioned but that he was sure that with a little added emphasis in these areas his citizen-soldiers would come through with flying colors.

I noted that Colonel Smith was more open to suggestions; he now reminded Welsh that he had spoken to him about these same two points at the last administrative drill. He followed up with the suggestion that he get together with me and with the recruiting and training people and come up with a plan. When Welsh said to get the G-1 (responsible for personnel and administrative matters) in on it for recruiting and the G-3 for training, I knew that Smith and I could at least get the ball rolling. Colonel Smith was a high school principal, and for nearly a year we were in daily contact, just to keep the ship afloat. During the 1960s, when the Army was feeding thousands of draftees into Vietnam, men subject to the draft had sought alternatives to stints in Southeast Asia. The U.S. Army Reserves and the National Guard had found America's bright, draft-eligible youth pounding at their doors. Often there were no vacancies; the units were full. With the draw-down in Vietnam and the signing of a peace accord, the knocks at the reserves' recruiting door became few and far between. Since mobilization of reserve units was very rare, after six months training John Doe Reservist could go back to school, stay at his job, be with his wife or girlfriend or whatever, and just give up a weekend a month and two weeks at camp in the summer. It was all legal. Now with no threat of being deployed to Vietnam, young Americans asked, "Why join the reserves?" Those already in the reserves asked, "Why remain?"

The chief of staff (Colonel Smith) and I put together an outline recruiting plan that we thought the G-1 could use for starters. The next day, Sunday (a drill day), the active-duty major who was the G-1 adviser was given the outline plan by the reserve G-1 and was asked to come up with a draft recruiting plan, which he did during the next week. When the major showed me the draft plan, I commended him but told him we were going to have to get the reserves to do this type of planning. To go full circle, I showed the plan to the ARCOM commander, and he agreed that the G-1 should have come up with it. General Welsh said he would speak to the G-1 on the matter and kept the plan.

A week later, after an evening administrative drill the G-1 adviser brought the draft recruiting plan in to me; he had found it in his in-box. In the upper right-hand corner had been written the word "Noted" and the G-1's initials. After notifying the chief of staff, I called General Welsh and told him that I didn't think that the G-1 understood that he was responsible for the recruiting program in the ARCOM. I strongly suggested that at the next administrative drill, the G-1 be told to present his recruiting plan to the general, chief of staff, the G-1 adviser, and the ARCOM chief administrator, a civilian.

A lengthy meeting a week later ended with the G-1 coming up with a final, detailed plan that would involve recruiters from every one of the ARCOM's units in a two-month campaign in malls, universities, community colleges, and even high schools. While the results were an improvement over previous recruiting drives, I recommended that the ARCOM maintain a body of recruiters, trained and used in a continuous drive lasting at least a year. Eventually recruiting became a continuing program.

While emphasizing recruiting, we also placed greater emphasis on planned training. Some units did a bang-up job of training, but there were more that didn't do as well. Without exception, training was accomplished on one weekend each month, for which the reservist received four days' pay for two days' duty. This meant the advisers had to be present on the weekends, assisting and evaluating the training. They also had to accomplish the day-to-day training coordination and preparation during the week, to ensure that weekend training could be conducted properly. While all reserve units trained one weekend a month, they did not all train on the same weekend; this would make for a seven-day workweek for advisers. I gave all my advisers Mondays off, but I worked seven days a week.

A case in point was the mechanized infantry brigade, with its headquarters in Horsham, Pennsylvania, and its battalions based elsewhere in the ARCOM area. The brigade was commanded by a reserve brigadier general, with his own staff and civilian administrators, who had responsibility for ensuring that the battalions conducted the prescribed training.

The assumption could never be made that reserve brigade and battalion readiness was equal or even close to that of active Army units; a comparison of available training time supported this. However, this was not the commonly accepted view within the higher active Army commands, who sought comparability. If the reserve officers, advisers, and civilian administrators all used their time wisely and emphasized training that promoted the highest possible warfighting capability commensurate with the time available, they could meet the basic goal, which was to produce units that could be made combat ready within a reasonable time by concentrated training provided upon mobilization.

I had observed the training of infantry and artillery units for a couple of months and could readily see that there was little or no advance planning for weekend field training. There was nothing more demoralizing for a reserve soldier than to travel in an open truck for a hundred miles and upon arrival stand around and wait while the officers and NCOs decided what they were going to do. I could readily see why General Powers was especially upset with the training conducted by the combat units. (It might be noted here that logistics units, say, quartermaster petroleum companies, could accomplish most of their training within their training centers.) After seeing some disastrously poor training weekends involving units of the mechanized brigade at Fort Dix, New Jersey, and Indian Town Gap Military Reservation, Pennsylvania, I advised General Welsh that I was going to hold a training-coordination session at brigade headquarters before each training weekend that was to be conducted in the field, and I suggested that the brigade commander be involved in the session. General Welsh agreed and passed along to the units the details, which I provided.

On the morning of the first training-coordination session, everyone was present except the brigade commander. I told Welsh about the "no show." We went on with the session, and the following weekend I saw some improvement in the training, with the one exception that the brigade commander again did not make an appearance. In my report of the training, I commented on the absence of the brigade commander and gave a copy of the report to General Welsh before sending it to General Powers.

On Monday noon, the brigade commander came into my office, took off his service cap, removed his star from it, handed it to me, and announced that he was retiring. I told him I didn't want his star, but he wouldn't take it back. He left the ARCOM headquarters, and I never saw him again. When I notified General Welsh, he said that he had asked the brigade commander why he hadn't visited his battalion in the field, and that had apparently prompted him to retire. General Welsh told me to put his star in an envelope and send it to his home address.

The next time I saw the chief of staff, he told me that some of the officers thought I was getting a bit tough, when things had been running so smoothly. What could I say? But as news of the brigade commander incident traveled throughout the ARCOM, I noticed an improvement in training, as did the other advisers.

It didn't take long to figure out that alongside the official means of communications in the ARCOM there was the personal telephone, and that a great many of the important decisions were incubated there. When the chief of staff was selected as the interim commander of the mechanized brigade, I recommended a Col. Richard Leitheiser, who commanded a well-trained transportation unit in Norristown, as chief of staff. I am quite sure that the telephone lines were buzzing in and around the Philadelphia area about promises that had been made concerning the chief of staff position. The major who was the G-1 adviser told me of several conversations that the G-1 had had with General Welsh on the matter, as well as names of prospective chiefs of staff.

I contacted General Powers and suggested that he interview "nominees" for the position. He replied that he wanted the names submitted of the normal minimum of three nominees and that he would interview them. Welsh submitted Leitheiser's name with those of two other reserve colonels, and he was selected. After I retired, he would become the ARCOM commander; eventually he was promoted to major general, U.S. Army Reserve.

I had a number of discussions with Brigadier General Eisenhower, especially during lunch on training weekends. I learned one thing from him that I never forgot: he did not want to be called "General"—in his mind, there was only one General Eisenhower. During one discussion with him he said that he thought that improvement in training had a direct bearing on retaining reservists in the program and that, in turn, reduction in turnover in personnel through reenlistment would lower recruiting needs. So, in a way, the G-3 became involved in the retention side of recruiting.

I still remember when John Eisenhower asked me if I knew the most difficult decision that his father had had to make. I immediately said it must have been the decision as to the timing of the Channel crossing for the invasion of the continent in 1944, when the weather had been so bad on the scheduled day. Wrong! He told me his most difficult decision had been whether or not to commute the execution in 1953 of Julius and Ethel Rosenberg (who had been convicted of espionage for the USSR). Several weeks later, he called me at noon at the ARCOM and asked me to have someone box up his flag, stationery, and other personal items. He had decided to retire. I saw him only one more time, after I had retired myself, when he invited me to lunch in King of Prussia, Pennsylvania.

In 1974, Lt. Hudson Berry visited us in Lansdale while Rosalind was home for Thanksgiving. He asked for her hand while we were all at dinner, at the Inflight Inn in Colmar. They were married at Holy Family Church in Stow the following April and returned to Galveston, where Hud was still in medical school. Our daughter Mary Lou and Sheri Anwar were married in California in October 1975. Sheri had recently received a master's degree in industrial engineering from Berkeley.

We had been looking for a house to buy since we arrived in Pennsylvania; our real estate agent had been combing the countryside. In May 1975 we finally moved into a new home, at Oxbow Meadows in Chalfont. This was the first home we had ever bought, so it was a new experience, in a way. We had already decided that I would retire within six months, so we used our last transportation authorization to move our household goods from Lansdale to Chalfont, a matter of about five miles.

Rick graduated from North Penn High School in Lansdale in 1975 and planned to attend Bowling Green State University in the fall. During the summer he hitchhiked to California and worked at entry level jobs in the San Diego area.

Colonel Smith had to give up the command of the brigade because of physical reasons following his active-duty training. The deputy brigade commander took over the command until a new commander was designated. A reserve colonel who had complained when he was not selected as the chief of staff was high on the ARCOM commander's list, along with two totally unqualified colonels.

About this time I received a telephone call from Col. Dean Meyerson, a 1949 graduate of the Military Academy, seeking information on position availability for reserve infantry colonels—that is, himself. Meyerson had served with me in the Eighth Cavalry in 1950; he had resigned in 1954 and then reverted to the Army Reserves. After advising him that there was an opening for a commander of a mechanized infantry brigade, I told him I'd get back in a day or so. General Welsh's recommendation had not gone forward, so I informed General Powers about Meyerson's interest in commanding the brigade. Powers wanted to interview Meyerson as a possible candidate for the position, and a date was arranged. I also informed General Welsh about Meyerson's request and told him Myerson had a solid infantry background, including combat. Welsh told me he would not send the recommendation forward until he had seen Meyerson, and again an interview was arranged.

Powers was very impressed with Meyerson. When Myerson arrived at the ARCOM to be interviewed, both the G-1 and I were in General Welsh's office. I soon sensed that the G-1 was asking Meyerson questions designed only to embarrass him. I suggested that the G-1 and I let Meyerson and the general continue the interview without us. The G-1 grudgingly left the office with me; when we got outside, he accused me of unfair tactics. My only response was that I had been exposed to some very good teachers. Later, when I asked General Welsh how Meyerson impressed him, I was told that Meyerson would be recommended for the position.

As I recall, in late 1975, about a month before my retirement, I received word that the FORCECOM inspector general would be at the ARCOM in early December to look into the selection process for the mechanized brigade commander. The word was out that I was being accused of using undue pressure to get a "friend" assigned as the brigade commander. (I hadn't seen or spoken to Myerson in over twenty years.) I was interviewed, as were others. The IG, an active Army colonel, asked me during his exit interview only one question: "If you had it to do over again, is there anything you'd do differently, Colonel?" My response was, "I wouldn't do anything differently, except perhaps send in Myerson's name as my written recommendation for the brigade commander!" The IG gave me a thumbs-up, and I never heard a thing more about it.

After a short leave, my replacement already on board, I retired from the U.S. Army on January 1, 1976. Subsequently, Colonel Meyerson was selected by General Powers and the First Army (First Army is next higher headquarters) commander who made the final decision on general officer positions. He was later promoted to brigadier general, USAR, and has since passed away. In the end, after thirty years in the army, I still wore the same size hat as when I was inducted into the army in 1943, but I had a much better appreciation of what was needed in the army, professionally.

# Epilogue

Having participated in a few of the nation's military operations during the past fifty-six years, I wrote this book with the notion of identifying the lessons I learned along the way that are relevant for the Army's institutional memory. In my view, the lessons of experience serve either as guides to future military endeavors or as warnings of traps to be avoided. In this respect, I have tried to avoid direct involvement in politics, if that is possible in this day and age.

From March 1943, when I first entered the Army, I found that the institution was challenging, that perseverance coupled with an element of humility were needed to meet its needs. My experience as an enlisted man and officer showed me that the Army consistently provides most of the tools needed for the trade but that there was and still is a need for field expedients and "make do" in combat.

If there is one lesson I learned during World War II, it was that the Army needed every ounce of leadership it could squeeze from its drafted forces, to match the high morale of the citizenry and industry. There is every evidence that it did this.

Concerning my Korean War service, I recall lessons I learned as a replacement platoon leader in Company C, Eighth Cavalry Regiment, but my first recollection was the Camp Drake Reception Center in Japan, where the supply system had failed to provide items necessary to fight effectively a powerful enemy. The capability of small units to communicate over extended distances, particularly during the Pusan-perimeter period, suffered because batteries had exceeded their shelf lives, there was insufficient field-telephone wire, and because telephone and radio equipment had been poorly maintained during peacetime. These inadequacies placed great stress on the Army's defensive capabilities, and they often required forces to lay field wire when on the offensive. The lesson was that continuous communications maintenance is a must, from the platoon to the highest levels.

If frontline units are to achieve the defensive and offensive capabilities that are intended for them, weapons must be assigned as prescribed by the tables of organization. In Korea the primary weapons of rifle squads were the M-1 rifle and the Browning automatic rifle (BAR); however, approximately half of the squads were armed instead with the shorter-range M-1 carbine, and the un-availability of BAR repair parts caused frequent downtime for this weapon. I learned that weapon-distribution plans must be followed and that preventive and higher-level maintenance must be enforced, both of which apparently had been lax in Japan before the Korean War.

It was my experience that offensive operations at company level were too often initiated as frontal attacks, with platoons moving up in column rather than in flanking or envelopment attacks and using the time-honored tactic of two platoons up and one to the rear (as a reserve, or exploiting, platoon). Frequently the rationale for this tactic was that ridges were too narrow. By attacking the flank of each objective using fire and maneuver, and assaulting using marching fire, I succeeded in seizing my objectives. The lesson (relearned) was to take advantage of opportunities for flanking attack, avoiding frontal attacks wherever possible.

For me, marching fire was an effective means of assaulting the flank of an enemy position. The tactic required training and practice in placing small arms fire on the "military crest" of an objective, taking over the effect of support fires with small arms. The lesson was simply to train platoons in the tactic of fire and maneuver and in the use of marching fire in the final assault—nothing new here!

Force multipliers should always be considered in the attack and the defense. While there is no way of certifying that bright bayonets, for instance, make enemy defenders less resolute and more likely to withdraw, prisoners told us that they had done just that. As to the defense, foxholes on the flanks proved to be critical during the Chinese attack at Unsan; they providing additional fighting positions for troops forward of us that withdrew and also for reinforcements sent forward. This force multiplier permitted us to hold our position for an extended period of time. In general, supplemental positions in the defense have to be prepared to meet changes in the original defensive situation.

An intelligence lesson learned in Korea was that leaders down to the platoon level need the information on the immediate situation that the prisoners they capture provide. That information should get back to them in a timely manner.

The Vietnam War differed greatly from the Korean War, but it offered many lessons as well. Perhaps the major one I learned during my service with the Second ARVN Division as a regimental and G-3 adviser was to respect the desire of the Vietnamese commander (just like that of any U.S. commander) "to save face," by giving advice and discussing unit affairs only in private. A major tactical lesson was that success in that military-political conflict was increased by long-term deployment of combat units to conduct random patrols, using the "saturation concept." That approach gave the commanders of ARVN regiments better understandings of the terrain and of enemy operations; eventually, it could have allowed government forces to control and pacify major areas, whole provinces.

Another major tactical-political lesson I learned as an adviser was that the military commander and the political commander (in this case, province chiefs) must coordinate their forces throughout the operational area, emphasizing the unity of command—that is, there must be single officer exercising operational control. Another significant lesson was that in regions laced with rivers, such as Vietnam, plans should incorporate river craft to support combat elements logistically and tactically.

Several years later, back in Vietnam, I drew lessons from my experience with the Fourth Infantry Division. One of them (which I could not discuss in earlier chapters because of classification) was that all intelligence available to the U.S. government concerning the immediate enemy situation in battalion areas of operation should be disseminated to those battalions, not only to brigade level, as was done during the Vietnam War.

An important lesson in the use of Army helicopter forces was that the closer their fuel and ammunition resupply points were to the operational area, the more continuous their employment in combat assaults and fire support could be.

Battalion commanders usually situated themselves in fire bases or in helicopters, overhead or at a distance. I learned that a light, mobile command post, with communications—the battalion commander, S-2 and S-3 assistants, plus radio-telephone operators—gave positive direction to the course of the battle. Positioning battalion commanders at fire bases was a carryover from the Vietnamese and French organization of the battlefield. Unfortunately, we had already lost the war when I learned this lesson. A mobile CP permits the battalion commander to maneuver tactical units directly, eyeball to eyeball, while the executive officer or the battalion M-3, normally majors, run the fire base.

I also learned that depth could be added to fire-base security by having the company used for that purpose conduct combat patrols, to include ambushes around the fire base. The defense of the base could be augmented by staff and artillery personnel.

Since my retirement, I have made my own assessment of the Army during the past twenty-four years, from the time of its low morale following the withdrawal from Vietnam. I am sure that most of us who retired from the Army nearly a quarter-century ago would need at least a one-year course to catch up with technical advances in communications, weaponry, and electronic battle-field devices. In addition, maintaining a war-fighting capability in an era of continuous peacekeeping would probably keep me awake at night, as would thinking about how the Army can meet its worldwide commitments with a steadily reducing active strength. That strength is now around 480,000 officers and men. In 1999, the active Army was at approximately 62 percent of its 1976 programmed strength of 779,000.[1]

I believe the Army's participation in peacekeeping and humanitarian operations is fully commensurate with the nation's responsibility as the single superpower. Such operations exercise the Army's deployment and operational muscles, probably better than would training at home stations or even at the National Training Center in California. It does, however, have an adverse impact on family life and personal morale, and that can affect the end-strength of the Army, in that it gives officers, NCOs, and enlisted people second thoughts about the Army as a career. There is a definite requirement to maintain the Army at a higher strength, to spread the operational requirements over a broader base—aside from taking advantage of Army Reserve forces, which may have new contingencies to meet in the future.

While the Army today seemingly has endless peacekeeping commitments, the world is not much safer than it was in the years of the well-known Soviet threat. In fact, there are indications that the world is less safe from nuclear, biological, and chemical catastrophe than it was when the USSR existed, especially since economic and political turmoil in Russia has destabilized that country. An unstable Russia is but one threat; the People's Republic of China, North Korea, Iran, Iraq, and others can also rise to the occasion with "weapons of mass destruction."

The Army must still contribute to NATO's conventional and nuclear capability, to thwart any renewal of the threat to Europe. This certainly calls for restoration of some deployable U.S. ground force and nuclear capability for Europe. An increase in Army forces and replenishment of prepositioned stocks in Europe is needed as soon as possible.

Recruitment needs more than slogans ("Be all you can be!"). There may well be solutions other than more pressure on recruiters. Greater emphasis must be placed on recruiting military and civilian personnel who can fill the high-tech needs of Army units and research-and-development programs. Inasmuch as eighteen-year-olds still register with the Selective Service (although there have been moves to stop funding it), it may be necessary for Congress to permit a draft lottery to make up the annual troop shortfall. In this connection, there should be special benefits and rewards to soldiers who serve with the combat arms (infantry, armor, artillery, engineers, signal corps, and aviation) but are not eligible for bonuses. I for one would be willing to pay the taxes that would be required to give each infantryman several thousand dollars upon each reenlistment.

Greater attention must also be paid to cadet selection for the U.S. Military Academy, ROTC scholarships, and other officer-producing programs, with the goal of selecting, training, and commissioning officers who desire long-term commitments. Greater emphasis must be placed on officer (and enlisted) leadership, on ability to solve military problems by field expedients rather than relying only on firepower, technology, and logistics. Finally, while junior officers often wish to earn master's degrees early in their careers, in-service study should be granted only in fields directly related to Army needs, and upon award of his or her degree, an officer should be assigned to work in that field. (An exception would be officers selected for Military Academy and ROTC assignments).

As the terrorism threat increases in the United States, it might be advisable to merge the current reserve forces—the National Guard and and the Army Reserve—into the National Guard, which would be given a definitive mission, by state, in a unified national counterterrorism program or command.

Steps should be taken to ensure that sophisticated battlefield information systems do not overburden soldiers in combat or restrict their capability to seize and hold terrain. In particular, attention must be paid to the continuous reduction in size and weight of such equipment as night-vision devices and "man-packable" computer systems.

The U.S. military leadership must apply the full spectrum of war-fighting capabilities, reduce service parochialism, and give military advice to the political leadership without regard to partisan allegiance. For instance, in the Persian Gulf War—after the largest military buildup, in the shortest time, since World War II—we didn't sufficiently reduce the Iraqis' military and unconventional capabilities, instead sought peaceful conformity through meaningless sanctions. From the start, our negotiators permitted Saddam Hussein to maintain strong air and ground forces, which now have to be policed from the air, a never-ending task, and by apologetic inspectors on the ground. The jury is still out on the bombing of Yugoslavia and Kosovo, and we are still in Bosnia.

Military equipment to clear the "fog of war" was available to the ground forces when I retired from the Army. Since then, year after year, new electronic

Granddaughter Alison Berrey, Marge, and Mack near Boston in 1984.

means have enhanced frontline combat leadership, ranging from the unmanned aerial vehicles that seek out the enemy to improved night-vision devices, to the Global Position System, to shoulder-fired antiaircraft systems. Still, we must be alert to the enemy's countermeasures.

We must also remember the spouses and children of soldiers. They accompany their husbands and wives, fathers and mothers, about the world, and often must wait for their safe return. They play a key role, providing vital support to their soldiers and our nation.

Finally, I want to express my gratitude to my wife, Marge, who assisted and encouraged me throughout my Army career and during the writing of this book. My four children are scattered to the winds; I commend them for their forbearance, for the many homes, schools, and friends they encountered and then had to leave each time I was reassigned.

To the youngest, Dr. Richard E. Mack, Jr. (a reconstructive surgeon practicing in California) and his wife Rene, a nurse practitioner: keep up the good work. To Elizabeth Mack, my youngest daughter, living in Minnesota, a graduate of

Syracuse University: I will never forget those long letters I received in Vietnam. To Rolly, with her master's in information systems, and her husband, Dr. B. Hudson Berrey, Jr. (a graduate of the U.S. Military Academy, a retired Army colonel, and now a professor and chairman of the Orthopedic Department, University of Florida School of Medicine): I commend you for the fine parenting of your daughters, Alison and Jillian. To my daughter Mary Lou, a graduate of San Diego State and a consultant on the arts: I have always appreciated your depth and wisdom. Sheri now is the president of an aircraft-parts manufacturing venture.

Finally, to all the soldiers I had the pleasure of serving with, thanks for the experience. You are all in my thoughts and prayers.

# Chronology of Military Service



March 15, 1943: Served in the U.S. Army as an enlisted man in a Tank Destroyer battalion and an ordnance battalion in the United States, Europe, and (through March 10, 1946) the Philippine Islands. Discharged as a Technician Fifth Class.

June 15, 1949: Appointed second lieutenant, Infantry, U.S. Army, upon graduating from Kent State University and the Army ROTC program. Assigned successively to the 526th Armored Infantry Battalion, Fort Knox; Ground General School, Fort Riley, Kansas; and the Infantry School, Fort Benning, Georgia.

August 6, 1950: Assigned as a rifle platoon leader to Company C, Eighth Cavalry Regiment, First Cavalry Division, in Korea. Promoted to first lieutenant, September 27, 1950. Wounded near Unsan, North Korea, on November 1, 1950.

November 1950: Hospitalized at Tokyo Army Hospital and the 161st Station Hospital in Sapporo, Hokkaido, until March 1951, and then assigned to Company 3, First Infantry Battalion at Camp Drake in Japan until June 30, 1951.

July 8, 1951: Assigned as First Cavalry Division Liaison Officer to the First British Commonwealth Division in Korea until November 18, 1951.

January 7, 1952: Assigned to the First Officer Candidate Regiment at Fort Benning, Georgia, as a company tactical officer, battalion adjutant, and information and education officer, in that order, until December 15, 1953.

January 12, 1954: Attended the Army Language School, Presidio of Monterey, California, completing the Russian-language course in December 1954.

April 27, 1954: Promoted to captain.

January 18, 1955:   Assigned as commander, Company B, Infantry School Detachment at Fort Benning until August 1955; attended the Infantry Officers Advanced Class, completing the course in June 1956.

July 15, 1956:   Assigned as commander of Company C, later Company D (Heavy Weapons), Sixth Infantry Regiment, in West Berlin. In April 1958, assigned as assistant secretary of General Staff, on the staff of the U.S. Commander of Berlin, until June 1959.

July 5, 1959:   Instructor, Army ROTC until August 1962. Promoted to major on September 6, 1961.

August 1962:   Student, Command and General Staff College, Fort Leavenworth, Kansas.

October 5, 1963:   Senior adviser with the Army of the Republic of Vietnam Fourth Regiment until July 1964; assigned as G-3 (operations) adviser, ARVN Second Division, until October 1964.

November 15, 1964:   Assigned to the Naval Amphibious School (NAMS) at Little Creek Naval Amphibious Base, Virginia, in the Intelligence and Communications Department. Promoted to lieutenant colonel in September 1965 and reassigned to the staff of the Amphibious Training Command, Atlantic (COMPHIBTRALANT), performing operations and training functions.

November 27, 1967:   Assigned to U.S. Army Europe (USAREUR) as manager of Army intelligence programs, in Heidelberg, Germany, until June 1968, when reassigned as a student at the U.S. Army War College at Carlisle, Pennsylvania.

July 15, 1968:   Attended the Army War College and upon graduation in June 1969 was assigned to the Third Brigade, Fourth Infantry Division in Vietnam's Central Highlands as the deputy brigade commander. Commanded the First Battalion of the Eighth Infantry Regiment and in April 1970 was assigned as chief of staff at the U.S. Army Headquarters Area Command. Promoted to colonel in July 1970.

September 10, 1970:   Assigned to the Strategic Studies Institute at Carlisle as a study team member until June 1963.

June 15, 1973:   Assigned to U.S. Army, South in the Canal Zone as the Deputy Chief of Staff for Operations, Plans, and Training.

September 10, 1974:   Assigned as senior adviser of the Seventy-ninth Army Reserve Command (ARCOM) in Colmar, Pennsylvania, until December 31, 1975.

January 1, 1976:   Retired from the U.S. Army in a ceremony at Fort Dix, New Jersey.


## AWARDS AND DECORATIONS

October 9, 1950:   Combat Infantryman Badge.

November 1, 1950:   Silver Star for action at Unsan, North Korea, and Purple Heart for wounds received at Unsan.

February 15, 1953: Awarded Airborne Badge after completion of training with Class 28.

March 24, 1964: Combat Infantryman Badge (second award).

July 27, 1964: Gallantry Cross with palm, per General Order 38, Armed Forces of the Republic of Vietnam.

September 23, 1964: Bronze Star for meritorious achievement in ground operations against hostile forces (October 1963–July 1964).

October 21, 1964: Bronze Star (first oak-leaf cluster) for heroism in ground combat in Ly Tinh Valley for evacuating an ARVN soldier under fire, on August 9, 1964.

June 18, 1968: Army Commendation Medal for meritorious service in Europe from November 1967 to June 1968.

November 25, 1969: Bronze Star (second oak-leaf cluster) for meritorious service in command of the Chu Pa Mountain Task Force during November 1969

December 8, 1969: Bronze Star (third oak-leaf cluster) for heroism in ground combat leading a ground assault on a suspected enemy base during the Chu Pa Mountain operation, November 9, 1969.

December 20, 1969: Air Medal for meritorious achievement (August 9–September 30, 1969).

December 20, 1969: Air Medal (second and third awards) for meritorious achievement (September 30–November 6, 1969).

April 13, 1970: Air Medal (fourth award) for heroism while participating in aerial flight on February 27, 1970.

June 11, 1970: Air Medal (fifth award) for meritorious achievement while participating in aerial flight (January 2–March 1, 1970).

July 13, 1970: Purple Heart (first oak-leaf cluster) for wounds received on April 17, 1970.

July 20, 1970: Legion of Merit for exceptionally meritorious conduct in the performance of outstanding services (August 1969–August 1970).

May 14, 1973: Legion of Merit (first oak-leaf cluster) for exceptionally meritorious conduct in the performance of outstanding services (August 1970–June 1973).

March 24, 1976: Legion of Merit (second oak-leaf cluster) for exceptionally meritorious service while serving as the senior adviser of the Seventy-ninth U.S. Army Reserve Command in Colmar, Pennsylvania, from September 1974 through December 1975.

# Notes

1. Reflections on Early Experiences

1. During the fall and winter of 1945–46, as a member of the 3166th Artillery and Fire Control Company, I hauled numerous tanks, half-tracks, and other combat vehicles to barges at Manila Bay; these vehicles were subsequently dropped into the water.

2. William Manchester, *American Caesar: Douglas MacArthur, 1880–1964*, p. 375.

3. Richard E. Mack, "Marching Fire," monograph, Infantry School Library, Fort Benning, Georgia, 1956.

4. Roy E. Appleman, *South to the Naktong, North to the Yalu*, p. 625.

5. Ibid., p. 19.

2. The Pusan Perimeter

1. Unknown to me at the time, on August 3, 1950, other alternatives lacking, the commander of the First Cavalry Division, Maj. Gen. Hobart Gay, ordered the bridge over the Naktong River to be blown up, reportedly with hundreds of refugees on it. NKPA infiltration via refugee columns had taken place. The First Cavalry Division, with only two battalions per regiment, rather than the three normally authorized, was placed under the constant jeopardy of refugee columns harboring NKPA units in disguise, gaining access to rear areas. Appleman, p. 251.

2. 57 mm recoilless rifle (RR): a shoulder-fired weapon capable of firing a small (but artillery-sized) high-explosive round effectively distances over a thousand yards. It had a twenty-five-yard bursting radius.

3. Withdraw and Attack

1. Kane was referred to as "Killer" because of his continuous presence on the front line with his men.

2. Appleman, p. 566.

3. Ibid., pp. 589–90.

4. Manchester, pp. 592–93.

5. Harold Evans, *The American Century,* pp. 401–2.

6. Appleman, p. 623.

## 4. A Final Thrust

1. Appleman, pp. 650–51.

2. Joseph C. Goulden, *Korea: The Untold Story of the War,* pp. 251–252.

3. Appleman, p. 661.

4. Ibid., pp. 661–63.

5. Ibid., p. 658.

6. Manchester, p. 601.

7. Appleman, pp. 675–76.

8. Ibid., pp. 677–81.

9. Discussion with B Company sergeant in a U.S. hospital in P'yongyang.

10. Appleman, p. 693.

11. Ibid., p. 694.

12. Ibid., p. 699

13. Ibid., pp. 700–707.

14. Ibid., pp. 707–8.

## 6. Assassination and Struggle

1. Stanley Karnow, *Vietnam: A History,* p. 136.

2. Richard E. Mack, "A Riverine Operation," in *A Distant Challenge: The US Infantry in Vietnam,* pp. 21–25.

3. Piers Brendon, *Ike,* p. 413.

4. Richard E. Mack, "Hold and Pacify," *Military Review (November 1967):* 91–95.

5. Popular Forces (PF), normally used for village and hamlet defense, normally remained in the villages where their members lived. The Regional Forces (RF) were recruited at the district and province level. The RF were full-time paramilitary forces that had both offensive and defensive capabilities and were organized like ARVN companies.

6. Karnow, p. 335.

7. Ibid., pp. 259–62.

8. Ibid., pp. 22, 366–73.

## 7. The Holding Pattern

1. Karnow, pp. 324–26, 345, 415–16.

2. See Mack's "Ambuscade," *Marine Corps Gazette* 51, no. 4 (April 1967); "Minbotrap," *Marine Corps Gazette* 51, no. 7 (July 1967); "Case for the Ruse," *Marine Corps Gazette* 52, no. 4 (April 1968); "Comprehensive View of Terrain," *Marine Corps Gazette* 52, no. 10 (October 1968); "Suspect," *Infantry* 58, no. 1 (January–February 1968); "Surprise," *U.S. Army Aviation Digest* 14, no. 1 (January 1968); and "Trap," *Infantry,* Combat Notes from Vietnam (July 1968).

3. Bresnahan, Richard. Biographical Sketches, USAWC Class of 1969, Student Section, Army War College, Carlisle Barracks, Penn.

## 8. America's War

1. G-1: The general staff officer responsible for matters such as personnel, promotions, discipline, law and order, and administration.

2. Flak vest: a vest that covered the upper torso, front and rear, for protection against small arms. It was heavy and sweaty, and because of its discomfort was not often worn. It was Fourth Division policy that it be worn in the field.

3. Harold Moore and Joseph L. Galloway, *We Were Soldiers Once . . . and Young: Ia Drang, the Battle that Changed the War in Vietnam,* maps for November 14, 1965.

4. Bouncing betty mine: a land mine that, when activated, sprang up waist high and exploded—a very lethal mine.

5. Civilian Irregular Defense Group (CIDG): Organized units of Montagnards (indigenous Vietnamese), commanded by ARVN officers and advised by the U.S. Army Special Forces Teams. Usually operated in the mountainous, remote western regions of South Vietnam.

6. Conex container: Large steel containers used by the shipping industry for material aboard containerships. Used by U.S. ground forces in Vietnam for field combat headquarters, particularly of battalions and brigades, to enhance mobility. Usually placed in ground recesses dug by "minidozers" and then covered by timbers and earth or sandbag.

7. Karnow, pp. 604–12.

## 9. The Cold War Continues

1. Strategic Studies Institute (SSI): This institute was assigned to the U.S. Army War College but received its tasking from the Office of the Deputy Chief of Staff, Operations (DCSOPS), Department of the Army. SSI conducted studies on issues as directed by DCSOPS related to the operations and procedures of the U.S. Army.

2. Graham Greene, *Getting to Know the General,* pp. 13, 20.

3. Ibid., pp. 19, 20.

## Epilogue

1. Harold Brown, DOD *Annual Report, FY 1980,* p. B-4, Table 4.

# References


Appleman, Roy E. *South to the Naktong, North to the Yalu.* Washington, D.C.: Department of the Army, Chief of Military History, 1961.

Bradley, Omar N., and Clay A. Blair. *A General's Life.* New York: Simon and Schuster, 1983.

Brendon, Piers. *Ike: His Life and His Times.* New York: Harper and Row, 1981.

Bresnahan, Richard, Col. USA, Biographical Sketches, U.S. Army War College, Class of 1969, Carlisle Barracks, Penn., 1969.

Brown, Harold. DOD *Annual Report, FY 1980.* Washington, D.C.: 1980.

Coleman, J. D. *Pleiku: The Dawn of Helicopter Warfare in Vietnam.* New York: St. Martin's Press, 1988.

Dupuy, Ernest R., et al. *Military Heritage of America.* New York: McGraw-Hill, 1956.

Evans, Harold. *The American Century.* New York: Alfred A. Knopf, 1998.

Goulden, Joseph C. *Korea: The Untold Story of the War.* New York: Times Press, 1982.

Greene, Graham. *Getting to Know the General.* New York: Simon and Schuster, 1984.

Hamilton, Nigel. *Master of the Battlefield: Monty's War Years.* New York: McGraw-Hill, 1983.

Harrison, James Pinckney. *The Endless War.* New York: The Free Press, 1982.

Hermes, Walter G. *Truce Tent and Fighting Front.* Washington, D.C.: Department of the Army, Chief of Military History, 1966.

Irving, Davis. *The War between the Generals.* New York: Congdon and Lattès, 1981.

Karnow, Stanley. *Vietnam: A History of the Vietnam War.* New York: Viking, 1983.

Kowet, Don. *A Matter of Honor: General Westmoreland vs CBS.* New York: MacMillan, 1984.

Mack, Richard E. "Black Power: To Build or to Burn." Student Essay, U.S. Army War College, Carlisle, Penn., February 18, 1969.

———. "Hold and Pacify." *Military Review,* November 1967.

———. "Marching Fire." Monograph. Infantry School Library, Fort Benning, Georgia, 1956.

———. "A Riverine Operation." In *A Distant Challenge.* Ed. Col. Ward M. Bradford. Fort Benning, Ga.: Infantry School, 1971.

McCullough, David. *The Path between the Seas.* New York: Simon and Schuster, 1977.

Manchester, William. *American Caesar: Douglas MacArthur, 1880–1994.* Boston: Little, Brown, 1978.

Montros, Lynn. *The Chosin Reservoir Campaign.* Washington, D.C.: Headquarters, U.S. Marine Corps, 1957.

Moore, Harold, and Joseph L. Galloway. *We Were Soldiers Once . . . and Young: Ia Drang, the Battle that Changed the War in Vietnam.* New York: Random House, 1993.

Petre, Peter, and H. Norman Schwarzkopf. *It Doesn't Take a Hero.* New York: Bantam, 1992.

Summers, Harry G., Jr. *On Strategy.* Novato, Calif.: Presidio, 1982.

Woodward, Bob. *Veil: The Secret Wars of the CIA, 1981–1987.* New York: Simon and Schuster, 1987.

# Index